Eight
Twentieth-Century
Russian Plays

Eight Twentieth-Century Russian Plays

Edited, translated from the Russian,

and with an introduction by

Timothy Langen and Justin Weir

Northwestern University Press

Evanston, Illinois

Northwestern University Press
Evanston, Illinois 60208-4210

Copyright © 2000 by
Northwestern University Press.
All rights reserved.

Published 2000

Printed in the United States of America

ISBN 0-8101-1373-2 (cloth)
ISBN 0-8101-1374-0 (paper)

Library of Congress Cataloging-in-Publication Data
Eight twentieth-century Russian plays / translated from the Russian and
with an introduction by Timothy Langen and Justin Weir.
       p.   cm.
    ISBN 0-8101-1373-2 (alk. paper) — ISBN 0-8101-1374-0 (pbk. : alk. paper)
    1. Russian drama—20th century—Translations into English.   I. Langen,
Timothy.   II. Weir, Justin.
PG3245.E38 2000
891.72'408—dc21   00-008680

Contents

Acknowledgments

We translated all the plays except *Elizaveta Bam,* which was translated by Andrew Wachtel and edited by us. At various points during our work we consulted Guy Daniels's *Complete Plays of Vladimir Mayakovsky,* George Gibian's *Man with the Black Coat: Russia's Lost Literature of the Absurd,* Eugene Lyons's *Six Soviet Plays,* and Harold B. Segel's *Twentieth-Century Russian Drama: From Gorky to the Present.*

This anthology would never have come to fruition were it not for the extraordinary patience of Susan Harris of Northwestern University Press and the persistent exhortations of Andrew Wachtel, who generously offered his advice and expertise throughout the project. Irina Dolgova spent countless hours explaining usage, derivation, and myriad other nuances of the Russian original texts; she deserves ample credit for whatever success we have achieved in these translations. Our thanks to Ilya Kutik, Gary Saul Morson, Caryl Emerson, Julie Cassiday, Charles Isenberg, and Lena Lencek for their encouragement and assistance. Reed College students Tatiana Martusev, Michael Kunichika, and Casey Revkin-Mauger helped with text formatting and other crucial tasks.

Our families supported us in ways too numerous to elaborate.

Timothy Langen and Justin Weir

Editors' Introduction:
Revolutions in Drama

The story of Russian life in the twentieth century is a story of revolution—at first suppressed, then achieved, institutionalized, and finally overturned. During the institutional phase, the Soviet Union was one of those countries where "revolutionary" paradoxically meant "pro-government" and "counterrevolutionary" meant "treasonous." Revolution was thus a privileged concept, parallel to the identity of the state itself. But the discourse of revolution preceded the 1917 Revolution and the Soviet regime. By the 1890s, the painful effects of rapid industrialization had combined with an already rich heritage of radical social critique to create a labor movement and a variety of pro revolutionary political parties. If one can speak at all of a "revolutionary tradition," then the foundations of such a tradition were firmly in place in Russia by the turn of the century, touching not only politics, but music, philosophy, and literature, as well.

When Russian authors entered onto the world literary stage in the first half of nineteenth century, they did so in a spirit of innovation and revolutionary iconoclasm. Indeed, these very traits became almost a point of national pride. Lev Tolstoy, seeking to justify the abnormal construction of his behemoth novel *War and Peace*, appealed to this sense of revolutionary tradition:

> [T]he history of Russian literature since the time of Pushkin not only affords many examples of such a departure from European form, but does not offer so much as one example to the contrary. From Gogol's *Dead Souls* to Dostoevsky's *Dead House,* in the recent period of Russian literature there is not a single work of artistic prose, at all rising above mediocrity, that quite fits the form of a novel, a poem, or a story.[1]

And by the end of the nineteenth century, this revolutionary spirit had intensified; writers and artists now more frequently displayed an intense desire to break decisively with the past, to change the state or nature of art itself, rather than merely to innovate in the manner of a Pushkin, Gogol, or Tolstoy.

The selections in this anthology illustrate the development of a revolutionary tradition—political and artistic—as manifested in the Russian theater. We begin with symbolism, the first major reaction against the tradition of literary realism that had dominated Russian writing for the better part of the nineteenth century. Though less influential abroad than their compatriot Anton Chekhov, the Russian symbolists (Zinaida Gippius, Dmitry Merezhkovsky, Valery Briusov, Konstantin Balmont, Fyodor Sologub, Andrey Bely, Alexander Blok, Vyacheslav Ivanov, and others) were among the first to declare that a revolutionary new art had reached the theater and, moreover, belonged primarily in the theater. They rejected the heightened mimesis of Konstantin Stanislavsky's ultrarealistic stagings of Chekhov—and Chekhov in turn ridiculed the excesses of their mysticism—but both Chekhov and the symbolists were responsible for making the stage a significant force in Russian aesthetics. This turn to the stage was itself a revolution of sorts, for the theater in Russia had not dictated cultural aesthetics to the extent that it did in France and elsewhere.

Drawing on the work of European symbolists as well as the philosophy of Friedrich Nietzsche, Vladimir Solovyov, and others, the Russian symbolists wanted to use drama as a way to transcend the ordinary experience of the world, rather than to duplicate or even merely to intensify it. Their rebellion against realism targeted both content and style—they wrote plays about strange and unlikely events, and they narrated those events in strange and unlikely ways. The topics of Russian symbolist drama included mystical or supernatural events; folklore; classical Greek and Roman themes; psychological decay; pseudoreligious, cosmic, or transformative spiritual experience; and so forth. The style was equally heterogeneous. In a symbolist play, speech-registers can shift abruptly with no explanation, scenery and costumes often fail to resemble the ordinary world, and the audience may be kept deliberately and perpetually off guard as to what is true, false, good, or bad. In short, the symbolist movement provided safe haven for a myriad of unconventional topics, so long as they were presented in an antinaturalistic way. Such assaults on traditional subject matter and style frequently appealed to an even older tradition (Greek tragedy, as interpreted by Nietzsche, or native pagan rituals); but most often the symbolist playwrights simply endeavored to represent a different kind of experience than was possible in the tradition of the nineteenth-century classics. When they succeed, it is by causing the audience to perceive the world in a whole new way; when they fail, it is because they seem *merely* bizarre and awkward.

With its aggressive mysticism and unusual characters, *Sacred Blood* (1901), the first play written by Zinaida Gippius (1869–1945), certainly qualifies as bizarre, and the dialogue often seems stiff and unnatural. But naturalism is clearly not the effect Gippius is after. Her characters—mermaids, hermits, and a witch—inhabit a world defined by its spatial, temporal, and conceptual separation from "our" world. One is hard pressed, for example, to identify exactly where and when the action of the play occurs. And the experiences of a young mermaid are presumably outside those of the average theatergoer.

Still, the main theme of the play offers a discourse on Christianity and paganism that is familiar in modernist representations of spirituality. This conflict was especially important for the Russian symbolists, whose two major philosophical inspirations were Friedrich Nietzsche and the Russian theological philosopher Vladimir Solovyov. The pagan world of the mermaids is unaffected by Christ's great sacrifice, as the young mermaid of the play complains: "The man, Christ, God, came only for people; He didn't come for us. He forgot us!" This non-Christian world displays some of the elements of Greek pagan life as described by Nietzsche: the cool, Apollonian moonlight and harmonious relations between characters on the one hand, and the Dionysian impulses of music and dissolution (either from sunlight or from the death that all mermaids face) on the other.

In the play's hermits, we see two versions of Christianity, which are sometimes associated with perceptions of a New versus an Old Testament God. The first, practiced by Father Pafnuty, is based on unbounded love—in accordance with Solovyov's theories—while the other, represented by Nikodim, relies on books and laws. The tension between these principles provides the main driving force for the play, as it had for Fyodor Dostoevsky's *Brothers Karamazov*. That novel presents a stark contrast between Father Zosima's truly Christian love and Father Ferapont's severe adherence to monastic rule. The figure of Dostoevsky loomed large over early symbolist thought. *L. Tolstoy and Dostoevsky,* a critical work by Gippius's husband, Dmitry Merezhkovsky, reveals as much about the symbolists' interest in Dostoevsky's religious ideas, for example, as it does about the novelists themselves. And the desire to borrow so many themes and images from earlier writers was itself characteristic of most of the symbolists.

Other important characteristics of early symbolism also permeate Gippius's play. The symbolists relished every opportunity to flout the somewhat Victorian attitudes toward sexuality that characterize much of nineteenth-century Russian fiction, and Gippius, in particular, is known for her subversion of traditional concepts of gender and sexuality. In *Sacred Blood,* the young mermaid is surely meant to be a sexually transgressive, though naive, character; and Nikodim, the representative of Law in the play, rightly perceives her as both a threat and a temptation. Should the audience dismiss Nikodim too readily, they will find him at least partially vindicated in the final scene, which if it represents a triumph of Christian love, then also represents its apocalyptic and blood-soaked antithesis.

After a time, the symbolists seemed to develop a sort of apocalyptic fatigue. Alexander Blok (1881–1921) belonged to the "second generation" of Russian symbolists, who took it upon themselves to locate the Beautiful Lady—later, the Unknown Woman—who would instigate a new era of culture and knowledge (as indicated by another of her names, Sophia, meaning "divine wisdom" in the Russian Orthodox tradition). Actually, Blok went one better: Having identified her as one Lyubov Mendeleyeva, he married her. Yet the world remained untransfigured, and even Blok's own personal life was not especially improved.

Blok, like many others who felt political revolution and spiritual revolution to be closely interrelated, displayed a combination of hope and disillusionment in response to the 1905 Revolution. Though the series of strikes and demonstrations won a number of concessions, most notably a national assembly and the promise of a constitutional monarchy, more grandiose hopes were disappointed, and a conservative backlash followed. The 1905 experience produced strong emotions and led to several extremely well known works of Russian writing, including Andrey Bely's modernist novel *Petersburg* and Vladimir Lenin's political critique *What Is to Be Done?* Thus, *The Unknown Woman* (1908) reflects an atmosphere of social, mystical, and political uneasiness. This play is the first example of a theme that will recur throughout this anthology: "So we've had our revolution... Now what?" With this play, Blok expresses a common symbolist response to mystical disappointment: self-mockery.

Blok had earlier developed the theme of disillusionment in a poem of the same name ("The Unknown Woman," 1906). The poem reads in part:

And every evening my only friend
Is reflected in my glass
And is, like me, subdued and stunned
By the tart and secret liquid.

And nearby, at adjoining tables
Sleepy waiters linger,
While drunks with rabbit eyes
Shout: "In vino veritas!"

And every evening at the appointed hour
(Or am I only dreaming it?),
The figure of a girl, swathed in silk,
Moves within the misty window.

Existential solitude as plain old loneliness, mysticism as inebriation, and the fated woman as no more than a punctual prostitute: such are the end results of Blok's deflated enthusiasm. And yet, in the play as well as in the poem, the final lines admit residual though ambiguous optimism. A "bright star" still burns in the sky at the end of the play, and the poem's protagonist, in closing, exclaims: "You're right, you drunken monster!/ I know: truth is in wine."

Though a supporter of the 1917 Revolution, Blok tempered this support with highly charged remnants of his former mysticism (as, for example, in the image of Christ in his poem of the Revolution, "The Twelve") and a carefully constructed, circumspect attitude toward his own and others' enthusiasm. As he writes in a 1918 essay, "The Intelligentsia and Revolution," "The revolution, like a whirlwind, like a snowstorm, always brings the new and unexpected. It cruelly cheats many. It cripples the worthy in its whirlpool. It often carries the unworthy to safety onto dry land." And indeed, the 1917 Revolution did not reward all the enthusiasms of those modernist and "revolutionary" writers who had called for it. Some felt betrayed; others, like Blok, developed a more complex amalgam of loss and achievement, detachment and zeal.

Still others attempted to place themselves fully at the service of the new order. Vladimir Mayakovsky (1893–1930) was one of these—a Bolshevik from early in life, he was in some ways more revolutionary than the revolutionaries. "I feel that 'I' is too small for me," he wrote in his early poetic tour de force "A Cloud in the Pants" (1915), and, indeed, he poured his "I" into every revolutionary activity he could find, until, as he put it, "love's boat smashed up against the daily grind," and he shot himself in the head. One of the poet's friends and great admirers, the literary critic Roman Jakobson, responded to Mayakovsky's suicide with an essay "On the Generation that Squandered Its Poets," which lays the blame on those who encouraged the ego-expansionism of Mayakovsky and his comrades.

But it is difficult to imagine what sort of writing Mayakovsky could have produced had his friends successfully prevailed on him to tone down the restlessness of his "I." For the inherent tragedy of ego-revolution is at the core of Mayakovsky's aesthetic practice. His cubo-futurist drama *Vladimir Mayakovsky: A Tragedy* (1913) is a series of variations on that very theme and an inadvertently ironic reflection of what would become the real tragedy of his life.

Several important tenets of futurism—and pet themes of Mayakovsky's—appear right away, in the play's Prologue. First and foremost is an attack on the literary tradition and its readership. "Can you understand," Mayakovsky asks in the opening line of the play, clearly doubting the mental capacity of his bourgeois audience. The end of a tradition also forms the mock tragedy of the play, for which Mayakovsky proposes to eliminate the "last poet"—that is, himself. Typically, the end here of traditional poetry is also an apotheosis of the new, a transition symbolized by the strangling of nature's rivers by steel bridges and by a drawing out of the body's tissues and nerves into "telegraph wires." As his reward, Mayakovsky asks only to be allowed to throw himself (à la Anna Karenina) under that hackneyed symbol of progress, the steam engine.

Mayakovsky could set off such fireworks of futurist imagery practically in his sleep. But his *Tragedy* speaks to another literary agenda as well, one which involved a rerouting of literary perception through his own highly aestheticized ego. The *Tragedy* is in this sense solipsistic, since everything gets filtered through the experience of the main character; yet Mayakovsky's solipsism is, paradoxically, a solipsism for everyone, an imagistic revolutionizing of mental categories and modes of perception. The real

Vladimir Mayakovsky recognized no distinction between his own revolution and that of society.

In 1923, Mayakovsky and an assortment of other artists and theoreticians formed a group known as LEF (the Left Front of Art), the purpose of which was to change objectively existing artistic practice. The group itself was novel in its attempt to fuse literary theory and practice, criticism and art, and many of the core group of cubo-futurists (Mayakovsky, Vasily Kamensky, and Aleksei Kruchenykh) joined, as did several formalist critics, constructivist artists, and filmmakers. One approach they favored was the generation of "literature of fact"—a paradoxical phrase that indicates their intent to shape the new, revolutionary society by forcing art and reality closer together. Though the LEF approach was not favored by the government, and eventually perished in a hostile climate, its practitioners considered themselves champions of the Revolution. They wanted to revolutionize art, and to use art to revolutionize society. Both of these goals were shared in principle by the Bolsheviks, although just how this was all to be done was another matter altogether. Revolution in society, revolution in art, and revolution in the relation between the two—in the 1920s these goals or slogans still awaited final definition.

Perhaps education would provide a means to revolutionize both art and society. In the period following the 1917 Revolution, troupes of actors toured the country performing "agitational drama" that was supposed to excite support and show the population how to conduct itself in the new regime. To be effective, these plays needed to appeal to a wide range of audience members, and the result was a collection of sometimes hilarious plays that satirized various forms of misbehavior. *The Case of the Entry Room,* by Victor Ardov (1900–76), was one of these. With its monomaniacal characters, its transparent scams, and its equation of the immoral with the ridiculous, the play combines features of the eighteenth-century comedy of manners and the twentieth-century aesthetic of the absurd. An agitational drama, designed to aid in the construction of a wholly new society, but containing so many old-fashioned elements—this paradox merely reflected a more general tension in postrevolutionary Russia.

Bound as it is to the nineteenth-century canon, Soviet "revolutionary" culture can seem remarkably *un*revolutionary and conservative in its literary tastes. *The Case of the Entry Room* ends with an unmistakable allusion to Nikolai Gogol's satirical play *The Government Inspector* (1836), in which a corrupt provincial mayor addresses the laughing audience near the end of the play: "What are you laughing at? You're laughing at yourselves!" Thus when the First Resident of *The Case of the Entry Room* similarly addresses the audience in the last line of the play—"Well, citizens, what's so funny, eh?"—he recalls not only Gogol, but also the moralizing tone of earlier Russian satire. The creation of a new, revolutionary culture required an often uncomfortable compromise. On the one hand was the desire to discard every rotten scrap of prerevolutionary life (perhaps to live in a state of "permanent revolution") and on the other a clear need to work with existing materials, be they physical or cultural.

The New Economic Program (NEP) of the twenties represented this second imperative: It was a major concession to what we might now call "the reality on the ground." The Civil War (1918–20) following the Revolution had left the country in a shambles, and in response, the government allowed elements of capitalism to reenter the economy. Those able to enrich themselves under the new regime became known as "Nepmen" (not a term of endearment). The concessions contained in NEP were supposed to be a temporary detour from the road to socialism, not a final destination; they were to be accepted grudgingly, not enjoyed.

This was a great time for literature. Artistic freedom was not nearly as limited as it would become a few years later, and the conflicts between Communist ideals and language, on the one hand, and the economic, social, emotional, and linguistic habits inherited from previous ages, on the other, provided many opportunities for dramatic and humorous conflict. *Squaring the Circle* (1928), a comedy written by Valentin Kataev (1897–1986) at the very end of the NEP period, makes the most of these opportunities.

The title of the play contains a pun that escapes translation. *Kvadratura Kruga* has the same meaning as the English expression "squaring the circle," but there is another meaning, too. *Kvadratura* can mean "area"—we might say "square footage"—and *Krug*, like the English "circle," can refer to a group of people. So the title, in addition to its meaning as a fixed expression, also means something like "the group's living space," which, in fact, is the focus of the play. While Soviet society as a whole is trying to square the circle (transform a messy hodgepodge into a well-regulated socialist economy), the mismatched lovers are trying to do more or less the same thing in their apartment: that is, make marriage out of mayhem.

So this is a play about revolution: Revolving spouses try to figure out how to revolutionize their domestic life in accordance with the broader ongoing social revolution. A resulting comic effect, used not only by Kataev but also by such authors as Mikhail Zoshchenko, Nikolai Erdman, and Andrey Platonov, is the misapplication of vocabulary and rhetoric from one sphere to another. In *Squaring the Circle,* the character Abram does this repeatedly. He uses the politically derogatory term "feudal" as a generalized negative epithet: He says "feudal bicycle," for example, where we might say "stupid bicycle." He even applies the Stalinist slogan "building socialism in one country" to domesticity: "building a household in one room."

The play gives us our first example of the direct equation of Communism with morality and of membership in the Communist Party and affiliated groups—such as the Communist Youth League (Komsomol) and the Young Pioneers—with moral activity. In the plays by Kataev, Kirshon, and Zorin, to be a Communist is exactly equivalent to being a moral person. Lyudmila's nonmembership in the Party speaks ill of her, for example, whereas the earnest bookworm Tonya judges everything by Communist standards. She may be somewhat overzealous, like Nikodim in *Sacred Blood,* but she is unquestionably reading the right books. In fact, many have argued that Communism was effectively a state religion in the Soviet Union, and, although the comparison is disagreeably broad, Communism, like many religions, set forth universal values that also purported to guide individual behavior. Thus, one might substitute the word "Christian," as it was used in America around the time these plays were written, for "Communist" and strike the same chord.

In other words, although the play is pro-revolutionary, it contains many essentially traditional elements. Some of these are predictable, such as love and morality. *Squaring the Circle* depends for its interest on questions the characters ask themselves, explicitly and implicitly, about the status in the new regime of things like love and morality. If these concepts have changed, how? If not, why not? And in its structure, *Squaring the Circle* is positively conservative—sometimes compulsively so, as in its methodical elaboration of symmetries. In the last scene, Kataev finally gives in to the obvious with the stage direction "Lyudmila copies Tonya's gesture with respect to Vasya and Tonya." But this copying has been going on from the beginning of the play, right from the opening stage directions that indicate the interchangeability of the right and left sides of the room. In fact, *Squaring the Circle* is even somewhat self-consciously conservative in form, as witness Tonya's rejection of Emelian Chernozemny as a "blatant decadent." Although her judgment is not always foolproof, Emelian's poetry is indeed bad, and, insofar as he stands in for "decadents" (a word used by the early symbolists to describe themselves and then used by the Soviets to describe any modernist they did not like), he makes them look bad.

Emelian's doggerel is tame, however, compared with some of the literary experimentation that survived through the end of the 1920s. The most experimental of all were the absurdist groups that went by such names as OBERIU (Association for Real Art) and Radix. And radical they were—in precisely the areas of literary form where *Squaring the Circle* is conservative. *Elizaveta Bam,* written by Daniil Kharms (the pseudonym of Daniil Yuvachev, 1905–42), is by far the OBERIU's most celebrated work. This play aspires to the condition of "drama as such," which the absurdists seem to equate with abnormality:

> If an actor who represents a minister begins to move around on the stage on all fours and howls like a wolf, or an actor who represents a Russian peasant suddenly delivers a long speech in Latin—that will be theater, that will interest the spectator, even if it takes place without any relation to a dramatic plot. Such an action will be a separate item; a series of such items organized by the director will make up a theatrical performance, which will have its plot line and its scenic meaning.
>
> This will be a plot which only the theater can give. The plots of theatrical performances are theatrical, just as the plots of musical works are musical. All represent one thing—a world of appearances—but depending on the material, they render it differently, after their own fashion.[2]

By all accounts, the OBERIU members practiced some of this theatricality in their daily lives as well, to the chagrin of others and to their own eventual detriment.

But theatricality was only part of the absurdists' program. Just as they wanted audiences to experience drama "as such," apart from any discernible plot, they used language in a way that draws attention to the words themselves, even at the expense of intelligibility. Thus after the "Entr'Acte-Cataract" that comes just after the beginning of piece 12, Mommy says "Oh, my legs are tired," Ivan Ivanovich responds with "Oh, my arms are tired," and Elizaveta Bam replies "Oh, my scissors are tired." In Russian, the word for scissors, *nozhnitsy*, is closely related to the word for legs, *nogy*, and so Elizaveta's response is not quite as random as it appears in English—but the connection is etymological rather than logical.

With such techniques, *Elizaveta Bam* destabilizes traditional cognitive processes and protocols. Anything might lead to anything else—or to nothing in particular. M. Meilakh, a Kharms scholar and the editor of the latest, most authoritative Russian-language edition of the play, identifies the theme of transformation as central to the play's aesthetic, and, indeed, transformation itself is one of the few constants afforded the audience, who witnesses a kind of permanent revolution taking place on stage—not just a social revolution, but a constant changing of everything.

The play's initial circumstance, that two men have come to arrest Elizaveta Bam without disclosing the reason, also conforms to the absurdists' general procedure of playing down logical "reasons." One cannot, however, help but compare this aspect of the play with Franz Kafka's *Trial* and other critiques of bureaucratic society. The play turns on the presumption of guilt, a presumption that came to dominate Soviet society in the purges of the 1930s. It would be wrong to ascribe special prophetic powers to Kharms, and *Elizaveta Bam* is certainly more an elaboration of absurdist thinking than a sustained social analysis. Still, both Elizaveta Bam and her creator Daniil Kharms are examples of those left behind by the now fully consolidated revolutionary society. Kharms was arrested in 1931 because he was supposedly distracting the populace from the work of industrialization (though one wonders how many people actually paid him enough attention to be distracted).

Another author who fell victim to the purges of the 1930s was Vladimir Kirshon (1902–38). His play *Grain* (1930) was anything but a distraction from industrialization, however, for it was dedicated to the Soviet notion that the countryside could be transformed into a gigantic agricultural factory. *Grain* describes the efforts during the first Five-Year Plan of a regional party secretary, Dmitry Mikhailov, as he collects grain from peasant villages and promotes the collectivization of agriculture into kolkhozes, or collective farms. The enemies of this process are the kulaks, peasants who were more wealthy than their neighbors, who hoarded this wealth instead of distributing it, and who were "liquidated as a class" by the Soviet collectivization process.

For many, the first scenes of *Grain* will have a disorienting effect. At first, it would seem that Mikhailov's old buddy Pavel Rayevsky must be the hero of the play. Good-looking, worldly, brave, and enthusiastic, Rayevsky seems destined to take the countryside by storm. Mikhailov, on the contrary, is an overly rational bureaucrat—not a "bean" counter, in this case, but a streetlight counter—and his wife almost immediately abandons him for the more dashing Rayevsky. By the end of the play, however, Mikhailov has proven himself the man of the future, a successful operator in a world where romantic notions of revolutionary activity are simply counterproductive and hopelessly anachronistic. Individualism in the play is thereby defeated in two of its most dangerous guises: as the kulak mode of agricultural production and as the obsolete romantic mode of revolutionary activity.

The time for tearing down the old has ended, the play seems to argue, and the construction of the new will be a collective and rational undertaking. The avant-garde of *this* sober project will be the "millions" of Mikhailovs revealed in the audience at the end of the play. Again we encounter the central paradox: Kirshon heralds the future with a recollection of the past. Just as in *The Case of the Entry Room,* the Gogolian appeal to the audience reveals a conservative, educational agenda in Soviet drama. In fact, as a member of the Russian Association of Proletarian Writers (RAPP) in the last half of the 1920s, Kirshon was among several authors who openly advocated literature's return to nineteenth-century realist models.

Grain is unmistakably the story of a campaign—in literature, public relations, and public policy—to integrate the entire country into a single institutionalized order. This political campaign degenerated into a series of purges throughout the 1930s that sent waves upon waves of people to death or to Siberian prison camps (and often to death in the camps)—including Daniil Kharms and Kirshon himself. The purges let up during the Second World War (what the Soviets called the Great Patriotic War), but did not really cease until the death in 1953 of Joseph Stalin.

The significance of our last play, *The Guests* (1954) by Leonid Zorin, comes largely from its status as one of the first literary works of the political and cultural "thaw" that followed Stalin's death. Works such as Alexander Solzhenitsyn's *Day in the Life of Ivan Denisovich*, which would never have seen the light of day under Stalin, were suddenly published, and diversity—even mild critique—now seemed possible. Though Zorin's play was subsequently condemned by the ministry of culture, it nonetheless gives one a good idea of the sorts of oblique criticism that were becoming permissible.

The play is decidedly *not* a critique of the 1917 Revolution, or of its goals, or of Communism. The dignified grandfather, Aleksey Petrovich Kirpichov, was a hero in the Revolution and serves as the play's moral touchstone. Indeed, characters are judged harshly for having *strayed* from the revolutionary ideals. Aleksey Petrovich's son, Pyotr Alekseyevich Kirpichov, personifies the decay of revolutionary spirit, the transformation from self-sacrificing to self-serving officialdom. When his son Sergey accuses him of wrongdoing, Pyotr defends himself by pointing out that he is a Communist (and thus, traditionally, a moral person). But Sergey replies indignantly, "You, a Communist?" the way an American might say "You, a Christian?" to a church-going cynic. The questions Zorin addresses are not "Is revolution good?" or "Is Communism good?" Rather, he asks "What was the Revolution really about?" and "What does it mean to be a true Communist?"

The Guests juxtaposes these issues of revolution and morality against a backdrop of intergenerational conflict. In so doing, it self-consciously recalls the classic literary treatment of this cluster of themes, Ivan Turgenev's novel *Fathers and Sons*. Zorin acknowledges Turgenev's importance to his play when he has Vera Nikolayevna call Sergey "Arkady," a reference to the zealous, impressionable son in Turgenev's novel. In this case, another son, Pyotr, builds his career on the unfair advantage of his last name; prestige trickles down from father to son, even though the latter may not deserve it. But Pyotr would have enjoyed another boost as well, though one not directly mentioned in the play. The loss of life in the 1930s and 1940s from famine, purges, and war was so massive that it depleted the party hierarchy and opened up career paths for a new generation of bureaucrats. Pyotr is one of these; he belongs to an ignoble group of men who benefited equally from their fathers' heroism and from the starvation and slaughter of their uncles.

One must keep in mind that *The Guests* is not a Western-style liberal critique of Soviet society. The dramatic obstacles in this play are bureaucracy and the bureaucratic runaround, which the character Pokrovsky has been trying to break through. Significantly, no one in the play expects or even proposes to solve Pokrovsky's problem by adjusting the legal or bureaucratic system to make it operate more fairly. Rather, Pokrovsky and his supporters try to establish and use a system of personal connections to right the wrong. Pyotr denounces this tactic as "protectionism"—we might call it "cronyism" or "the old-boy network"—and it is hard to disagree with his point. The positive characters want him to intercede on their behalf, whereas he insists on the inviolability of the system and of those who (like him) uphold it. Pyotr's orientation toward procedure indicates his guilt. Process, in this play, distracts and dilutes; the positive characters exhibit the impulse, not to perfect it, but to avoid or dismantle it.

They also want to tell the unvarnished truth, no matter whom it may hurt. Trubin, a friend and something of a mentor to Sergey, is, significantly, a journalist. And the play ends with the dramatic revelation that the morning paper will carry an exposé of some of the corrupt dealings of Pyotr's friends and associates. A revolution needs to correct itself, the message seems to be, and the tool for the job is the press—not necessarily a "free" press in the Western sense of the word, and by no means an adversarial press, but certainly an honest one.

The Guests thus ends with a sort of promise (and in the Soviet context it is a "revolutionary" promise) of openness. In fact, it took more than thirty years for the openness established by the Gorbachev presidency to fulfill that promise. Much of what we now associate with the *glasnost* in the 1980s, however, had precursors in Zorin's play and other "thaw" literature: for example, reformation of the press, the movement against institutionalized bureaucracy, and the "purification," or return to origins, of revolutionary ideology. Such interaction among art, society, and politics had been a hallmark of Russian life since long before the period covered by our anthology. But as the plays in this book demonstrate, in the twentieth century, Russia's cultural energy turned toward the artistic, the social, and the political proposition of revolution.

Eight
Twentieth-Century
Russian Plays

Sacred Blood

Zinaida Gippius 1901

Young Mermaid
Old Mermaid
Witch
Father Pafnuty
Nikodim
Mermaids

SCENE 1

Even before the curtain rises, the distant, thin ringing of a bell is heard. Deep in the woods. A small lake—smooth, placid, and bright. On the right shore, overgrown with rushes, is a clearing, and beyond it, a dark forest. A waning moon hangs quite low in the sky but casts a dim, somewhat reddish light onto the lake and clearing. A swarm of pale, wan, naked MERMAIDS are holding hands, and moving very slowly in a circle around the clearing. Their melody is also slow and regular, but not sad. It drowns out the bell, which rings continuously—but when the MERMAIDS fall silent for a few moments, the bell becomes much more audible. Not all the MERMAIDS are dancing: some of them, older ones, sit on the bank, their feet dipped into the water; others make their way through the rushes. At the edge of the clearing, near the forest itself, sits a rather fat, OLD MERMAID beneath a large tree, combing her hair in a slow and businesslike manner. Next to her is a very YOUNG MERMAID, almost a child. She sits motionless, her bare knees grasped in her thin arms, stares at the clearing without looking away, and listens closely. The hour is very late. Yet the thin moon does not descend, but climbs. Over the water a fog congeals as if alive.

OLD MERMAID (*sighing*). You're tangling, tangling your hair all up in a whorl, and you won't be able to comb it out. (*Falls silent, to the* YOUNG MERMAID.) What are you sitting for, instead of dancing? Go on and play with the others.

(*The* YOUNG MERMAID *keeps silent and stares out at the clearing, not moving.*)

(*Indifferently.*) Stuck again! What kind of child is she! As if the moon doesn't even warm her.

(*She continues to comb her hair. The quiet and slow song of the* MERMAIDS *is heard in time with their rhythmical sliding movements.*)

MERMAIDS.
We're the radiant lake's white daughters,
born of its purity and cool.

The foam, the mire, and the grass all pamper us,
we're caressed by the light, idle rush;
under ice in the winter, like greenhouse glass,
we sleep, and dream of summer.
        Everything's a blessing: life! and reality! and dreams!

(*The song breaks, the movement of the circle is silent for a moment, nei-ther quickened nor slowed. The bell is more audible.*)

We don't know, haven't seen
the deadly burning sun;
but we know its reflection,
we know the quiet moon.
Damp, sweet, meek, pure,
golden on a silver night,
she's kind, like a mermaid....
        Everything's a blessing: life! and us! and the moon!

(*Again the movement of the circle is silent for a few moments. The bell sounds.*)

On the bank, in the rushes,
a pale fog slips and melts away.
We know: Summer yields to winter,
winter—to spring, many times,
and the secret hour will arrive,
like all hours—blessed,
when we'll melt into the pale fog,
and the pale fog will melt away.
And there will be new mermaids,
and a moon will shine for them—
and they too will melt into the fog.
        Everything's a blessing: life! and us! and the world! and death!
OLD MERMAID (*painstakingly smoothing her disentangled, sparse hair with a comb*). What, you're not going to sing the songs? Go on. Especially since the moon is late today. It'll start to fade.

YOUNG MERMAID (*not averting her gaze*). I don't want to, Auntie. The song is so boring.

OLD MERMAID (*displeased*). What do you mean, boring! It's a good song. What sorts of songs do you want?

YOUNG MERMAID. Here's what I wanted to ask you about, Auntie: Our songs say we live, look at the moon, and then melt into the fog, as if there had been no mermaid at all. Why is it like that?

OLD MERMAID. What do you mean, why? The hour for each of us comes, and, well, we melt away. Our lifetime is easy, long: We live three, four hundred years.

YOUNG MERMAID. And then into the fog?

OLD MERMAID. And into the fog.

YOUNG MERMAID. Nothing more?

OLD MERMAID. Nothing. What more do you want?

YOUNG MERMAID (*after deep thought*). Is it like that for all living creatures, Auntie?

OLD MERMAID (*with conviction*). For all of them. (*Silence.*) No, wait, I forgot. Not all. I heard from my own aunt that it's not like that for all of them. There are people. I've seen them. And you've seen them, too, from afar. Well, it's said that they don't float away into the fog. They have an immortal soul.

YOUNG MERMAID (*opening her eyes wide*). They never die?

OLD MERMAID. No, no! They die. And their time here is—terribly short; they don't live a hundred years even. Their bodies disintegrate in the earth, but they don't mind, because humans have an undying soul; it just keeps living. I think that after a human's death, it's even better, easier. Their bodies are thick, full of blood, heavy.

YOUNG MERMAID. But their soul is light, like us?

OLD MERMAID. Well, perhaps lighter. For us there's still death, but not for the soul.

YOUNG MERMAID (*after a silence, suddenly, imploringly*). Auntie! Dear! Tell me everything that you know about us, about people, about their soul! You know, you're old, but I was born just recently. Perhaps I'll just melt into the fog, and not find out, but I do want to know!

OLD MERMAID (*with surprise*). What a child! What's wrong with you? I'll tell you. Just give me a chance to remember. I heard very long ago.

(*Stops. The* YOUNG MERMAID *turns and stares at her face as intently as earlier she had stared at the clearing.*)

I don't know much, little one. Now I heard that before, long ago, there had always been people in the world, and various other living creatures, and mermaids, and others. People had heavy bodies, with blood, with short lives and death, but we mermaids and other water, wood, meadow, and desert creatures had light and immortal bodies.

YOUNG MERMAID. Immortal bodies? But people had an immortal soul?

OLD MERMAID. No, wait, don't confuse things. At that time people didn't have immortal souls. And time passed. People knew that we alone were immortal, and they respected us and were humble before us. But it was no good for them, with such short lives and death, too, and they only acted as if they were humble; but secretly they grumbled and thought something else. Then a Man was born among them, whom they called God, and He spilled his own blood for them and gave them an immortal soul.

YOUNG MERMAID. Blood?

OLD MERMAID. Yes, his own blood.

YOUNG MERMAID. For them? For all of them?

OLD MERMAID. Well, yes, for all people. But since then we've learned that we're not immortal, and we've begun to die. Our time is long, our death easy, but we don't have an immortal soul.

YOUNG MERMAID. That means, He, this Man, or, how did you say it, God—brought us death, but them life? Why do we have to die because of His blood?

OLD MERMAID. Blood for blood. We don't have blood.

YOUNG MERMAID. Auntie! Are people better than us? Do they live better?

OLD MERMAID. Well, I don't know! I heard that they're evil, that there is animosity among them, jealousy, hatred.... You don't understand, we have nothing of that. We are kind.

YOUNG MERMAID. Then why did the Man bring them life and us death, if we're better?

OLD MERMAID. I really don't know. My aunt told me that they have something besides anger and hatred, and that's the reason why; but what it's called—I've forgotten the word. Now "hatred" I remember—but that other word I don't recall. We don't have it either. Yes. My memory's gone bad.

(*Silence.*)

The moon's paled a bit. I'll bet morning's coming soon. It'll be time to rest.

YOUNG MERMAID (*as if waking up*). Auntie, dear! Don't you know any more?

OLD MERMAID. I guess not.

YOUNG MERMAID. But don't you know whether... it's somehow possible... that one of us... say, a mermaid... could make it so she also had a human immortal soul?

OLD MERMAID. I don't know. What a persistent thing you are! You're born a mermaid, wonderful, so live out your time. What else do you want?

YOUNG MERMAID. Then there's no way? It's impossible?

OLD MERMAID. I'm telling you—I don't know! Wait, I've heard something about that, too, but I don't remember at all.

YOUNG MERMAID. But who does remember? Who knows?

OLD MERMAID. If you're that anxious to know—ask the Witch. She lives in the woods; she was a person; I hear she sold her soul to someone for a long life; by now she's five hundred years old. She knows everything. She comes creeping here to our lake every night to drink. We don't see her, because she drags herself along just at dawn, when the sky's already pink. That's a dangerous time for us, because we don't dare see even a sliver of the sun.

YOUNG MERMAID. Is it then that the fog is strongest?

OLD MERMAID. Yes, the fog's there then. When I was younger, I was also brave. I'd sit 'til the very last minute. And I saw the Witch. She's no sun; she can't harm us. So, if you're not afraid—stay, wait for the Witch. She'll tell you everything. But it's time for me to rest, into the water and the mire. My old bones ache. We're all dropping into the water already.

(*One after the other, the* MERMAIDS *disappear into the water. The moon grows white, then pink. The fog is livelier and denser.*)

(*Rising with difficulty.*) I'm going. Morning's near.

YOUNG MERMAID. I'm not afraid, Auntie. Maybe, the Witch will come. I'm staying for sure.

OLD MERMAID (*indifferently*). She'll come, she'll come. Go ahead, stay.

(*She leaves. Picks her way through the rushes, which bend and crackle. A splash in the water is heard. The* YOUNG MERMAID *sits closer to the tree, nestles up to the trunk and waits, motionless, her knees grasped in her arms. The bell has fallen silent. It is quiet. The sky grows more and more pink, the fog rises higher. An old woman, small, wrapped up, and stooped over, walks out of the woods without a sound, as if she were crawling. She has her large, yellow face turned toward the ground. Crawling up to the lake, she lies on the bank and drinks at length. Not a sound is heard. Finally, the old woman rises slowly, sniffs the air and looks around. The* YOUNG MER-MAID *has gotten up and she is standing, holding onto a branch. The old woman turns toward her and lifts a hand to her eyes, protecting them from the pink light of the sunrise.*)

YOUNG MERMAID (*timidly*). Hello, Auntie.

WITCH. Hello. Only I'm not your auntie. I'm a witch.

YOUNG MERMAID. I know, Auntie Witch. I'm, well, here....

WITCH. I see that you're here. I see what sort you are, little fish. Why are you so late? The sun will soon rise. And it's harsh for you, the sun is. You'd best not misjudge it.

YOUNG MERMAID. You're late, Auntie Witch. And I was waiting for you.

WITCH. For me? But why would you wait for me? Do you need me for some reason? Speak quickly, don't hem and haw. The sun is about to come up.

YOUNG MERMAID (*hurrying*). I will right away, Auntie. You see, today I heard different things about us, about mermaids, and about people.... That apparently we die—we turn to fog, and there's nothing more. But people, it seems, have an immortal soul, because blood was spilled for them. Is that true?

WITCH. It's true. What else?

YOUNG MERMAID. And I just wanted to ask you—surely you know—is it possible to make it so that a mermaid could also have an immortal soul? Tell me, Auntie, dear! You know!

(*The* WITCH *looks at her and suddenly begins to laugh silently, her body shaking. The* YOUNG MERMAID *is silent, holds her gaze, and is frightened.*)

Why are you laughing? Why are you laughing? Is it impossible?

(*The* WITCH *laughs.*)

(*Trembling and raising her voice.*) So there's no way? It's impossible?

WITCH. It's possible, it's possible! Ooh, you are funny, little fishie! I haven't laughed in a long time. I've waited a long time for a little fish like you. What do you mean, impossible? Hold on, I'll catch my breath.

YOUNG MERMAID (*with happiness and entreaty*). Auntie! Dear! So it is possible? Teach me! And then whatever you'd like....

WITCH. Wait, wait. I said it's possible, so it's possible. I'll teach you. And I don't need anything from you for the lesson.

YOUNG MERMAID. You are good, Auntie Witch.

WITCH. No, what's so good about it? I'm helping you for my own amusement. I help everyone. Both little fishies like you, and also people, when there's occasion to. Somebody wants something—I'll give it right to them—here you go! And I don't ask anything for it: I have a little fun, and that's all I need. And I'll teach you how a mermaid can get an immortal soul, since you want one. Sit down, little girl, on my old lap. The sun will wait.

(*They sit down on the bank near the reeds.*)

(*Groaning and wrapping herself up.*) It's cold this morning. The fog's high. It'll be a bright sun.

(*Silence.*)

All right, little fishie, so you really want an immortal soul?

YOUNG MERMAID (*lifting her eyes*). Yes.

WITCH. Does it bother you that... he spilled his blood for people, but not for you creatures?

YOUNG MERMAID (*thinking*). I don't know.... It should bother me.

WITCH. Well, then, listen, young lady: I'll teach you. You must approach people.

YOUNG MERMAID (*frightened*). People? I don't know where people are.

WITCH. Listen when you're spoken to. I know. There are people not far away from here. You go through the clearing in the forest, and there you'll see a cell, a little wooden sort of house, a human living place. And nearby, on a little hill, there's a chapel that you'll recognize by its high bell tower. You go there tomorrow night. Don't go at this time, but earlier, when it's darker. Just make sure that the bell is not ringing. If the bell is ringing, it means they're celebrating morning services, not sleeping.

YOUNG MERMAID. Auntie, I'm afraid. Are there many of them? And how will I talk to them?

WITCH. If you're afraid, that's your business, don't go. I'm only telling you how to do it. There are two people there: an old one and a young one. At first you won't have to talk with them. You just go into the little cell, make sure they don't see you, that they're asleep, and nestle up to one of them, close, warm yourself, have him breathe on you, touch him. He'll wake up and think he's seeing things; he'll start to say words over you, to drive you away, and perhaps he'll start to beat you—pay no attention, endure it, don't leave. He'll breathe on you and touch you—and you'll have a body, like people do, with blood. And then you'll be able to see the sun.

YOUNG MERMAID (*loudly*). And I'll have an immortal soul?

WITCH. Come, come, how hasty you are! You won't have an immortal soul. And your blood won't be warm, like people's, but cold.

YOUNG MERMAID (*despondently*). Then why am I doing all this?

WITCH. Because for a human soul you need a human body. Without a body that looks human, people won't let you among them, and the Man who spilled his warm blood won't give you a soul.

YOUNG MERMAID. Well, all right, Auntie, but once I have a body—what else do I need?

WITCH. You need the people to baptize you.

YOUNG MERMAID. What is that, Auntie—baptize?

WITCH. A sort of sign. The people will take you in, your blood will become warm, and the Man will give you an immortal soul.

YOUNG MERMAID. People are kind, aren't they? Then tomorrow I'll ask them to baptize me.

WITCH. Hold on, you little fool. Kind or not, they won't baptize you. To them you are—unclean.

YOUNG MERMAID (*sadly*). Unclean?

WITCH. Yes. Because they know so little, they're always afraid. Don't say anything to them at first, don't tell them anything, so they won't be afraid, and they'll get used to you. And keep living with them, warm yourself, and get a body. And then when one of them is... when one starts to be very kind to you, and you to him—then reveal yourself to him and ask to be baptized.

YOUNG MERMAID. I'm kind to everyone.

WITCH. Well, that doesn't count. It's when you start to be especially kind, to one in particular.

YOUNG MERMAID. And then he'll agree to baptize me?

WITCH. I don't know. Perhaps he still won't agree. Then you won't get an immortal soul.

YOUNG MERMAID. Auntie Witch! Dear! What do you mean? If he doesn't agree—then there's no other way at all?

WITCH. Quiet! You even scared a frog. And don't interrupt me, because we barely have a minute left. I didn't tell you he wouldn't agree. I'm just saying—it may happen.... Well, and then there is another way....

YOUNG MERMAID (*joyfully*). Truly? Is there? Is there?

WITCH. Only it's not for you. I know you, my kind little fishies. I won't tell you that other way just now. Try this one first. What, are you all afraid?

YOUNG MERMAID. No.

WITCH. Obviously, you want warm blood and a human soul very much?

YOUNG MERMAID. Yes.

WITCH (*laughs at length and silently, finally stops*). Fine. You're very funny, little fishie. Go tomorrow. Remember: Warm yourself, warm yourself up next to them! They'll start asking where you're from—say you forgot. When they start to tell you things—listen.

YOUNG MERMAID. You say—there's two of them in the cell. Which one should I approach first, the old one or the young one?

WITCH. It doesn't matter. (*After thinking.*) Better go to the younger one, he sleeps more deeply, you'll be able to breathe him in. And he's strict about temptation. He won't cut you any slack. He'll wake up and beat you mercilessly. But that's just what you need. As long as he doesn't beat you to death. (*Laughs.*)

YOUNG MERMAID (*considering it, seriously*). He won't kill me. Thank you, Auntie Witch.

WITCH. Don't thank me, don't thank me! My fun is dear to me. In case you need something, little girl, I'm not far away. I gather herbs in these parts. Oh! I nearly forgot! If he really wants to kill you—cross yourself, he'll calm down.

YOUNG MERMAID. But how do I do that? What is it?

WITCH. It's also a sign. I can't show you how. But I can tell you. Take three fingers.... Not those, those! Yes, that's it. Then put them to your forehead, then to your chest, then to your right shoulder, then to your left. How odd you are! Here... like this, and like this.... Again. Good. Don't forget. And now, my dear little fishie, hurry along. Right away, here's the sun.

(*The birds have raised a din. The sky is red. The bell is heard more often and a little louder than during the night. The* YOUNG MERMAID *still wants to say something, but the* WITCH *waves her hand, and the* YOUNG MERMAID *jumps into the water and disappears. At that very second the sun rises. The* WITCH *watches the circles of ripples expanding in the water and laughs silently, shaking.*)

See how she jumped, just like a little frog! A very funny little girl. Well now, what will my little monks say. I always help them. Show them the path. Let them save their immortal souls. That's their business.

(*Drags herself into the forest, continuing to laugh and mumble something. The bell grows louder and louder.*)

(*The curtain falls quietly.*)

SCENE 2

Early morning, foggy, with no sun. The woods. A clearing in the forest. On the right—a wooden cell. Beyond it the corner of a chapel is visible. On the left—a narrow path at the end of which a lake barely glitters. Between the open door to the cell and a wall, in the corner, lies the YOUNG MERMAID, *curled into a ball. Her face is covered by fairly short, disheveled hair. Near her, bent over, stands* FR. PAFNUTY. *He is wearing an old monastic cassock and on his head is a skullcap. His face is small, bright, with wrinkles. He has a sparse, gray, wedge-shaped beard.* NIKODIM, *a novice, stands at some distance, in consternation. His face is young and pale, like a rock, with sunken cheeks. His eyebrows are thick and furrowed.*

FR. PAFNUTY. Alive! A living girl, Nikodim! You nearly killed a child! She's barely breathing. She's awfully cold. But a girl, a girl!

(*The* YOUNG MERMAID *is silent.*)

(*Bending closer and moving her hair aside.*) Truly, you almost killed her. What if we had destroyed a baptized soul! Really, Nikodim. What came over you? Were you half asleep?

NIKODIM (*flatly*). I was tempted.

FR. PAFNUTY. Tempted! What are we, saints! Temptation must yet be earned from the Lord. We're no match for those holy men who've been tempted! But you grew proud—and nearly killed a child, an innocent girl, a living human being! Look what a glorious girl she is! She's very frightened.

NIKODIM (*taking two steps*). Father Pafnuty, pray cover her.

FR. PAFNUTY. Go, go, in the cell on the peg I have an old, short cassock. Bring it here.

(NIKODIM *exits.*)

Don't be afraid, little girl. We won't do you any harm. Tell me, whose little girl are you?

(*The* YOUNG MERMAID *slowly raises her eyes to him and is silent.*)

What's your name? Are you baptized?

(NIKODIM *returns with the cassock.* FR. PAFNUTY *clumsily and tenderly tries to clothe the* YOUNG MERMAID. NIKODIM *turns away.*)

NIKODIM. She doesn't have a cross.
FR. PAFNUTY. Well, she probably lost it. We'll give her a cross.
NIKODIM. We mustn't, if she's not baptized.

(*The* YOUNG MERMAID *looks and listens. At the last words it seems she has remembered something and, raising her hand, she tries to make the sign of the cross.*)

FR. PAFNUTY (*joyfully*). You see, you see, she's crossing herself, she's baptized! Her soul is God's. I told you! But you nearly destroyed her in your pride. Sit down, sit down, little girl. Don't be afraid. It's all right now.

(*The* YOUNG MERMAID *embraces* FR. PAFNUTY *and presses close to him.*)

She cuddles like a small child. She doesn't speak at all. Perhaps she's feeble-minded. She probably cuddled up to you, in a childlike sense, and you go on about temptation! Are you mute, little girl? Can you speak?
YOUNG MERMAID (*barely audible*). I can.
FR. PAFNUTY (*cheerfully*). That's wonderful. Tell us—don't be afraid—where did you come from?
YOUNG MERMAID. I... don't know.
FR. PAFNUTY. What do you mean, you don't know?
YOUNG MERMAID. I don't remember.
FR. PAFNUTY. And you don't remember who you belong to?
YOUNG MERMAID. I don't remember.
FR. PAFNUTY. But what is your name?
YOUNG MERMAID. I don't remember.
FR. PAFNUTY. Well, everything's "I don't remember"! You try and remember. What were you called? Annushka or something?

YOUNG MERMAID. Yes.

FR. PAFNUTY. Very well, so it's Annushka. We'll start calling you that, too. Now, remember some more.

NIKODIM. Phantasm.

FR. PAFNUTY. Enough with your phantasm! This is God's child. God didn't give her reason; He made her one of the holy fools. She makes the sign of the cross, and all you can say is "phantasm"! (*To the* YOUNG MERMAID.) Don't be afraid, Annushka. Let me stroke your little head. That cassock isn't too long, is it?

NIKODIM. Father Pafnuty, pray ring for mass.

FR. PAFNUTY. Hold on, hold on! Don't we have some bread left in there? Could you bring it: Perhaps she wants to eat. Would you like to eat, Annushka?

(NIKODIM *disappears silently and brings the bread. The* YOUNG MERMAID *takes the bread from the hands of* FR. PAFNUTY *and eats it greedily.*)

NIKODIM. She eats without crossing herself.

FR. PAFNUTY. Do you know how to pray to God, Annushka?

YOUNG MERMAID. To whom?

FR. PAFNUTY. To God. Can it be you don't know who God is?

YOUNG MERMAID. God? No, I know. The one who spilled his blood for people?

FR. PAFNUTY (*joyfully*). Do you hear that, Nikodim? She knows of Christ, our true God. She knows that He, the Lord, spilled His blood for us. My little holy fool, you don't remember your own name, but you remember that. Do you know how to pray to Him, do you know any prayers?

YOUNG MERMAID (*softly*). I don't know. Teach me, tell me.

FR. PAFNUTY. I'll teach you, teach you, little girl. One must pray to our Heavenly King. Since you've lost your way, we'll give you bread, teach you a prayer, and then take you home, if you remember where you lived.

YOUNG MERMAID. I don't remember! I don't know! I didn't live anywhere. I want to live here, with you. You'll teach me to pray.

NIKODIM. We should send her off into the forest.

FR. PAFNUTY (*with reproach*). There you go again! What do you mean, send a child off into the forest? Christ said: "Do not prevent the children from coming to Me," and I'm going to drive a hungry, cold child off into the forest? As you like, Nikodim, but I can't bring myself to do so. We should take the child in, warm her, teach her. As she doesn't have a home—let her live with us in the glory of our Heavenly King, for His is the Kingdom, Power, and Glory.

NIKODIM (*flatly*). Amen.

FR. PAFNUTY (*stroking the* YOUNG MERMAID's *head*). If you have no shelter, little girl, live here, and may God be with you.

NIKODIM. Pray, Father Pafnuty, ring for mass.

FR. PAFNUTY. Wait a little. (*To the* YOUNG MERMAID.) So you don't know any prayers, Annushka? What do you know? Can you do anything? Try to remember.

YOUNG MERMAID. I... know songs. I sang different songs in the meadow. I'll sing them for you later.

NIKODIM. Instead of prayers—she knows festival tunes.

FR. PAFNUTY. So what? Song is also prayer. To each his own. All is pure for a pure soul. Do you think a lark in the heavens does not pray to the Creator? You know how sonorously and cheerfully its songs pour forth. All earthly voices are praise to God. Go, Nikodim, Lord be with you, ring the bell.

(NIKODIM *approaches for the blessing without glancing at the* YOUNG MERMAID *and leaves in the direction of the chapel.*)

Annushka, you really don't remember your father and mother?

YOUNG MERMAID. My father and mother? I don't know. We have all aunts.... (*Quickly.*) I had an auntie.

FR. PAFNUTY. I see. And where is she now?

YOUNG MERMAID. I don't know.

FR. PAFNUTY. Poor child! You don't know a parent's caress.

YOUNG MERMAID. We also had grandpas.... They were old, like you. Only you are better, kinder! There weren't any like you—so kind! I'll always be with you. And you teach me to pray, Grandpa! And I will teach you my songs, if you want, I'll teach you!

FR. PAFNUTY (*laughs*). Hah, what a sharp one! We have our own songs, liturgical ones. (*Thinks for a moment.*) Don't be afraid of Nikodim, Annushka. He has committed his soul to Christ. The path he has taken is severe. He fulfills an order of obedience, and, no doubt, is more pious than his own superiors. The Lord in his wisdom is revealed to him, he reads the holy books, every word of God is known to him. Whereas I praise my God simply. Blades of grass emerge from the earth, I am attentive and rejoice in life, and think about the Creator. Perhaps the Lord will forgive me my simplicity.

(*The strike of the bell sounds.* FR. PAFNUTY *crosses himself, the* YOUNG MERMAID *looks at him and also crosses herself. The bell rings more and more loudly, powerfully, and often.* FR. PAFNUTY, *without noticing himself, begins to sing with a shaky, old, and soft voice. Toward the end, the* YOUNG MERMAID *sings just audibly with him, looking at him and trying to learn the words.*)

We praise Thee, Creator of heaven and earth,
We sing Thy glory, Almighty One.
May Thy blessed mercy, strength,
and power be forever;
light, hope, and life are in Thee,
Thy name will cover the earth,
we praise Thee, Creator of heaven and earth.

(*The bell rings.*)

(*Curtain.*)

SCENE 3

The same place in the woods, near the cell. In the heat of the afternoon. FR.
PAFNUTY *sits near the wall of the cell on a stone serving as a bench and
laboriously weaves a bast shoe.* NIKODIM *stands at the edge of the clearing in the forest and, putting his hand to his eyes, looks attentively into the
distance, in the direction of the lake.*

FR. PAFNUTY. What are you looking at, Nikodim? What is there to see? Is
someone coming?

NIKODIM (*after a silence*). No, no one. It's just that she seems to be bathing
again.

FR. PAFNUTY. Annushka? Let her bathe, Christ be with her. It's hot.

NIKODIM. No matter when you look over there, there's always something
white on the lake. She's always bathing. She's always hot. She even bathes
after vespers. Yesterday the stars had already started to glow, the dew had
fallen, and she—sets off for the lake.

FR. PAFNUTY. There is no sin in God's water. Let the child swim in the
glory of the Lord. The thoughts you have, Nikodim. I can't make them
out, only there's something wrong with them. Enough, is it not the enemy who disturbs you? Temptations are delivered invisible, from our
heart.

NIKODIM (*is silent, stares, then lets his hand drop and takes two steps toward* FR. PAFNUTY). No, Father.... But just yesterday I was thinking
about us. We used to live in the village.... People would come to you. You
helped them, prayed with them. And the Lord loved you for your holy
life, gave you the power to heal the sick....

FR. PAFNUTY (*frightened, waving his hands*). What are you saying, what
are you saying! Stop! It's a sin! Me, a holy man? I am a great sinner.

NIKODIM (*not listening*). And you chose the most difficult path. You
wanted to withdraw from people, cut yourself off from them, so that
your prayer would go more directly to the Lord. I, too, burned with the
desire for that path. You didn't reject me, and I took a vow of obedience.
We lived in peace, and we labored. But now people have found us, and
there is no longer the same sweetness and severity in our path. What are
your thoughts on this, Father?

FR. PAFNUTY (*sets aside the bast shoe*). Are you talking about Annushka? (*Grows silent.*) This is what I will say to you, Nikodim. Forgive me, I'll tell you simply. Now, you say that I wanted a path and so withdrew to the cell. I don't know, Nikodim. I wasn't thinking about that, but people became horrible to me, it was horrible to live with them. What kind of holy man am I? How could I dare to heal? I can do little more than pray for the forgiveness of my sins. Here my heart is cheerful, and there is no labor for me here, but great ease. Perhaps you know better, perhaps it's a sin, but my heart simply loves the sun, and the water, and the tiny blade of grass, and the Lord God, Who created all, to Him Alone belongs eternal praise.

NIKODIM. Amen. Father Pafnuty, people are also His creation. And if you have cut yourself off from the people not in the name of the most burdensome labor....

FR. PAFNUTY. I was not cutting myself off from men, Nikodim. I'm telling you—it was horrible for me with them. It was horrible, there were so many of them. And they distanced themselves from the Lord, and I, unworthy as I am, did not have the strength to teach and admonish them. It was Christ who brought the sword to the earth, and I am only his slave; I am not a teacher. My heart has languished greatly. Perhaps it was not from my strength, but from my weakness, and love, that I went out into the desert. The Lord created my soul without cleverness, so He will not punish me for my weakness.

NIKODIM. I took my vow of obedience not out of love, but out of zeal.

FR. PAFNUTY. I know, Nikodim, I know. Your path is severe. You are, perhaps, much more worthy than I. The Lord is revealed to you through reason. Every word of God is known to you from books. You begrudge no effort for the Lord. And much is asked of you, because much is given to you. Observe the severity of your path, Nikodim.

NIKODIM. We must seclude ourselves in God and avoid all the temptations of people. But another came to us, whom you took in.

FR. PAFNUTY. Are you speaking of Annushka again? Is she really an ordinary person? She's a child of God. She lives like a blade of grass and rejoices in the stars and the water. Is she that awful? She's no ordinary person.

NIKODIM. Perhaps she's not a person at all.

FR. PAFNUTY. What did she ever do to you? Why are you driving away a child? No, you have bad thoughts, Nikodim. I am a great sinner before my Lord, but the child has a pure soul. I will not let you harm her. How in God's name could I drive her away? You yourself know that it is said: I want mercy, not sacrifice.

NIKODIM. It is also said: He who will not leave his own mother and father and his own home to follow—he is unworthy of Me.

FR. PAFNUTY (*sadly*). The books of reason open wider to your mind than to mine. But do not harm my Annushka. Let her be.

NIKODIM. Pray, Father Pafnuty, let us go to the well for water.

(*Presently the* YOUNG MERMAID *runs up, cheerful, with her wet hair down over her shoulders. She is wearing the same old cassock; in her hair are seaweed and flowers. She is holding a garland woven from round, yellow water lilies. She doesn't notice* NIKODIM *and throws herself right at* FR. PAFNUTY.)

YOUNG MERMAID. Grandpa! My kind grandpa! Are you weaving bast shoes? I was at the lake. And, look, Grandpa, I made you a... (*Suddenly she sees* NIKODIM *and stops, not daring to continue.*)

FR. PAFNUTY (*hurriedly*). Go on, then, for the water, Nikodim. The pail's at the well. In the name of the Father, and the Son, and the Holy Spirit!

NIKODIM. Amen. (*Approaches for the blessing and withdraws.*)

FR. PAFNUTY (*tenderly*). Well, Annushka? What were you thinking?

YOUNG MERMAID (*follows* NIKODIM *out with her eyes, then speaks quietly*). I'm afraid of him, Grandpa.

FR. PAFNUTY. Enough, what is there to fear? He wouldn't harm anyone. We're not clever, but he understands the word of God. It is not given to us to understand, but to him it is.

YOUNG MERMAID (*thoughtfully*). I don't know about that, Grandpa. It's just that his eyes—they're like two wax candles, like the ones you have in the chapel that barely glimmer. But your eyes, Grandpa, are just like two little stars at night. I don't fear you, but I fear him.

FR. PAFNUTY. Fear God.

YOUNG MERMAID. But I don't fear God. You yourself said many times that God is kind, kinder than all people. If he is kinder than you—why be afraid of him? (*She sits near* FR. PAFNUTY *and begins to arrange the flowers. Then suddenly she jumps up with the garland of yellow water lilies in her hand.*) Grandpa! I forgot! I wove this for you at the lake! See, isn't pretty?

FR. PAFNUTY. It's pretty, it's pretty. Beautiful. God's little flowers.

YOUNG MERMAID. But try it on! Let me put it on you.

FR. PAFNUTY (*laughing*). What, what are you doing, you joker! A garland on my skull cap!

YOUNG MERMAID. You said yourself—they're God's flowers. Look, how wonderful! With the flowers, you're like one of my own! And your skull cap is visible. The water lilies are along the edge of it. Can you smell them?

FR. PAFNUTY. It smells of water and mud. Hmm, it smells good.

YOUNG MERMAID. And now I'll sing you a song. Shall I? The water and the seaweed really made me want to sing.... (*She gets up and stands before him.*) Here is my little song, Grandpa. I think I've sung it to you before. You join in after me. (*She sings, first quietly, then more and more loudly, with slow easy movements, as the* MERMAIDS *did in their dance.*)

The water sparkles through the reeds.
In the sky green stars have caught fire.
The moon rises above the woods.
Look, sisters, the stars are going out!
The fog coils, as if alive....
The fog is—our watery soul.
It thins and, melting, disappears....
The fog is—our life and our watery death.
Tonight we are alive and joyful,
Our joy is like the moonlight.
Let us call to one another,
We'll lend our voices to each other!
We of the lake, river, wood,
valley, desert,
underground and aboveground,
great and small,
shaggy and bare,
We'll all let each other know we're here!
O-ye! O-ye!
Answer, brothers! Answer, sisters!

(*At the end of the song* NIKODIM*'s singing is heard; he is returning with the pails of water. At first* FR. PAFNUTY *and the* YOUNG MERMAID *do not hear him.*)

NIKODIM (*offstage*).

      Eternal praise and glory,
To our One Lord,
Just and Fearsome!
Eternal praise and glory!
Blessed is His searching mercy,
Blessed is His punishing right hand,
Thy slaves serve Thee, Heavenly King,
Singing to Thee praise and glory.
To the Father—who sent His Son to death,
To the Son—who brought battle and division,
To the Spirit—that descended on the foolish—
      Glory for all eternity!

(*The* YOUNG MERMAID *falls silent, listening.*)

YOUNG MERMAID (*timidly*). Is he singing of that God you told me about?
NIKODIM (*closer*).

To Thee, Who brought not peace, but a sword,
To Thee, Who defeated death with Thy blood,
To Thy coming in power and glory,
To Thee, our Christ and God,
      Praise now and forever!

YOUNG MERMAID. He defeated death with His blood, Grandpa? Tell me again about Him and about how He gave people an eternal soul. Grandpa!

(NIKODIM *enters with the full pails. His eyes are lowered. But at the door to the cell he raises them, looks at* FR. PAFNUTY *and stops.*)

FR. PAFNUTY. What's wrong, Nikodim?
NIKODIM. The flowers...

FR. PAFNUTY (*smiling and removing the garland with slightly shaking hands*). It was she... the little joker... she adorned me. God's little flowers. She was singing me her childish songs. And she adorned me.

(NIKODIM *silently looks at the* YOUNG MERMAID. *She draws close to the old man and hides her face on his shoulder.*)

NIKODIM. I heard the songs. I wasn't far away.

FR. PAFNUTY. You heard? Well, good. What's wrong, Annushka? What are you hiding for? That's enough, sit down. What shall I tell you.... And you, Nikodim, go about your chores with God.

(NIKODIM *exits.* FR. PAFNUTY *strokes the* YOUNG MERMAID*'s head. She rises a bit and sits by the old man's feet.*)

(*After a silence.*) Yes. Don't be afraid, little girl. There's no sin in your singing songs. You're just a silly child. You praise God however you're able. (*Falls silent.*) It's just that your songs, from what I've heard of them, are all somehow... night songs.

YOUNG MERMAID (*sadly*). Yes, mine are all night songs.

FR. PAFNUTY. Well, learn some prayers, too. We'll start to sing prayers. God loves those such as you.

YOUNG MERMAID (*with surprise*). Love? What is that, Grandpa?

FR. PAFNUTY. What is what? Christ loved people and spilled His blood in order to save them.

YOUNG MERMAID. I know about blood, Grandpa, and you've told me a lot about Christ; but somehow I just haven't heard that one word; and I don't understand.

FR. PAFNUTY (*laughs*). You don't understand love? My silly little blade of grass! If you understand why Christ spilled His blood for you, then you also understand love.

YOUNG MERMAID (*sadly and seriously*). He didn't spill His blood for me, Grandpa.

FR. PAFNUTY. What? What are you saying, silly? That is a great sin. What do you mean, He didn't spill His blood for you?

YOUNG MERMAID (*looking aside*). Blood for blood only.

FR. PAFNUTY. I can't understand you. Let's sing a prayer instead.

YOUNG MERMAID (*decisively*). No, Grandpa! First tell me this: If I hadn't been baptized, would I have an immortal soul?

FR. PAFNUTY. Come now? And what about stillborn infants? They fly as angels to the throne of God. A human is born with an immortal soul. By His death Christ conquered human mortality.

YOUNG MERMAID (*as though to herself*). Human! (*To* FR. PAFNUTY.) But just the same, would you baptize me, Grandpa, if you knew I was unbaptized?

FR. PAFNUTY. But you *are* baptized. You make the sign of the cross; your name is Christian.

(*The* YOUNG MERMAID *cries.*)

(*Frightened.*) What are you worried about, Annushka? Hmm? What's wrong, child? In the time you've been living with us, you've sometimes been sad, but I've never seen a single tear. What is it?

YOUNG MERMAID (*through tears*). I don't know what it is myself, Grandpa. Don't leave me. Talk to me.

FR. PAFNUTY (*trying clumsily to dry her eyes with his wide sleeve*). Come now. Would I leave you, little girl? I've grown to pity you so, pity you so, just as if you were my own child. It's nearly a sin, because we are hermits, Nikodim says; we must cut ourselves off from all that is earthly. But I cannot overcome my joy. And you've grown in my heart, little girl, as my own God-given little daughter! You lack human cunning, it's not horrible to be with you. Don't cry, little girl. Tell me what's wrong. And I'm ready to give up my soul to you.

YOUNG MERMAID (*suddenly hugs him impetuously*). Your soul? Your soul, to me? What did you say, Grandpa?

FR. PAFNUTY (*smiling uncertainly*). And just why do you want my soul? You have your own.

YOUNG MERMAID (*softly*). I don't understand you, Grandpa. I wasn't asking about your soul. I thought, how kind you've become toward me, especially compared to everyone else, and I thought that you would agree to give me your soul. Because I don't have a soul, Grandpa.

FR. PAFNUTY. Don't have a soul? The power of the cross be with us! What do you mean, Annushka? What do you mean, dear?

YOUNG MERMAID. I don't have a soul! Do you understand? I don't! The man, Christ, God—came only for people; He didn't come for us. He forgot us! No, he didn't forget, because He brought us death with His death! We used to be immortal, but as soon as His blood fell on us—we began to die. As if it had scorched us!

(FR. PAFNUTY *watches her in horror and crosses himself.*)

(*Continuing.*) Why are you afraid of me? Don't be afraid. You have an immortal soul, and I don't. Perhaps, like you, I, too, would give up my soul to you, because you're also—dear to me; so dear that I cannot even say your name.... But only I have no soul, and no one to give it to and nothing to give it for. I don't have an earthly *or* a heavenly father.

FR. PAFNUTY. I do not fear you, child. As I said, so it is. You've grown in my heart. Tell your father everything that you think and know.

YOUNG MERMAID. Yes, I'll tell you. I must tell you. Listen.

(NIKODIM *enters and stops at the door. Neither the* YOUNG MERMAID *nor* FR. PAFNUTY *notice him.*)

The blood—scorched my soul, but it did not scorch the desire in me. I was born (*points to the clearing in the woods*) there, at the lake, I came from the water, from the mire. There are many of us there, living creatures, dying our deaths, bloodless. People despise us, call us unclean. You see, we melt away into the fog, and it's the end for all of us. The Lord despised them, people think, how can we not despise them? But just tell me, if God wanted to kill us, why did He leave us the desire for an immortal soul? And such a desire, such a will, that it's impossible to resist?

FR. PAFNUTY (*softly*). Impossible? Is it possible, then, that it is *His* will? Can it be it's not your will but His? Can it be He is calling you to come meet Him? How could He, the Blessed One, make it so that there would be no answer to His will? If it is His will that you should desire an immortal soul, He must want to give you one. Pray to Him, child.

YOUNG MERMAID (*joyfully*). Grandpa! It's just as I thought! You told me about Him, and then I thought and thought. And you taught me how to pray. In fact, I came from there, from the lake, so that you would teach me to pray. But they told me—and it's the truth—that I wouldn't have an immortal soul until a man... one just like you... gave me the sign. And as soon as he puts the sign on me—my blood will become warm like his, and I will receive an immortal soul.

FR. PAFNUTY (*sternly and seriously*). What sign are you talking about?

YOUNG MERMAID. Baptize me... Grandpa.

NIKODIM (*takes several steps forward*). The Lord is just and terrible. And His ways are inscrutable.

(*The* YOUNG MERMAID *moves away in horror.*)

FR. PAFNUTY (*confused*). You were here, Nikodim? Did you hear what the silly child was saying? Perhaps she dreamed it. Well, well. Your works are miraculous, Lord. But we mustn't assume it is so. She herself doesn't know what she is saying.

NIKODIM. Father Pafnuty, all that she was saying about herself is the truth. It has long been revealed to my mind. Do you not believe me?

FR. PAFNUTY (*with effort*). So what? Even if it is the truth—is our path not clear? How can we fail to do the will of the One who sent her and us?

NIKODIM. What are you saying, Father? Who dares take in one rejected by the Lord? Or did He not know what He was doing when He brought men life and sent the unclean creatures into the darkness? How can we transgress heavenly laws? Would you really dare to baptize a cur? Even a cur is more pure than the issue of Satan marked with death by the Lord Himself. Do you know what the holy books say about that?

FR. PAFNUTY. I don't know, Nikodim. I don't know the books. I don't have the mind for the sacred books. But it just seems to me one must not condemn a soul that asks to be born to God. It must be saved.

NIKODIM. In the books it is said of God's reason that he who has transgressed the law will die. And if you blaspheme the mystery of baptism—your soul will perish. There is no forgiveness for one who has transgressed the law.

YOUNG MERMAID (*in despair*). Grandpa! What is he saying? You will destroy your own soul? You won't have a soul? Grandpa, my dear...

(*She wants to throw herself at him, but* NIKODIM *raises his hand and stops her.*)

NIKODIM. In the name of the One Heavenly King, who died for us on the cross and was resurrected on the third day, I adjure you, creation of the enemy, depart from this place. You were unworthy of the Lord in flesh and in spirit.... It is not for us, His servants, to judge and correct His deeds.

FR. PAFNUTY (*rising*). Brother Nikodim! The vow of obedience has not been lifted, and you submitted yourself to it of your own will. Your zeal is great; the wisdom of the books is revealed to you. But why do you fret about my soul? Am I myself not free to think of it? Am I not free to lose it, if I consider it just? I do not recall all of God's words, but these I recall: Those who seek to save their own soul will lose it. Leave us now, brother. Go. In the name of the Father, and the Son, and the Holy Spirit.

NIKODIM (*after a silence, with effort*). Amen.

(*He exits slowly, without taking his eyes from the* YOUNG MERMAID, *who is trembling.* FR. PAFNUTY *follows him out with his eyes, then sits on the stone, saddened, and falls to thinking.*)

YOUNG MERMAID (*simply*). Grandpa, don't be afraid of me. Only tell me, is it true?

FR. PAFNUTY. What, my dear?

YOUNG MERMAID. That God will take away your soul, if you save mine? He just said...

FR. PAFNUTY. I don't know. Nikodim knows, the word of God is revealed to him, he understands the scriptures. But I judge according to my simple reasoning. It is not given to me to read in the books. Perhaps he is right.

YOUNG MERMAID. Is that what you believe? Well, then it's the truth.

FR. PAFNUTY. Perhaps I will destroy my soul.

YOUNG MERMAID. No, Grandpa. If it's true, then I'd better go. I'll go just where he told me.

FR. PAFNUTY (*rouses himself*). Where, silly?

YOUNG MERMAID (*motioning with her hand to the right*). There, to the lake. You mustn't baptize me. You mustn't destroy your soul.

FR. PAFNUTY (*clearly*). Listen to me, child. Here's what I'm going to tell you, plain and simple. What the truth is—I don't know, if I destroy my soul—that's His holy will! But I just can't let you go. I pity you so much that I have no strength left whatsoever. And do not go against me, child. I can't help giving up my soul, if God takes it. I pity you very much. I am going to baptize you, child.

(*The* YOUNG MERMAID *wants to say something, but cries.*)

(*Continuing.*) I told you about Christ, I taught you how to pray to Him; it's not for me to drive you away from Him.

(*The clap of the bell is heard. The* YOUNG MERMAID *shudders.*)

Well, what's wrong? That was Nikodim ringing for vespers. It's time. Now, little girl, don't go to the chapel; stay here awhile. Sit in the cell if you like. And later, when the service has ended, go with God to the chapel. Take care not to be late. I'll wait there. After vespers I'll baptize you. (*Hugs and kisses her.*) Now, there's no need to cry, daughter. Let's rejoice. And let His holy will be done. Let me bless you. In the name of the Father, and the Son, and the Holy Spirit. There. Say "amen."

YOUNG MERMAID (*barely audible*). Amen.

(*Kneels and kisses his hand, crying. When* FR. PAFNUTY *withdraws, she falls face-down on the ground. Her hair covers her face. The bell rings thinly and regularly. It grows dark. A young, still rose-colored moon is seen between the trees. The* WITCH *comes through the opening in the forest, wrapped up, her long yellow face moving about. In her hands she has a little bag of coarse cloth with herbs that she stoops over from time to time to cut. She comes closer to the prone* YOUNG MERMAID, *stops above her and loses herself in silent laughter.*)

WITCH. What a funny one! It's really caught on now, smoking and crackling. (*Louder.*) Greetings, little fishie! Recognize me?

YOUNG MERMAID (*raising herself a bit and pushing aside her hair, frightened*). Who's there? Are vespers over? Is that you, Grampy?

WITCH (*laughs*). Not Grampy but Witchie! You're not too bright. What do you need Grandpa for? It's not time to be baptized yet. Nikodim's still ringing.

YOUNG MERMAID (*sits and looks around*). Ah, it's you, Auntie Witch. I almost didn't recognize you. It's dark already. I'm not *going* to be baptized. Vespers aren't over yet. I'll still make it.

WITCH. Make it?

YOUNG MERMAID. Leave.

WITCH. Where are you planning to go, little girl?

YOUNG MERMAID. To the lake.

WITCH. You'll probably drown in the lake now. You're not as you were, little fishie. Your blood isn't warm yet, but your flesh *is* firm. You got that from people. Be careful of the lake.

YOUNG MERMAID. I don't care.

WITCH (*laughs*). Don't try to pull one over on me, you won't fool me! You've made up your mind, then? You don't want an immortal soul anymore? And who told you that your grandpa would lose his soul for sure if he baptized you? That, my friend, is impossible to know for sure. So you don't want a soul anymore?

YOUNG MERMAID (*with despair*). Why do you torment me? What do you want? I don't want to, I can't, if it isn't certain that he won't lose his soul, if he *might* lose it! Why didn't you tell me this before?

WITCH. Because if I'd have told you then, "Look, the man who agrees to baptize you might lose his soul for yours"... then you'd have said to me, "What are you talking about; he's so kind!" But now.... How foolish you are! Don't you think I see how upset you are? I came to help you, and you reproach me.

YOUNG MERMAID (*mistrustfully*). Help? How will you help me?

WITCH. Just look how proud you've become! You learned from people about the Man, and so you don't want to believe me any longer.

YOUNG MERMAID. Well, hurry up and tell me, if you have something to say.

WITCH. Don't get smart with me, little girl. If it weren't amusing for me, I'd leave you here halfway. If you're going to swagger—I'll leave you immediately.

YOUNG MERMAID. Tell me, Auntie Witch.

WITCH. I see, I see everything. He's agreed to baptize you…. But you should go to the lake. Obviously you don't need an immortal soul quite so much….

YOUNG MERMAID. Why do you keep tormenting me for no reason?

WITCH. Well, I'll stop, I'll stop. Remember, little girl, I said that if the old man doesn't agree to baptize you, then there's another way? Even without baptism it is possible to receive an immortal soul.

YOUNG MERMAID. And Grandpa's soul won't perish?

WITCH. No-no! It will be sheltered by the crown of the One… the Man. That's what all the people will say.

YOUNG MERMAID (*folding her arms*). Auntie! Teach me! I'm not scared of anything now. I'm ready for anything.

WITCH (*laughs*). I see that you've changed a lot, little fishie. But make sure you don't thank me too soon. Perhaps you will be scared. I've gathered the means for you. I have it here with me, in this little bag. Just wait. I nearly forgot. It isn't good for every situation. Tell me first, do you truly love this old man?

YOUNG MERMAID. What do you mean… love?

WITCH. Well, the way people love. They love their children, they love their fathers, mothers, brothers… each other, sometimes.

YOUNG MERMAID. I don't understand that word, Auntie.

WITCH (*with surprise*). Could the old man really not have explained it to you?

YOUNG MERMAID. No, he said the word. He says Christ loved people…. I didn't understand.

WITCH. Now-now, don't you name that… that Man… to me. What a stupid old man! He didn't explain a word like that. I guess I'll have to interpret. Listen. To love—that's when another becomes more dear to you than you are to yourself. You look at him—and you feel joy, and if he is happy and cheerful—then you are happy and cheerful.

YOUNG MERMAID (*listens greedily*). Yes, yes!

WITCH (*continuing*). And if you love someone, you don't begrudge him anything, you take from yourself and give to him. And if he hurts—then his pain hurts you even more. And if death comes for him—you yourself take his death, so that he won't die.

YOUNG MERMAID. Auntie! Dear! Thank you! I understand everything! I know it all, exactly...., I just didn't know the word. And what is more, Auntie... (*softly and distinctly*) moreover, if I love someone, and I hear— He is calling me, wants me... I must go to him!

WITCH (*confused*). Well that... now you're back... about the One. I was speaking to you of human love. So there, now you know, so tell me, do you love the old man? Because if you don't love him—just as I was saying, so that if a speck of dust fell on him it would cause you pain—then this way won't work.

YOUNG MERMAID. Not love Grandpa? You know, Auntie Witch. What are you asking for! Aren't I going into the lake, because if I don't go, his soul will die? I always want to call out to him as I sit with him and listen; it's quiet and pleasant for me to be with him, and just then I'm unable to call out, and that's painful. I am a part of him, as if I had been born of him, and what's good or bad for one of us is good or bad for both. And if it happens that something bad for me will be good for him—then will I not take the bad upon myself, and will it not become good for me?

WITCH. Well, fine. You've become happy. I've opened the floodgates for you. How do you like that, you've gotten used to people and started loving. And it's all the better for you. Here is the means, little girl. (*Not hurrying, she pulls from the little bag a knife with a long, thin blade. The blade is flexible, of steel, and gleams reddish and bright.*)

YOUNG MERMAID. What is that?

WITCH. A knife. And such a glorious one. Amazing, even. Here. You take it, and after vespers go to the chapel. When does the old man want to baptize you, after vespers? That means he'll wait for you at the entrance. He's a stubborn old man, too. You won't talk him out of it. He said he wants to baptize you, and he'll baptize you and not look back. And, who knows, he might lose his soul for your sake.

YOUNG MERMAID. I said I won't be baptized by him! Well, what then, Auntie? I don't understand....

WITCH. You don't interrupt me. Listen. Walk up to your old man—don't let him start talking—and stab him immediately with this knife. What strong hands you have there. Stab him so that the knife goes in deeply, and as his blood splatters on you, everything in you will immediately change; you'll become as people are, warm, and a soul will enter your body. Well, do you understand? Why are you staring? How dumb you are!

YOUNG MERMAID (*slowly*). That is... in order to... kill Grandpa?

WITCH. Well, yes. So that his blood, spilled by your hand, touches you. His soul, you see, cannot be killed with a knife. This will make things even easier for his soul. It will be hard on yours, perhaps. People say that... He does not forgive the one who spills blood. He will even torment your soul as punishment. So people say.

YOUNG MERMAID. No.... It's probably not like that. Torment for what? Wasn't His blood spilled for the sake of people?... And if it were human blood—for His sake?

WITCH. Well, I don't know anything about it. That's what people say. I've told you—after that, it's not my business. Choose as you like. Be baptized, or else go to the lake without a soul. You know best.

YOUNG MERMAID (*looking aside*). Well all right.... But it's just that... Auntie! Have pity on me! (*Nearly screams.*) How can I kill him, when his pain—is more painful for me than my own? How can I enter into such torment myself? You see I love him, as if I were part of him, as if I were born of him, as if his blood were my blood! But no, that's not it! I don't have the right word for that pain! (*Throws the knife; it quietly and harmoniously rings.*) No, I'm better off going to the lake. (*After a moment of silence.*) Now I feel better.

WITCH (*laughing quietly*). I know you feel better, little fishie. It's much easier to go to the lake. I told you that, about the knife. I know how difficult this is; not a single person nor any other creature has been able to take it upon themselves. Creatures, who were in the lake just like you, could not, because they do not know love. People know love—but they cannot because of the torment. But without love, these means are of no use.

YOUNG MERMAID (*repeating*). Of no use?

WITCH. No. If you want eternal life—you must earn it through unbearable torment. And perhaps, as people say, it will be eternal torment, if there is no forgiveness for blood.

YOUNG MERMAID. I don't care about that. I don't know. And if He wants my eternal soul in order to torment it—what does that matter? He wants it.

WITCH. He didn't give the strength. Because no one has such strength to carry it out. But there are means. Means that are just. Blood for blood. Blood was not spilled for you, and you have neither blood nor life. Blood will flow—and consume your death. But earthly creatures simply haven't the strength for it.

YOUNG MERMAID (*slowly picks up the knife and stares at it. She speaks softly, almost to herself*). He blessed me.... I will baptize you, child, he said. And don't cry. Let us rejoice, he said....

WITCH. Well, give the knife here. I must admit, I really just brought it here, because I wanted to have a look at you. I've seen the likes of you before, too. Give it to me. If you're going to the lake, then we're traveling the same path. It looks like your sisters and aunties are already coming out. (*Looks closely.*) An early moon. (*Falls silent.*) Then go get baptized. The ringing stopped a long time ago.

YOUNG MERMAID (*not listening and taking several steps about the stage with the knife in her hands*). And he also said something else as he was leaving. He said it and right afterwards he blessed me. His hand is so thin, so old.... What was it he said?

WITCH (*laughing*). How amusing! You're not at all yourself, little girl. Who knows what you're muttering. Give the knife to me, I say.

YOUNG MERMAID (*joyfully cries out*). I remember, I remember what he said! "Let His holy will be done!"

(*She runs out to the right. The* WITCH *watches her with disbelief and stops laughing.*)

WITCH. What a worthless girl! What's come over her? She'll lose the knife over there somewhere, and that's no joke. Such a nice little knife. I'll just wait and see if she comes back. Nothing doing! Now the old man will certainly baptize her. She didn't go straight to the lake, so she won't go. And the way she swaggered. (*Sits on a knoll.*) I'll just rest a moment. Will she go to him or not? Too bad about the knife. It's a nice little knife, brand-new.

(*She sighs, not laughing. She wraps herself up in her rags from time to time. The sky grows very dark, but on the ground it is light with cool shadows from the golden young moon. In the distance something white flashes vis-*

ibly. Something is carried in the wind, barely audible, not quite a song, not quite the rustling of the leaves.)

SONG (*very quietly*).
>Get up! Get up!
>Hurry! Hurry!
>The sky's above the lake.
>The sky's in the lake.

Where's the end to the sky above?
Where's the end to the sky below?
>Hurry! Hurry!

(*The barely audible sounds are drowned out by* NIKODIM*'s voice, also very far away, but a little clearer, and from the opposite side.* NIKODIM *is almost not singing, but speaking.*)

VOICE OF NIKODIM.
Thou art merciful, Lord,
long-patient and ever-merciful,
but the hour of Thy wrath shall come,
those not knowing Thee shall fall before Thee,
and Thy fury shall rain upon them.
Thou shalt reach out Thy right hand
and destroy earth and heaven....

(*Stops. Immediately the song from the lake, like the rustling of leaves, is heard.*)

Where's the end to the sky above?
Where's the end to the sky below?

WITCH (*angrily wrapping herself up*). There's no peace around here. And that one isn't coming! What's with her, is she mad? This is getting worrisome. Amusing indeed! And the noise all around. Perhaps the owls are yelling. (*Silence.*) She's dragging her feet. Let her fly to pieces, the little scoundrel!

(*The* WITCH *stands up. From the depths to the right, the* YOUNG MER-MAID *emerges very slowly. Her face is calm, her hands empty.*)

Where's the knife? Give me the knife!

(*The* YOUNG MERMAID *is silent. The* WITCH *takes a good look at her and steps back.*)

You...

YOUNG MERMAID (*calmly*). I cannot speak with you. Leave.

WITCH. I'm leaving. I'm leaving. (*Wrapping herself up in her rags and recoiling.*) The Man... has conquered.

(*She crawls off behind a tree and immediately disappears there. The* YOUNG MERMAID *stands motionless, listening carefully. As* NIKODIM *enters she turns toward him.* NIKODIM *is walking quickly, but he suddenly stops in the right corner of the stage, far from the* YOUNG MERMAID.)

NIKODIM (*loudly, his voice breaking*). Have you committed an evil deed? Have you spilled blood?

YOUNG MERMAID. I have.

NIKODIM. You killed the father?

YOUNG MERMAID. His soul is alive.

NIKODIM. The blood of the martyr cries out to the heavens. You will be henceforth and forever be da—

(*The* YOUNG MERMAID *raises her hand.* NIKODIM *stops.*)

YOUNG MERMAID. Now I'm—like you. It was *not my* will that was done. Blood was spilled for me.

NIKODIM. The cup of the Lord's patience overflows. Holy blood...

YOUNG MERMAID. Yes, holy blood. And the blood spilled by God for you—wasn't that holy?

NIKODIM. There is no forgiveness for your soul. There is no limit to the Lord's wrath. Eternal torments await you.

YOUNG MERMAID. Will He, whose will was done by me, give me eternal torment for my own torment? Because for His sake I spilled blood which was dearer to me than my own? He knows—dearer than my own! Where is the man who would fear torment after my torment? I am afraid of nothing. I went to the One Who called me, Who gave me the most difficult of paths, and He met me.

NIKODIM (*turning away and covering his face, impassively*). Let my hand not touch you. But tomorrow...

YOUNG MERMAID (*joyfully*). Do you hear the bell? No? But I hear it. There's no one to ring it. He's ringing it himself.

(*Very weak clangs of the bell are mingled with the distant song at the lake, so distant that the words cannot be heard.*)

NIKODIM. Tomorrow the people will learn of the death of the holy man, and they will come here. Blood calls out for vengeance. The people will kill you. Torment awaits you—your body and your soul.

YOUNG MERMAID (*looking him in the eye, clearly*). I don't care.

(*Curtain.*)

The Unknown Woman

Alexander Blok 1906

The portrait depicted a woman of truly unusual beauty. She was photographed in a black silk dress, of an extremely simple and elegant cut; her hair, evidently dark-blond, was done in a simple, domestic style; her eyes were dark, deep; her brow thoughtful; the expression on her face was passionate and somehow arrogant. Her face was somewhat thin, perhaps, and pale....

—Dostoevsky

"But how did you know it was I? Where have you seen me before? Really, what's going on here, apparently I've seen him somewhere?"...

"I have apparently seen you somewhere, too?"

"Where? Where?"

"I have definitely seen your eyes somewhere.... But this cannot be! I'm just... I've never even been here. Perhaps in a dream...."

—Dostoevsky

CHARACTERS

The Unknown Woman
Sky-Blue
Astrologer
Poet
Patrons and guests at a tavern and in a drawing room
Two doormen

THE FIRST VISION

A streetside tavern. The dull-white light of an acetylene lamp flickers in its crumpled shade. The wallpaper depicts completely identical ships with enormous flags. Their bows cut through sky-blue water. Outside the door, which opens often to admit patrons, and outside the large windows, decorated with ivy, pass pedestrians in fur coats and young women in scarves— under the sky-blue evening snow.

Behind the bar, onto which has been hoisted a barrel with a gnome and the inscription "Mug-Goblet," are a pair who look completely alike: each with a tuft of parted hair and in a green apron; but the PROPRIETOR's *mustache curls downward, while his brother's, the* WAITER's, *curls upward. By one window, at a small table, sits a drunken* OLD MAN—*the spitting image of* VERLAINE; *by the other, a clean-shaven, pale man— the spitting image of* HAUPTMANN. *Several drunken groups. Conversation in one group.*

ONE. I bought this fur coat for twenty-five rubles. But there's no way I'm giving it to you, Sashka, for less than thirty.

ANOTHER (*earnestly, having taken offense*). You're full of it!... To think that... I'll give you....

A THIRD (*with a mustache, shouts*). Quiet down! Stop fighting! Another bottle, my good man.

(*The* WAITER *runs up. The gurgling of beer can be heard. Silence. A lone patron rises from the corner and approaches the bar with an unsure gait. He begins to pick through a shiny plate full of boiled crayfish.*)

PROPRIETOR. Excuse me, sir. You can't do that. You're picking through all our crayfish. No one will eat them.

(*The patron, mumbling, walks away. Conversation in another group.*)

SEMINARIAN. And she danced, I'm telling you, my friend, like a heavenly creation. I'd just love to take her by her little white hands, I'm telling you, and kiss her right on the lips.

DRINKING COMPANION (*laughs shrilly*). Wow, our little Vaska's been daydreeeeaming, and he's blushing like a poppy! And what kind of love is she for you? What kind of love?... Huh?...

(*Everyone laughs shrilly.*)

SEMINARIAN (*completely red*). And, I'm telling you, my friend: It's not right to laugh. I'd take her just like that, and carry her away from immodest gazes, and she'd dance before me on the street in the white snow... she'd fly, like a bird. And whatever it took to get my wings—I'd fly after her, over the white snows....

(*Everyone laughs loudly.*)

SECOND DRINKING COMPANION. Look here, Vaska, you're not gonna be flying much across the snow....

FIRST DRINKING COMPANION. A little frost'd be better for you, or else you'll end up right in the mud with your sweetheart.

SECOND DRINKING COMPANION. Dreeeamer.

SEMINARIAN (*very drowsy*). Ugh, friends, you don't study in a seminary, so you don't understand delicate emotions, I'm telling you. However, another beer would...

VERLAINE (*mutters loudly to himself*). To each his own. To each his own....

(HAUPTMANN *makes expressive signs to the waiter. Enter a* RED-HEADED MAN *and a* YOUNG WOMAN *in a scarf.*)

YOUNG WOMAN (*to the* WAITER). A bottle of porter, Misha. (*Continues speaking rapidly to the man.*) But she went out, honey, and—darn it!—forgot to buy her landlady a beer. So now, back she goes, but he's already opened the dresser, and he's digging around; he's gone through everything, everything, thinking: She won't be back soon.... She screams, honey, but he stops up her mouth, honey. Well, anyway, the landlady runs in, also screaming, and calls the doorman. So now he's at the police station, honey.... (*Breaks off quickly.*) Give me twenty kopecks.

(*The* REDHEADED MAN *gloomily pulls out a twenty-kopeck piece.*)

YOUNG WOMAN. You gotta problem with that?
REDHEADED MAN. Just drink and shut up.

(*They are silent. They drink. A* YOUNG MAN *runs in and joyfully rushes up to* HAUPTMANN.)

YOUNG MAN. Kostya, my friend, she's waiting by the door!...
HAUPTMANN. Fine. She'll hang around a little longer. Let's drink.
VERLAINE (*mutters loudly*). To all people, their own pursuits.... And to each his own trouble.

(*Enter* POET. *Calls the* WAITER *over.*)

POET. Can I treat you?
WAITER (*a born comedian*). A great honor, sir... from such a famous personage....

(*Runs out for beer. The* POET *takes out a notebook. Silence. The acetylene hisses. Pretzels crunch. The* WAITER *brings the* POET *a bottle of beer and sits opposite him on the edge of a chair.*)

POET. You just listen. To wander the streets, to catch fragments of unknown words. And then—to come here and to speak one's heart to a surrogate.
WAITER. Incomprehensible, sir, but highly refined, sir....

(*Darts away from the chair and runs to a patron's call. The* POET *writes in his notebook.*)

YOUNG WOMAN (*sings*).
How I love her....
And all for love, she...

(*The* WAITER *returns to the* POET.)

POET (*drinks*). To see many women's faces. Hundreds of eyes, large and deep, blue, dark, bright. Narrow, like the eyes of a lynx. Wide open, childlike. To love them. To desire them. There can be no man who does not love them. You must love them, too.

WAITER. I'm listening, sir.

POET. And amidst this flame of gazes, amidst whirlwinds of gazes, there arises suddenly, as if blooming beneath the sky-blue snow—one face: the uniquely beautiful countenance of the Unknown Woman, beneath a thick, dark veil... The feathers sway atop her hat.... Her slender hand, drawn tight in her glove, holds her rustling dress.... Now she slowly passes.... She passes.... (*Drinks greedily.*)

VERLAINE (*mutters*). And everything passes. And to each—his own concern.

SEMINARIAN (*slurring*). She danced, I'm telling you, like a heavenly angel, and you devils and thieves aren't worth her little finger. However, let's drink.

DRINKING COMPANION. Dreeeamer. That's why you drink. And we're all dreeeamers. Give me a kiss, my friend.

(*They embrace.*)

SEMINARIAN. And no one will love her as I will. And we will live out our sad life on the white snow: she—dancing, and I—playing the barrel organ. And we'll take flight. And we'll fly right beneath the silver moon. And, damn it, you won't butt your stupid dirty noses in there, I'm telling you, my friends. But just the same, I love you very much and regard you highly. Those who haven't drunk a bottle to the end can never be true friends.

(*Everyone laughs.*)

DRINKING COMPANION. That's right, Vaska. Very well put. Give me a kiss, my friend.

YOUNG MAN (*to* HAUPTMANN). But come on. Why should she have to wait so long in the cold? She'll freeze completely. Let's go, Kostya.

HAUPTMANN. Drop it. If a man indulges a woman's whims, then there's nothing left of him—just to spit in his face. Let her hang around, and we'll sit for a while.

(*The* YOUNG MAN *obeys. The patrons all drink and get tipsy. A man in a torn yellow coat, sitting alone, stands up and addresses everyone.*)

MAN IN COAT. My dear sirs! I have a small trinket—a highly valuable miniature. (*Pulls a cameo from his pocket.*) Here, sirs, want a look: On one side—an emblem, and on the other—a pretty lady in a tunic sits on the globe and holds a scepter over it: "Submit," she says, "obey"—and that's it!

(*Everyone laughs approvingly. Several approach and inspect the cameo.*)

POET (*drunk*). The eternal fairy tale. It's She—the World Ruler. She holds a scepter and commands the world. We are all enchanted by Her.

MAN IN COAT. Glad to serve the Russian intelligentsia. I'll sell it cheap, although I didn't get it cheap, but only, as they say, out of friendship. I see that you're a cultivated man. So, let's shake on it.

(*The* POET *gives him a coin. He takes the cameo and inspects it. The* MAN IN COAT *sits back down where he was. Conversation continues only between two people, sitting at a separate table.*)

THE FIRST (*picks up a humorous magazine*). Now it's time to have some fun. Hey, Vanya, listen. (*Ceremoniously opens the magazine and reads.*) "Affectionate spouses. Husband: 'My dear, drop by your mom's today and ask her...'" (*Laughs in advance, desperately.*)

THE SECOND. Hah! Devil take it, that's great!

THE FIRST (*continues to read*). "... and ask her... to give Katenka a doll...." (*Laughs violently.*) "Wife: 'What's with you, dear! Katenka's almost twenty years old. (*Barely able to read from laughter.*) What she needs now is a suitor, not a doll.'" (*Laughs thunderously.*)

THE SECOND. That's really great!

THE FIRST. Now that's what I call telling him off!

THE SECOND. Devil take 'em, they know how to write!...

(*The lone patron fumbles with the dish again. He drags some red crayfish out by the claws. He holds them and sets them down. And again the* PRO-PRIETOR *drives him away.*)

POET (*inspects the cameo*). The eternal return. Again, She envelops the earth's sphere. Again, we are subject to Her charm. Now She whirls the sparkling scepter. Now She whirls me.... And I whirl with Her.... Beneath the sky-blue... beneath the evening snow....

SEMINARIAN. Dancing.... Dancing.... Me on the barrel organ, and her dancing to the barrel organ. (*Makes drunken gestures, as if trying to catch something.*) I didn't catch her.... I didn't catch her again.... But you, Devils, you won't catch her, if I can't catch her....

(*Slowly, slowly the walls of the tavern begin to whirl. The ceiling tilts; one end stretches endlessly upward. The ships on the wallpaper, it seems, are sailing closer, but they can't quite make it. Amidst the confused general murmur the* MAN IN COAT, *having sat down next to someone, cries out.*)

MAN IN COAT. No, sir, I am a cultivated man! I love sharp cheese, you know, the round one! (*Makes circular gestures.*) I forgot the name.

INTERLOCUTOR (*hesitantly*). And you've... tried it?

MAN IN COAT. Tried it? You think I haven't. I've partaken of Rockford!

INTERLOCUTOR (*whose stool rocks under him*). You know... Luxemburger... it smells so bad... and it quivers, quivers.... (*Smacks his lips and rubs his hands.*)

MAN IN COAT (*stands, inspired*). Swiss!... That's the one, sir! (*Snaps his fingers.*)

INTERLOCUTOR (*blinks and wonders*). Well, you won't surprise anyone with that....

MAN IN COAT (*loudly, like a gunshot*). Brie!

INTERLOCUTOR. Well that... that... you know...

MAN IN COAT (*threateningly*). Know what?

(INTERLOCUTOR *is annihilated. Now everything spins, it seems, and turns over. The ships on the wallpaper sail, foaming the sky-blue water. For a minute, it seems, everything is upside down.*)

VERLAINE (*mutters*). For each his own time.... And it's time for everyone to go home....

HAUPTMANN (*shouts*). She's a harlot, so let her hang around! And we'll drink!

YOUNG WOMAN (*sings in the man's ear*). Farewell, my beloved...

SEMINARIAN. The snow dances. And we dance. And the barrel organ cries. And I cry. And we all cry.

POET. Blue snow. Swirls. Falls softly. Blue eyes. Thick veil. She passes slowly. The heavens have parted. Appear! Appear!

(*The whole tavern seems to plunge somewhere. The walls give way. Finally the tilted ceiling opens the sky: wintry, blue, and cold. In the sky-blue evening snow opens—*)

THE SECOND VISION

The same evening. The end of a street on the outskirts of the city. The last houses, coming to an abrupt end, give way to a broad vista: a dark empty bridge across a large river. On both sides of the bridge, quiet boats with signal lamps are slumbering. Beyond the bridge stretches an endless avenue, straight as an arrow, framed by chains of streetlamps and trees white with frost. Snow flutters and sparkles in the air.

ASTROLOGER (*on the bridge*).
> The night is filled with stars, ablaze
> We've but two wings to speed our gaze
> Impossible to count the stars—
> The Milky Way tonight grown dark,
> And gaze impoverished, fading out....
> Who is this drunken lout?

(Two DOORMEN *are dragging the drunken* POET *by the arms.*)

TWO DOORMEN (*enraged*).
> He spent the evening at the inn,
> But now we'll make short work of him.
> Hey, Vanka, give his nose a flick!
> Hey, Vaska, give his back a kick!

(*They drag the* POET *away.*)

ASTROLOGER.
> A new star rises to her crest.
> More brilliant she than all the rest.
> The darkened water growing clearer,
> Reflects a star within its mirror.
> The star is falling, flying near....
> Fly over! over! over here!

(Describing a slow arc, a bright and heavy star slides down across the sky. A moment later a beautiful woman in black with a startled look in her wide eyes is walking along the bridge. Everything becomes fairy-tale-like: the dark bridge and the slumbering sky-blue boats. The UNKNOWN WOMAN *freezes by the rails of the bridge, still retaining her pale fallen glow. The snow, ever young, clothes her shoulders, covers her figure. Like a statue, she waits.*

SKY-BLUE, *just like her, ascends the bridge from the dark avenue. He is also in snow, also beautiful. He flickers like a gentle blue flame.)*

SKY-BLUE.

Thawing in the winter's nighttime glow,
Turn your countenance to me.
Quietly you breathe the airy snow,
Make the gentle snow a gift to me.

UNKNOWN WOMAN (*turns her eyes to him*).

Eyes are stars whose lives have come undone,
Who have wandered from their course.
Over you, my lightly breathing one,
I have grieved from high above.

(His sky-blue cloak is strewn with snowy stars.)

SKY-BLUE.

Deep within your azure cold
Are many stars.
At my iron hand I hold—
A shining sword.

UNKNOWN WOMAN.

Loosen from your iron hold
The shining sword.
Countless in my azure cold
The many stars.

*(*SKY-BLUE *dozes in the pale light. Against the backdrop of his cloak shines a ray, as if he were leaning on a sword.)*

SKY-BLUE.

Centuries have flowed past, like dreams.

Long have I waited for you on earth.

UNKNOWN WOMAN.

Centuries have flowed past, like moments.

As a star I have passed through the skies.

SKY-BLUE.

Your radiance gleamed from the heights,

Down here on my sky-blue cloak.

UNKNOWN WOMAN.

You were looking into my eyes.

Do you often regard the heavens?

SKY-BLUE.

I can't lift up my gaze any longer:

For you, as you fell, captured my gaze.

UNKNOWN WOMAN.

Can you speak to me terrestrial words?

Why are you all in sky-blue?

SKY-BLUE.

Too long I watched the heavens above:

Hence the sky-blue in my eyes and cloak.

UNKNOWN WOMAN.

Who are you?

SKY-BLUE.

A poet.

UNKNOWN WOMAN.

What is your song?

SKY-BLUE.

Only of you.

UNKNOWN WOMAN.

You've waited for long?

SKY-BLUE.

Hundreds of years.

UNKNOWN WOMAN.

Are you living or dead?

SKY-BLUE.

I know not.

UNKNOWN WOMAN.

Are you young?

SKY-BLUE.

I am splendid

UNKNOWN WOMAN.

This falling-star woman
Wants terrestrial speech.

SKY-BLUE.

Only for mystery have I words,
Only in words that are solemn I speak.

UNKNOWN WOMAN.

Know you my name?

SKY-BLUE.

I know not and prefer not to know.

UNKNOWN WOMAN.

See you my eyes?

SKY-BLUE.

Yes I see. They are like unto stars.

UNKNOWN WOMAN.

Do you see, then, my slender shape?

SKY-BLUE.

Yes. You are dazzling.

UNKNOWN WOMAN (*an earthly passion awakens in her voice*).

Do you wish to embrace me?

SKY-BLUE.

I haven't the courage to touch you.

UNKNOWN WOMAN.

You may touch my lips.

(SKY-BLUE's *cloak flickers, disappearing under the snow.*)

Do you know passion?

SKY-BLUE (*quietly*).

My blood does not stir.

UNKNOWN WOMAN.

Do you know wine?

SKY-BLUE (*even more quietly*).

Celestial nectar is sweeter than wine.

UNKNOWN WOMAN.

Do you love me?

(SKY-BLUE *is silent.*)

The blood in me sings.

(*Silence.*)

Poison has filled my heart.
I'm more slender than all of your girls.
I'm more lovely than all of your ladies,
More impassioned than all of your brides.

(SKY-BLUE *dozes, all covered in snow.*)

How sweet is your life on the earth!

(SKY-BLUE *has vanished. A sky-blue snowy column begins to swirl, and it seems as though there hasn't even been anyone at this place. But then, beside the* UNKNOWN WOMAN, *a passing* GENTLEMAN *tips his bowler.*)

GENTLEMAN.

Were you speaking with someone?
But here there is no one to see.
Your enchanting voice sounded
In the empty expanse....

UNKNOWN WOMAN.

Where is he?

GENTLEMAN.

Oh, yes, there's no doubt you were waiting

Here for someone just now!
Allow an indelicate question...
Who was your invisible friend?

UNKNOWN WOMAN.

Splendid he was. In a sky-blue cloak.

GENTLEMAN.

How romantic the heart of a woman!
Go outside and you might even see
Men wearing sky-blue cloaks!
But what was his name?

UNKNOWN WOMAN.

He said he was a poet.

GENTLEMAN.

I'm also a poet! I'm also a poet!
Or at least when I'm looking
At your eyes bright and charming,
I could sing you a couplet:
"Oh, you're such a darling!"

UNKNOWN WOMAN.

Do you want then to love me?

GENTLEMAN.

Oh, yes! And very much so.

UNKNOWN WOMAN.

Are you able to hold me?

GENTLEMAN.

I'd like to know
Why couldn't I hold you?

UNKNOWN WOMAN.

And, touching my lips,
Will you caress me?

GENTLEMAN.

Let's go, my beautiful one!
"Your wish is my command"
As old man Shakespeare put it...
Now you see, dear, that poetry
Is far from a stranger to me!

(*The* UNKNOWN WOMAN *submissively gives him her hand.*)

What is your name?
UNKNOWN WOMAN.
                    Be still.
Let me think. In the sky, among stars,
No name did I bear....
But here, on the blue earth,
I'm fond of the name "Maria."...
"Maria"—you'll call me.
GENTLEMAN.
As you wish, my beautiful one.
After all I need only be right,
In my whispers to you at night.

(*Leads the* UNKNOWN WOMAN *away by the hand. The sky-blue snow covers their tracks. The* ASTROLOGER *is on the bridge again. He is in anguish. He stretches his hands toward the sky. His eyes are raised.*)

ASTROLOGER.
The beautiful star is no more!
The dark-blue abyss is deserted!
I've lost the rhythms
Of my astral songs!
Unpleasant henceforth to my ear
The jangling celestial songs.
In my tower today
I will enter with sorrowful hand
In my lengthiest scrolls
News of the fall of the brightest star....
And gently I'll call her
By a faraway name,
By a name, that caresses the ear:
"Maria"—let that be her name.
In yellowing scrolls
The words shall be traced

By my lonely hand:
"Maria has fallen—a star.
She'll not gaze in my eyes any more.
The astrologer is left all alone!"

(*Cries quietly. The* POET *goes up from the avenue onto the bridge.*)

POET.

O, I entreat you by all that is holy!
By your grief!
By your bride, if and when
You decide you will marry!
By the way, have you seen
A tall woman in black?

ASTROLOGER.

People are crude! Please leave me alone.
I haven't set eyes on a woman
Since my star fell down from the sky.

POET.

Your sorrow is known to me.
I also, like you, am alone.
And, surely, like me, you're a poet.
By chance, did you happen to see
An unknown woman in the sky-blue snow?

ASTROLOGER.

I cannot remember. Here many pass by.
And I sincerely regret
That I failed to recognize yours....

POET.

O, if you had seen her—
You would have forgotten your star.

ASTROLOGER.

Who are you to be speaking of stars?
You are too much a featherbrain,
I'd request of you kindly to keep
Your nose out of my profession.

POET.

I'll bear all your insults!
I've been humbled, believe me,
Not one little bit less than you....
O, if I hadn't been drunk,
I'd have followed right after her!
But two people were dragging me,
When first I caught sight of her....
And then I collapsed in a snowbank.
They decided to dump me,
And went away, cursing....
I've forgotten how long I slept....
When I woke, I remembered that snow
Had covered her tender tracks!

ASTROLOGER.

I dimly recall what for you
Is a sorrowful thing.
In fact, they were carrying you,
They pushed you and kicked you,
And you were unsure of your step....
Then, through a dream I remember,
A woman ascended the bridge,
And was approached by a sky-blue gentleman....

POET.

Oh, no!... A sky-blue gentleman....

ASTROLOGER.

I don't know what they talked about.
No more did I look at them.
They probably left after that....
You see I was minding my own....

POET.

And snow has covered their tracks!...
I will never again come across Her!
Encounters like this
Occur but once in a life....

(Both cry beneath the sky-blue snow.)

ASTROLOGER.

 Is it worth it to cry over that?
 My sorrow runs so much deeper;
 I've lost the astral rhythm!

POET.

 I've lost the rhythm of my soul,
 I hope that that's more important!

ASTROLOGER.

 The grief shall be logged in my scrolls:
 "A star has fallen—Maria!"

POET.

 "Maria"—A wonderful name!
 In verse I'll compose these lines:
 "Maria, you're gone!
 I can't see the dawn."

ASTROLOGER.

 Well, grief like yours will soon pass!
 For you need only to write
 Your verses as lengthy as possible!
 What do you have to cry about?

POET.

 And as for you, Mr. Astrologer,
 All you need is to take your scrolls
 And inscribe for the schooling of students:
 "Maria has fallen—a star!"

*(Both mourn beneath the sky-blue snow. They vanish in it. Even the snow
mourns. It has already covered both the bridge and the boats with its powder. It has formed white walls against the canvas of trees, along the walls of
houses, on the telegraph wires. In the distance land and river rise up like
white walls, so that everything is white, save the signal lamps on the boats
and the lighted windows of houses. The snowy walls grow denser. They
seem close to each other. Little by little there opens—)*

THE THIRD VISION

A large drawing room with white walls, on which electric lights burn brightly. The door to the anteroom is open. The delicate ringing of a bell frequently announces the arrival of guests. The hosts and guests are already sitting on sofas and chairs; the HOSTESS *is a middle-aged lady as stiff as a board; in front of her is a basket of biscuits, a vase filled with fruit, and a cup of steaming tea; across from her a deaf* OLD MAN *with a stupid face is chewing and gulping. Some of the young men, in impeccable dinner jackets, are speaking with the other ladies, and the others cluster in herds in the corners. A general rumble of meaningless conversation.*

The HOST *meets the guests in the anteroom and first bellows to each in a wooden voice "A-a-a!" and then utters banalities. At present he is thus occupied.*

HOST (*in the anteroom*). A-a-a! Well, you're sure all wrapped up, my dear fellow!

GUEST'S VOICE. It's cold out there, let me tell you! I'm in a fur coat, and I froze just the same.

(*The* GUEST *blows his nose. Since the conversation in the drawing room has flagged, one can hear the* HOST *speaking confidentially to the* GUEST.)

HOST. Where was it made?

GUEST. At Chevalier's.

(*The tails of the* HOST'*s frock coat are sticking through the door. The* HOST *examines the fur coat.*)

HOST. And what did you pay?

GUEST. A thousand.

HOSTESS (*trying to drown out the conversation, screaming the words*). Cher Ivan Pavlovich! Come quick! We were just waiting for you! Arkady Romanovich promised to sing for us today!

(ARKADY ROMANOVICH, *walking up to the* HOSTESS, *makes various gestures intended to show that he doesn't have a high opinion of himself. The* HOSTESS, *also with gestures, tries to show him the opposite.*)

GEORGE (*a young man*). Your Serpantini is an utter fool, Misha. To dance the way she did yesterday is perfectly shameless.

MISHA (*a young man*). George, you understand absolutely nothing! I'm utterly in love. That's only for the few. Think what a thoroughly classical figure she has—arms, legs....

GEORGE. I went there for the purpose of enjoying art. I can look at legs elsewhere.

HOSTESS. What are you talking about over there, Georgii Nikolaevich? Ah, Serpantini! Horrible, isn't it? In the first place, to interpret music—that's already an affront. I love music so passionately, and will not, will not put up with outrages against it. And then—to dance without a costume—that's... that's I don't know what! I took my daughter away.

GEORGE. I completely agree with you. But Mikhail Ivanovich here is of a different opinion....

HOSTESS. Mikhail Ivanovich! It seems to me that on this matter there can be no difference of opinion! I understand, it's natural for young people to get carried away, but at a public concert... performing Bach with the legs.... I'm a musician myself.... I love music passionately.... You can say what you want....

OLD MAN (*sitting across from the* HOSTESS, *unexpectedly and simply blurts out the word*). Brothel.

(*Continues to gulp tea and chew biscuits. The* HOSTESS *blushes and turns to one of the ladies.*)

MISHA. Ah, George, none of you understand anything! Really, Serpantini—an interpretation of music? Serpantini is music incarnate. She swims on waves of sound, and seems to take one swimming after her. Don't you think that the body, its lines, its harmonious motion, can also sing, just as sounds do? Anyone who truly feels music cannot be offended by her. You relate to music abstractly....

GEORGE. Dreamer! Now you're started. You build some theory and don't see or hear anything. I'm not even talking about music, and when it comes right down to it, I don't give a damn! And I'd be very happy to see all this in a private room. But you must admit that not to announce on the poster that Serpantini will be wrapped up in only a rag—means placing everyone in a most awkward position. If I had known, I wouldn't have taken my fiancée there.

(MISHA *absentmindedly gropes around in the basket of biscuits.*)

Listen, leave the biscuits alone. After all, it's disgusting to eat them, if you've touched them all. Look how your cousin is looking at you. And it's all because you're absentminded. Ugh, dreamers.

(MISHA, *mumbling confusedly, retires to another corner.*)

OLD MAN (*suddenly, to the* HOSTESS). Nina! Don't move. The back of your dress is unfastened.
HOSTESS (*flushed*). Uncle, that's enough, not in front of everyone! You're too... candid.... (*Tries to fasten her dress without being noticed.*)

(*A young* LADY *flits into the room, and after her walks an enormous* RED-HAIRED GENTLEMAN.)

LADY. Ah, hello, hello! Here, allow me to introduce you: my fiancé.
RED-HAIRED GENTLEMAN. Pleased to meet you. (*Retires sullenly to a corner.*)
LADY. Please, don't pay any attention to him. He's very shy. Ah, just imagine what happened!...

(*Hurriedly drinks tea and in a whisper tells the* HOSTESS *something piquant, judging by the fact that both fidget on the sofa and giggle. Suddenly turns to her fiancé.*)

Do you have my handkerchief?

(*Fiancé sullenly pulls out a handkerchief.*)

Do you have a problem with that?

RED-HAIRED GENTLEMAN (*unexpectedly sullenly*). Just drink and shut up.

(*They are silent. They drink. A* YOUNG MAN *runs in and joyfully rushes up to another. The latter is clearly the one who led the* UNKNOWN WOMAN *away.*)

YOUNG MAN. Kostya, my friend, she's waiting by the doo...

(*Falters in midsentence. Everything becomes extraordinarily strange. As if everyone suddenly remembered that these very words in this very order had been spoken somewhere.* MIKHAIL IVANOVICH *casts a strange glance at the* POET, *who enters at that moment. The* POET, *pale, bows to everyone from the threshold of the hushed drawing room.*)

HOSTESS (*with a strained look*). We were just waiting for you. I hope you will read us something. This evening is most strange. Our friendly conversation is not getting on.

OLD MAN (*blurts out*). As if someone died. Gave his soul up to God.

HOSTESS. Oh, Uncle, stop it! You'll end up scaring everyone.... Ladies and gentlemen! Let's renew our conversation.... (*To the* POET.) You will read us something, won't you?

POET. With pleasure... if it will interest...

HOSTESS. Ladies and gentlemen! Silence! Our wonderful poet will read us his wonderful poem—again, I hope, about the wonderful lady....

(*Everyone quiets down. The* POET *stands at the wall, directly opposite the door to the anteroom, reading.*)

POET.
The snows commenced their downward flow,
The rooftops shone, undressed,
When in the church's dark recess,
Her pearls began to glow.
And from the icon she descended,
In tender roses, slow....

(*The delicate ring of the bell in the anteroom. The* HOSTESS *imploringly clasps her hands in the direction of the* POET. *He interrupts his reading. Everyone glances with curiosity toward the anteroom.*)

HOST. Just a moment. I beg your pardon. (*Goes out to the anteroom, but does not bellow "A-a-a!" Silence.*) What can I do for you?

(*A female voice answers something. The* HOST *appears on the threshold.*)

Ninochka, some lady. I can't figure out a thing. It's probably for you. Excuse me, ladies and gentlemen, excuse me....

(*Smiles confusedly all around. The* HOSTESS *goes to the anteroom and locks the door behind her. The guests whisper.*)

YOUNG MAN (*in the corner*). This can't be....
ANOTHER (*hiding behind him*). You can be sure.... What a scandal!... I heard her voice....

(*The* POET *stands motionless opposite the doors. The doors open. The* HOSTESS *leads in the* UNKNOWN WOMAN.)

HOSTESS. Ladies and gentlemen, a pleasant surprise. My enchanting new acquaintance. I hope we will accept her with joy into our friendly little circle. Maria... excuse me, I didn't quite catch.... What's your name?
UNKNOWN WOMAN. Maria.
HOSTESS. But... your patronymic?
UNKNOWN WOMAN. Maria. I call myself Maria.
HOSTESS. All right, darling. I will call you Mary. There is something eccentric about you, isn't there? We'll enjoy the evening all the more with our delightful guest. Isn't that right, ladies and gentlemen?

(*Everyone is confused. Awkward silence. The* HOST *notices that one of the guests has slipped into the anteroom and goes out after him. Apologetic whisper and the words "Not feeling too well" are heard. The* POET *stands motionless.*)

HOSTESS. Well then, perhaps our wonderful poet will continue his interrupted reading? Mary, my dear, when you came in our famous poet was just reading us... reading to us.

POET. Forgive me. Allow me to recite it some other time. I apologize.

(*Nobody expresses dissatisfaction. The* POET *walks up to the* HOSTESS, *who for some time has been making imploring gestures but soon stops. The* POET *calmly sits down in the far corner. Looks contemplatively at the* UNKNOWN WOMAN. *The maid carries around the usual things.*)

GUESTS' VOICES (*through the meaningless general conversation breaks a guffaw, individual words, and whole phrases*). No, how she danced! You listen here! The Russian intelligentsia...

ANOTHER GUEST (*especially loudly*). You'll never get it! You'll never get it!

(*Everyone has forgotten about the* POET. *He slowly rises from his seat. He runs his hand across his forehead. Takes a few steps back and forth across the room. One can tell from his face that with agonizing effort he is trying to recall something. At this time the words "Roquefort" and "Camembert" are heard above the general conversation.*)

FAT MAN (*suddenly, in a terrible fit of enthusiasm, making circular gestures, jumping out to the middle of the room, shouting*). Brie!

(*The* POET *stops immediately. That instant it seems that he has remembered everything. He takes several quick steps in the direction of the* UNKNOWN WOMAN. *But his path is blocked by the* ASTROLOGER, *in a sky-blue uniform, who enters from the anteroom.*)

ASTROLOGER. Please excuse my uniform and late arrival. I've come straight from a conference. I had to give a paper. Astronomy.... (*Raises a finger upward.*)

HOST (*approaching*). Oh, we were just speaking of gastronomy. Ninochka, isn't it time to eat?

HOSTESS (*stands*). Ladies and gentlemen, follow me!

(*All exit after her. The* UNKNOWN WOMAN, *the* ASTROLOGER, *and the* POET *remain awhile in the darkened drawing room. The* POET *and the* ASTROLOGER *stand at the door ready to exit. The* UNKNOWN WOMAN *lingers in the background near the dark half-opened window curtain.*)

ASTROLOGER. Again we happen to meet. I'm very glad. But let the circumstances of our first meeting remain between us.

POET. I ask the same of you.

ASTROLOGER. I just gave a paper at the astronomical society—about that which you involuntarily witnessed. A startling fact: a star of the first magnitude....

POET. Yes, that's very interesting.

ASTROLOGER (*enthusiastically*). Yes! I entered a new paragraph in my scrolls: "The star Maria has fallen!" For the first time science.... Ah, forgive me, I haven't asked you about the results of your search....

POET. My search had no result. (*He turns toward the depths of the room. Stares hopelessly. On his face—anguish; in his eyes—emptiness and gloom. He reels from the terrible strain. But he has forgotten everything.*)

HOSTESS (*on the threshold*). Gentlemen! Come to the table! I don't see Mary.... (*Shakes her finger at them.*) Ah, young men! Have you hidden my Mary somewhere? (*Peers into the depths of the room.*) Where is Mary? So where is Mary?

(*There is no one by the dark curtain. A bright star burns outside the window. Sky-blue snow is falling, the same sky-blue as the uniform of the vanished* ASTROLOGER.)

Vladimir Mayakovsky

A Tragedy

Vladimir Mayakovsky 1913

Vladimir Mayakovsky
  poet, twenty to twenty-five years old
His acquaintance
  five to six yards tall; she doesn't talk
Old man with skinny black cats
  a few thousand years old
Man missing an eye and a leg
Man missing an ear
Man missing a head
Man with an elongated face
Man with two kisses
Ordinary young man
Woman with a small tear
Woman with a tear
Woman with an enormous tear
Newspaper vendors, boys, girls, and others

PROLOGUE

V. MAYAKOVSKY.

Can you understand,
for what reason I,
tranquil,
like the threat of a jeer
carry my soul on a plate
to the dinner of passing years.
Down unshaven plaza-cheeks
flowing like an unneeded tear,
I
may be
the last poet.
Have you noticed—
swinging
in the cobblestone tracks
the striped face of hanged boredom,
and across swirling rivers
on lathered-up necks
the iron bridges wring their cold hands.
The heavens cry
impetuous,
resonant;
and a cloud
has a scowl on its wrinkled countenance,
as if a woman expected a baby,
but god flung her a half-blind dunce.
With fat red-haired fingers
the sun caressed you like a stubborn gadfly—
in your souls there's an overkissed slave.
I, undaunted,
carried my hatred for rays of daylight through centuries;
with soul drawn out taut, like telegraph nerves,
I
am king of lights!

Approach me all you
who tore the silence,
who roared
because the nooses of noon were too tight—
I will reveal to you
with words
that are simple, like lowing,
our new souls,
glowing
like the arcs of streetlights.
I'll lightly touch your heads with my fingers,
and you
will grow lips
for enormous kisses
and a tongue,
to all nations native.
And I, hobbling on my mean soul,
will depart for my throne
with starry holes hung across the tattered vault.
I'll lie down,
bright,
in my clothes of sloth,
on a soft bed of bona fide dung,
and quiet,
kissing railroad-tie knees, the steam engine wheel
will grab my neck and squeeze.

ACT 1

Cheerful. The stage is a city, a cobweb of streets. A beggars' feast. V.
MAYAKOVSKY *is alone. Passersby bring him food—an iron herring from*
a signboard, an enormous golden breadroll, folds of yellow velvet.

V. MAYAKOVSKY.
Ladies and gentlemen!
Stitch up my soul
so the void can't ooze out.
I don't know if spit's an insult or not.
I'm as parched as a stone statue.
They milked me dry.
Ladies and gentlemen,
would you like
an extraordinary poet to dance before you?

(*Enter* OLD MAN WITH SKINNY BLACK CATS. *Strokes them. He's all*
beard.)

V. MAYAKOVSKY.
Seek the fat in their home-shells
and beat delight on their tambourine tummies!
By the feet seize the deaf and the dummies
and blow in their ears as in a flute's nostrils.
Break by their bottoms the barrels of malice,
I eat hot cobblestones of thought, you see.
Today to your loud-lifted chalice
I will marry my insanity.

(*The stage gradually fills.* MAN MISSING AN EAR, MAN MISSING A
HEAD, *and others. Stupid. They've become disorderly; continue to eat.*)

A barefoot diamonder of faceted lines,
fluffing up feather beds in foreign chalets,

today I'll set a worldwide feast ablaze
of beggars so motley and fine.
OLD MAN WITH CATS.
Enough.
What good are rattles to the wise?
I am a man of a thousand years.
But in you I see tormented cries
laid out on a cross of jeers.
An enormous sorrow sat on the city
and hundreds of miniature sorrows.
And candles and lights in a stormy brawl
obscured the whispers of nightfall.
After all, soft moons have no power over us,
streetlight flames are more elegant and scathing.
Named masters of cities on earth, soulless things
are making their way to destroy us.
From heaven looks a god gone mad
at the wail of the human horde.
Our hands are in roads corroded by mud,
in the tattered rags of his beard.
He is god,
but he screams of cruel reckoning,
while your little souls emit haggard sighs.
Get rid of him!
Go and stroke—
stroke the cats, skinny and black!
You'll boastfully grasp your enormous bellies
and inflate your shining jellyroll cheeks.
Only in cats,
their coats with a ravens' gleam,
will you catch the flashes of electrical eyes.
The entire catch of those flashes
(it will teem!)
we will pour through the wires,
through those muscles tight—
the trams will start galloping,

the blaze of lights,
like victory banners, will set sail through the night.
In greasepaint the world will start to stir,
flowers will peacock in every window,
people will be dragged along rails,
and behind them
all the cats, the cats, the black cats!
We'll pin suns to sweethearts' dresses,
from the stars we'll forge silvery brooches.
Get rid of your flats!
Go and stroke—
stroke the cats, skinny and black!

MAN MISSING AN EAR.

That's true!
Over the city
—where weathervanes sit—
a woman
—black cave eyelids—
takes aim,
hurls at the sidewalk gobs of spit—
and the gobs grow into enormous cripples.
Someone's guilt brought vengeance on the city—
people flocked together,
they ran in a herd.
And there,
on the wallpaper,
amid shadows of wine,
a wrinkled old fogy wails at the piano.

(*They circle round.*)

Over the city a legend of torment lingers.
You seize a note—
and bloody your fingers!
And the musician can't wrench his hands free
from the white teeth of furious keys.

(*All are agitated.*)

And just
today
since morning
a Charleston's cut lips
into a soul.
I wandered, twitching,
stretching my fingertips,
and everywhere stovepipes danced along the roofs,
their knees all kicked up forty-four!
Gentlemen!
Stop!
Can this really be?!
Even alleys roll their sleeves up for a bout.
And my sorrow grows,
incomprehensible, uneasy,
like the tear on a crying dog's snout.

(*Still more agitated.*)

OLD MAN WITH CATS.
There, you see!
We must hack things to pieces!
I was right to see in their caress an adversary!
MAN WITH AN ELONGATED FACE.
But, perhaps, we must love things?
Perhaps their soul is unordinary?
MAN MISSING AN EAR.
Many things are sewn inside out.
Their heart doesn't harden,
it's deaf to all hatred.
MAN WITH AN ELONGATED FACE (*cheerfully agrees*).
And where a man's mouth is sliced out,
many things have an ear darned on!

V. MAYAKOVSKY (*has walked into the middle, hand raised*).
Don't smear your heart-ends with hatred!
You,
my children,
I'll teach with a rod and a slap.
All of you, people,
are just bells
on god's cap.
I
on feet swollen from my quests,
in a domino and mask of darkness,
walked through
both your dry land
and some other countries, too.
I sought
her,
invisible soul,
to hold on my wound-lips
her healing flowers.

(*He stops.*)

And again,
like a slave
in a bloody sweat,
my body swoons with insanity.
However,
one time I found her—
soul.
She emerged
in a light-blue dressing-gown,
and said:
"Sit down!
I've been waiting for you.
Would you like a cup of tea?"

(*Stops.*)

I'm a poet,
I've collapsed the spaces
between ours and others' faces.
In the puss of morgues I sought sisters.
I kissed leper-blisters.
And today,
hiding sea-tears deeper,
I will hurl both my sisters' shame
and gray mothers' creases
onto a yellow flame!
On plates of halls licked clean,
centuries we'll gorge on you, meat!

(*Tears away a cover.* ENORMOUS WOMAN. *Timid. The* ORDINARY
YOUNG MAN *runs in. He bustles around.*)

V. MAYAKOVSKY (*aside, quietly*).
Ladies and gentlemen!
They say
that somewhere—
in Brazil, I think—
there is one happy man!
ORDINARY YOUNG MAN (*runs up to each person, clinging to them*).
Ladies and gentlemen!
Stop!
Ladies and gentlemen!
Sir,
Sir,
Tell me quickly:
Do they want to set fire
to mothers here?
Gentlemen!
Human brains aspire to,
but bow before, the world's secrets;

and you're making a pyre
of the treasures of knowledge and books!
I invented a gadget for chopping cutlets.
I'm no dunce!
I have an acquaintance—
for twenty-five years he's
been working
on a trap to catch fleas.
I have a wife,
about to give birth to a son or daughter,
and you—speak filth!
Cultured people!
Really, it's almost offensive.

MAN MISSING AN EAR.

Young man,

Get up on this box!

CROWD.

Better yet on this barrel!

MAN MISSING AN EAR.

Or no one will see you!

ORDINARY YOUNG MAN.

But there's nothing to laugh at!
I have a brother,
a little thing,
you'll come and gnaw on his bones.
You want to eat everything!

(*Alarm. Sirens. Shouts of "Pants, pants!" backstage.*)

V. MAYAKOVSKY.

Stop it!

(*They surround the* ORDINARY YOUNG MAN *on all sides.*)

If you hungered as I do—
You
would chew

the distances of east and west
as smoked factory faces
chew the bone of the firmament!

ORDINARY YOUNG MAN.
What—
so love means nothing?
I have a sister, Sonechka!

(*On his knees.*)

Kind people!
Don't spill blood!
Dear people,
you don't need an inquisition!

(*The alarm has intensified. Gunshots. A drainpipe begins slowly to drawl
out a single note. The iron roofs have begun to drone.*)

MAN WITH AN ELONGATED FACE.
If you loved as I do,
you would lynch love
or find a scaffold
to ravish
the rough sweaty sky
and milky-virginal stars.

MAN MISSING AN EAR.
Your women don't know how to love;
they're swollen from kisses like sponges.

(*Enter the stomping of a thousand feet on the taut belly of the square.*)

MAN WITH AN ELONGATED FACE.
But from my soul
you could also sew
such elegant skirts!

(The excitement cannot be contained. All crowd around the ENORMOUS WOMAN. *They lift her onto their shoulders. Carry her.)*

TOGETHER.

We're going—
where for piety
they crucified the prophet,
and we'll give up our bodies to an undressed dance,
on the black granite of sin and iniquity
we'll erect a monument to red meat.

(Carry her to the door. Hurried steps away from there. MAN MISSING AN EYE AND A LEG. *Happy. Insanity breaks out.* ENORMOUS WOMAN *is dropped.)*

MAN MISSING AN EYE AND A LEG.

Stop!
On the street,
where everyone's face,
like their burden,
is the same,
old mother time has now given birth
to a gigantic
crooked-mouthed revolt!
Antics!
The old-timers have gone dumb
before the snouts of fallen years
and on the foreheads of cities
spite now appears,
swelling rivers—
thousand-mile veins.
Slowly,
in dread,
shoots of hair
stood up on time's bald head.

In a flash
all things
rushed,
screaming themselves hoarse,
to cast off the rags of threadbare names.
Liquor-shop windows,
at a snap of Satan's fingers,
splashed on the bottoms of flasks.
To a tailor's surprise
his pants disappeared.
They escaped—
by themselves!
without human thighs!
A drunken dresser—
its black jaws agape—
tumbled out of the bedroom.
From the signboards "Robes et modes,"
Corsets crawled down, afraid of heights.
Every galosh is inaccessible and stern.
Stocking-courtesans
narrow their eyes in delight.
I flew, like foul language.
My other leg's a block back,
still trying to catch up.
What,
you,
yelling that I'm a cripple!
You old,
greasy,
flabby enemies!
Today
in the whole world you won't find a man
with
two
identical
legs!

ACT 2

Boring. A square in a new city. V. MAYAKOVSKY *has changed into a toga. A laurel wreath. Behind the door are many feet.*

MAN MISSING AN EYE AND A LEG (*obligingly*).
Poet!
Poet!
They've proclaimed you prince.
Your subjects
are crowding at the door,
sucking their thumbs.
Some silly vessel
is placed before each on the floor.
V. MAYAKOVSKY.
Alright,
let them come!

(*Timidly, women with packages. They bow a lot.*)

THE FIRST.
Here, this is my tear—
take it!
I don't need it.
Go ahead.
It's right here,
white,
in a silk cloth
of my eyes' grieving thread!
V. MAYAKOVSKY (*unsettled*).
I don't need it,
what for?

(*To the next one.*)

Are your eyes swollen, too?

THE SECOND (*carefree*).

It's nothing!
My son is heaving his last gasp.
There's nothing to do.
Here's another tear.
It can go on your shoe.
It'll make a pretty clasp.

(V. MAYAKOVSKY *is frightened.*)

A THIRD.

Don't worry
that I'm
dirty.
I'll wash up—
I'll be cleaner.
Here's my tear,
empty,
a huge drop.

V. MAYAKOVSKY.

That's enough!
There's already a mountain.
And I've got to go.
Who's that charming brunette?

NEWSPAPER VENDORS.

Figaro!
Figaro!
Matin!

(MAN WITH TWO KISSES. *Everyone looks him over. They speak all at once.*)

ALL.

Look—
what a savage!
Back off.

It's dark.
Let me by!
Young man,
don't cough!

MAN MISSING A HEAD.
Eeeeeeee....
Uuhhhh....

MAN WITH TWO KISSES.
Clouds abandon themselves to the sky,
nasty and old.
The day was dying.
Sky-girls also have a weakness for gold;
all they need is money.

V. MAYAKOVSKY.
What?

MAN WITH TWO KISSES.
Money and money!

VOICES.
Quiet!
Quiet!

MAN WITH TWO KISSES (*a dance with balls full of holes*).
A big and dirty man
was given two kisses.
The man was inept,
didn't know
how they were kept,
or where they should go.
The city,
all in celebration,
raised up alleluias in cathedrals,
the people went out and put on their best.
But inside the man it was cold,
and in his soles were little ovals of holes.
He chose
the bigger kiss,
and put it on, like galoshes.

But the frost was malicious,
bit him on the toes.
"What the hell"—
the man became vicious—
"I'm going to throw these useless kisses out!"
He did.
And suddenly
little ears sprouted from a kiss,
it started to move about.
"Mama!"
it screamed in a thin little voice.
The man was frightened.
He wrapped the shivering little body in the rags of his soul,
and brought it home,
to put in a little blue frame.
He rummaged through a dusty trunk
(he was searching for a frame).
Looked round—
the kiss was lying on the bunk,
enormous,
round,
grown,
laughing,
going crazy!
"Lord!"—
cried the man—
"I never thought I'd feel so lazy.
I should hang myself!"
And while he hung,
vile,
pathetic—
in boudoirs, women
—factories without smoke or stacks—
manufactured kisses by the millions,
all sorts,

large,
small—
with fleshy lever-lipped smacks!
BABY KISSES WHO HAVE RUN IN (*playfully*).
They turned us out by the crate.
Take these!
       Soon the rest will come.
       For now—eight.
       I
       am Mitya.
       We're begging you, please!

(*Each sets down a tear.*)

V. MAYAKOVSKY.
Gentlemen!
Listen—
I can't!
Things are fine for you,
but what about my pain?
THREATS.
You just talk a little more over there!
We'll make you into ragout,
like a rabbit!
OLD MAN WITH A PLUCKED CAT
You alone know how to sing songs.

(*Gestures toward the pile of tears.*)

Carry them off to your beautiful god.
V. MAYAKOVSKY.
Let me sit!

(*They don't.* V. MAYAKOVSKY *clumsily stamps about, gathers tears in his suitcase. Stands with the suitcase.*)

Very well!
Let me by!
I thought—
I'd be happy.
With glistening eyes
I'd retreat to my throne,
an effete-bodied Greek.
Lies!
Never,
dear roads,
will I forget
your skinny legs
and northern rivers' gray hair!
And so through the city—
today I'll depart,
leaving my soul,
shred after shred,
on the spears of houses.
The moon will pass nearby—
there,
where the firmament is ripped apart.
It will come up,
and try my hat on for size.
With my burden
I
will go,
stumble,
grope
further
north,
there,
where
in the clutches of an endless grief,
with the fingers of his waves
the ocean-pervert
forever

claws his breast.
I'll crawl—
tired,
in a final frenzy
I'll fling your tear
to the dark god of thunder
at the source of bestial belief.

(*Curtain.*)

V. MAYAKOVSKY.
  I wrote all this
  about you,
  poor rats.
  I felt bad—I didn't have a breast:
  I'd have fed you like a good little nanny.
  Now I've gotten sort of scrawny,
  I'm—a bit blessed.
  But, all the same,
  who
  where would
  give the mind
  such an inhuman domain!
  It is I
  who pointed blindly to the skies,
  proved:
  he—is a thief!
  Sometimes I fantasize
  I'm a dutch rooster,
  or
  a Pskov king.
  But sometimes
  I just like the ring
  of my own name,
  Vladimir Mayakovsky.

The Case of the Entry Room

Victor Ardov 1929

CHARACTERS

People's judge

People's jury

Neburchilov, plaintiff
a stingy and sullen man

Wife of the plaintiff
a pudgy woman

Sister-in-law of the plaintiff
wearing a scarf, coquettish and testy

Kharpiliuk, defendant
passes himself off as highly educated and is therefore somewhat foppish

Mother of the defendant
old, spiteful

Kashkin, Chairman of the Residents' Association
when he speaks, all of his attention strains to make a "speech," and he therefore expounds the actual substance of his thoughts with difficulty

Morepanov, first resident
a failed singer, is distinguished by his elevated self-respect; takes everything in the world personally

Strekach, second resident
a huffing and puffing swindler, deals exclusively in scams and, as a consequence, stockpiles documentation and certificates for everything

Lepekhin, resident of the basement
a merchant of peasant stock, so overcome by the thought of his flooded apartment he cannot think about anything else at all

Sapusko, female resident
a onetime student, now an utter philistine

The bench of the People's Court. Public benches. The PLAINTIFF, *the* WIFE OF THE PLAINTIFF, *the* SISTER-IN-LAW OF THE PLAINTIFF, *the* DEFENDANT, *the* MOTHER OF THE DEFENDANT, *the* CHAIR-MAN OF THE RESIDENTS' ASSOCIATION, *the* FIRST RESIDENT, *the* RESIDENT OF THE BASEMENT, *and the* FEMALE RESIDENT *buzz in groups, discussing the case. One can hear:*

The court will decide....
I'm going to put it to 'em straight....
You say I taught you how to....
Mama, *I* know that....
Now we're flooded: it's pouring from overhead and leaking from the bath pipe and the toilet....
You can bet the court will decide if horses are supposed to be put in rooms or if they're not supposed to be....
Pursuant to which I warned not to bring dogs into the cubic space....
I'm going to put it to 'em straight....
What is there to be shy about, dearie....

(*Everything dies down.*)

JUDGE. The case of the entry room in apartment number 3, building number 15, on Zigzag Street, between citizens Neburchilov and Kharpiliuk. Citizens Neburchilov and Kharpiliuk, are you here?
PLAINTIFF. Neburchilov, here.
DEFENDANT. Kharpiliuk. I'm here.
JUDGE. Approach the bench. Have any witnesses turned up?
ALL. (*in unison*). They have.... They came.... Here they are—us....
JUDGE. Excellent. Citizen witnesses, leave the courtroom.

(*The* CHAIRMAN OF THE RESIDENTS' ASSOCIATION, FIRST RESIDENT, RESIDENT OF THE BASEMENT, *and* FEMALE RESIDENT *exit; the* JUDGE *looks over the case. To the* PLAINTIFF.)

What is your complaint, citizen Neburchilov? In other words, what is your suit about?

PLAINTIFF. The entry room, of course. That's what the argument and complaint's about.

JUDGE. Just what do you mean?

PLAINTIFF. I mean that, of course, I want to use it. But him and his mama.... won't let me; they claim they're the legal tenants and that the room is theirs.

JUDGE. And what do you need it for?

PLAINTIFF. Pardon me, of course, there's no place to put anything or to put my sister-in-law.

SISTER-IN-LAW OF PLAINTIFF. I don't need any place of yours at all!

PLAINTIFF (*to* SISTER-IN-LAW). Of course—don't say that, Varya. Of course, you've got to be put somewhere. (*To the* JUDGE.) It's with that goal that I am making my complaint, of course.

JUDGE. Well, what's in the room now?

PLAINTIFF. Right now it's whatever junk of theirs. Then there's the stench.

JUDGE. The what?

PLAINTIFF. The stench. The stench there, the smells, of course, fan out. Since he's a vet, as far as dogs and horses, the liniment whirls around, because of which, of course, you can't breathe.

JUDGE. I see. Other than that, then, the room isn't being used?

PLAINTIFF. Besides that there's sometimes livestock passing through.

JUDGE. What's that?

PLAINTIFF. I, like I said, he's a vet, as far as animals, so, of course, he has visiting hours. And it's fine if there are dogs or cats that come to get treated. But a horse? And, of course, geldings visit two days a week. Not to mention the ox that got stuck on the stairs, that he barely pulled out by the horns. And it's from ten to five every day.

PLAINTIFF'S WIFE (*to* PLAINTIFF). Why don't you say anything about those dogs? I bet they've bit everyone, and you don't say a thing.

DEFENDANT'S MOTHER (*to* PLAINTIFF'S WIFE). How do you like that, bit them! If you didn't poke them with a stick, I bet you wouldn't get a single dog biting you....

JUDGE (*rings*). Citizens, come to order. Quiet....

PLAINTIFF. But the dogs—that's for sure. The dog being treated by him, by Kharpiliuk, living in that room, of course, bites at you. What's more, just when you get used to one dog, he's taken another one in. Again the biting, until you get used to that one.

JUDGE. Now, what can you tell the court, citizen Kharpiliuk?

DEFENDANT. It's a result of ignorance and, mostly, lack of education that the complaint's been made. And as for the stench, it's impossible to control because of—chemistry. And on that I personally have the qualifications of a veterinary doctor's assistant.

MOTHER OF DEFENDANT. And they tease the dogs, citizen Judge, from morning 'til night. They tease them any old way: tease them by spitting, tease them with a coat, tease them—with a stick. A dog—is a person too, citizen Judge, heaven knows it has feelings too.

WIFE OF PLAINTIFF. Oh yes, and it bit my nose because I was teasing it with my nose, right?

MOTHER OF DEFENDANT. Even with your nose, even with your nose. I expect anything out of you devils.

JUDGE (rings his bell). I have not permitted you to speak; keep quiet.

WIFE OF PLAINTIFF. Shut up, you stupid old woman! See, the Judge rang his bell on you.

JUDGE. You both be quiet, or I'll have you removed. (To DEFENDANT.) In other words, you actually keep animals there? And so there's no place for the citizen to put his things.

DEFENDANT. Pardon me, there's one problem: What little things are those? If it's a small suitcase or table, then how can it be that there's no space? But if you want to put a billiard table in the entry room, what kind of passageway's going to be left over after that? It has to be regulated beforehand. All the more since the Neburchilovs' car's already sitting in the hallway.

JUDGE. Citizen Neburchilov, do you, in fact, want to put a billiard table in that room?

PLAINTIFF. Pardon me, citizen Judge, but what am I supposed to do? Of course, in the lean years I got it in exchange for flour—the billiard table. And I traded only for the sake of the cloth, so that the whole family would have green clothes. I can't very well throw something like that out, now, can I? So we live around the billiard table. And, of course, even before then it was so crowded in those years that—here, ask my wife, I built a chest of drawers two stories high. On the floor, of course, there's one chest of drawers, and on top of it another. Climbing up to the top, I jumped so hard that I got hurt—I wound up with a floating kidney. So can I really scrap the billiard table now?

JUDGE. Well, and where did you get the car and why?

PLAINTIFF. I bought it last year on Palm Sunday. And if it wasn't all rusty, I'd find a buyer right away. And now, pardon me, of course, there's nowhere to put anything, not even my sister-in-law...

(SISTER-IN-LAW OF PLAINTIFF *snorts.*)

JUDGE. Call in the chairman of the Residents' Association.

(*The* CHAIRMAN *enters.*)

Are you the chairman of the Residents' Association of building number 15 on Zigzag Street?

CHAIRMAN. The citizen-members, who honored me with their trust and, by the way, pursuant to which I was elected, as regards my being chairman, at the current, present moment—yes.

JUDGE. In that case, state for the court the point of view of the Residents' Association on this matter. According to the blueprint of the apartment, it is clear that the room under discussion is joined to the entrance. So your entrance is closed off, then?

CHAIRMAN. Pursuant to their fear of theft-disappearance, many members—the residents, and, moreover, the insufficiency of resources to hire doormen, that for some eight years, it would appear—yes.

JUDGE. I see. The entrance, it seems, is closed. And is the Residents' Association aware that citizen Kharpiliuk brings animals into the entry room, even a horse?

CHAIRMAN. All the more so, whereas it would appear, we the governing body, to wit, at the current, present moment, definitively—yes.

JUDGE. And so the governing body of the Residents' Association does not object to this? What, do you consider it—acceptable—to fill a room with animals?

CHAIRMAN. Of course, pursuant to which I spoke, to wit, more than once, that yes, in actuality—the animal that in the Residents' courtyard is unnecessary, it would seem, so during the present crisis—no.

JUDGE. Well, then. So you consider it—unacceptable. Why haven't you put an end to it?

CHAIRMAN. It is imperative to circumvent the party, which pursuant to the animals constitutes an apparent majority—to wit, dogs, pursuant to which have bit me from childhood and with which I do not like to associate, which expressly howl, among which citizen Kharpiliuk, too.

MOTHER OF DEFENDANT. Our dogs howl, and your chickens don't howl? And your goat doesn't howl? You ask him, citizen Judge, about the goat. What blocks the entrance, if not the goat?

JUDGE. Quiet, citizen. Citizen chairman, do you really have a goat in the entrance?

MOTHER OF DEFENDANT. There's a good thirty chickens—just chickens—in the entrance.

JUDGE. Quiet!

CHAIRMAN. Pursuant to that which I was already saying, they're afraid of theft-disappearance and, moreover, the insufficiency of resources to hire doormen, while the roof leaks, so that not only is the laundry hung out to dry, but so, too, expressly, I allowed chickens— yes.

MOTHER OF THE DEFENDANT. And where'd you put the goat?

CHAIRMAN (*to her*). Well, the goat, too. (*To* JUDGE.) Which doesn't bite and doesn't wreck the stairs, like a bull, as it were, so that at the present moment—why not?

JUDGE. That's enough. Now call in citizen Lepekhin.

(*The* RESIDENT OF THE BASEMENT *enters.*)

Are you citizen Lepekhin?

RESIDENT OF THE BASEMENT. Exactly.

JUDGE. What do you know about the case of the entry room in apartment number 13?

MOTHER OF DEFENDANT (*to* WIFE OF PLAINTIFF). He's going to straighten you out. This isn't the Residents' Association.

(*The* JUDGE *rings bell.*)

RESIDENT OF THE BASEMENT. I can't say for sure about the room but, since we live in the basement, just that it turns out we've been flooded again. It's pouring there—from overhead, and leaking from the bath pipe and the toilet.

JUDGE. What does that have to do with the case?

RESIDENT OF THE BASEMENT. Pardon me, citizen Judge, but, how can I put it, we warned citizen Neburchilov and his wife: don't wash. But just because it doesn't leak on them, they go ahead and keep clean. And now it's pouring from overhead, and from the bath pipe and the toilet, and we've been swimming for three days.

WIFE OF PLAINTIFF. So we're the only ones in the apartment who wash, right?

RESIDENT OF THE BASEMENT (*turns to the* WIFE OF THE PLAINTIFF). What a stupid woman you are—I told you not to wash. And not to use the can. But you're all ready to dump water on people. All over people!

WIFE OF PLAINTIFF. You're a bumpkin yourself, an ignorant boor.

JUDGE (*rings bell*). Quiet! Citizen Lepekhin, you will tell the court what you know about the entry room in apartment number 3, but this has no relation to the case.

RESIDENT OF THE BASEMENT. Pardon me, citizen Judge, but what do you mean, no relation? Kashkin, the comrade chairman—sitting over there (*points to the* CHAIRMAN OF THE RESIDENTS' ASSOCIATION) promised, says he'll fix it all up. Lepekhin, he says, I'll rig up a new tap. Come to find out he only gave the repairman two rubles, so he twisted it a bit and left. And once again, turns out, it's flooding. It's pouring there, from overhead, from the toilet pipes, and from the bath. And so what if because we're merchants, two hundred rubles were also taken from us, and citizen Kashkin promised that the residents wouldn't find out it was without authorization.

JUDGE. Ah, so that's it? It seems you moved in without authorization, after paying the chairman of the Residents' Association two hundred rubles?

CHAIRMAN (*approaches the bench again*). Pursuant to that which I was already saying, comrade Judge, it would seem citizen Lepekhin is mistaken, and nothing of the sort, pursuant to two hundred rubles and without authorization, so that there was nothing, both in general and at all. Expressly not.

RESIDENT OF THE BASEMENT (*to the* CHAIRMAN OF THE RESIDENTS' ASSOCIATION). Now don't just lie, Nikolai Epifanovich, you're just talking nonsense! That we paid two hundred rubles, that's—the God's truth, and that now we're flooded, you yourself puttered around with the tap and promised the maintenance man two rubles. (*To the* JUDGE.) So naturally it's flooding again. It's pouring from overhead, from the toilet pipes, and from the bath.

JUDGE. Enough! The court already understands your case.

CHAIRMAN (*to the court*). That there was nothing of the sort, it would seem, insofar as what Lepekhin says, about the two hundred rubles. I highly submit that there wasn't. And ask the residents, insofar as the basement is no good, the idle merchant was therefore installed. I highly submit it.

JUDGE. Enough, citizen Kashkin. The court has heard you out.

CHAIRMAN. Pursuant to which, citizen Judge, take my word, there was nothing at all....

JUDGE. Take your seat!

(CHAIRMAN OF THE RESIDENTS' ASSOCIATION, *groaning, sits on the public bench.*)

Call the witness Morepanov!

FIRST RESIDENT (*enters and stops at the* JUDGE'*s bench*). You called me?

JUDGE. Yes. Citizen Morepanov, tell the court what you know in relation to the entry room of apartment number 3.

FIRST RESIDENT. What is there to say? Nothing of any interest at all. Just a disgrace. That's it.

JUDGE. I am asking you to tell what you know.

FIRST RESIDENT. Well, I know that they curse. From inside the room, no less. I have to work from morning on. I myself am a teacher of singing. Students arrive, you're singing exercises, but there they are, cursing; it's downright indecent. Imagine, you're conducting a court session, and they go swearing up a storm. Where's the good in that? You can't hear what note you're hitting. And that's it.

JUDGE. And does citizen Kharpiliuk really keep dogs and other animals in the entry room?

FIRST RESIDENT. Well, and where's the good in that? Eh? Suppose there's a dog in the room, a completely unfamiliar dog, and let's say that you, for example, come in, and it tears up your pants. Now, it's really uncomfortable for you to judge wearing torn-up pants, right? It's the same for me. I have students. There's nothing funny about it at all. It's embarrassing to wear torn-up pants, isn't it?

JUDGE. All right. That's enough! Take your seat!

FIRST RESIDENT. But there's nothing funny about it at all! And a dog can tear up your pants, just the same as it can tear up the pants of those— people's jurors. What's so funny about that? And they did tear them up.

(*Walks away to the public bench and continues the conversation with the* SISTER-IN-LAW OF THE PLAINTIFF; *she plays the coquette.*)

JUDGE. Call in the witness Sapusko!

(*The* FEMALE RESIDENT *enters.*)

RESIDENT OF THE BASEMENT (*approaches the bench again*). So what, are we just supposed to get lost now, citizen Judge? It's pouring there now, from overhead, and through the bath pipe and the toilet....

JUDGE. I did not give you the floor; take your seat!

RESIDENT OF THE BASEMENT. And because we're merchants, two hundreds of rubles were taken. It's not proper to leak, even on merchants.

JUDGE. I know.... Take your seat! (*To the* FEMALE RESIDENT.) Your name is Sapusko? Good. Tell me, what do you know in relation to the entry room?

FEMALE RESIDENT. What I know is that there's no entry at all in the entry room. What sort of entry could there be past dogs that, without the slightest shame, and not thinking who's going there or why—immediately start biting. That citizen (*points to the* DEFENDANT) has a poodle, not a poodle but shaggy like one, that tears your pants into pieces, you know. And then I'm picking them up, picking them up, sewing and sewing, no way of figuring out which is the right leg, which is the left leg, which....

MOTHER OF THE DEFENDANT. Why are you lying, Marya Timofeevna? Well, your man stood up for them because he's mixed up with the sister-in-law, fair enough, but why you, huh? You ought to be ashamed!

FEMALE RESIDENT. What do you mean, with the sister-in-law? (*Turning to the* FIRST RESIDENT.) Well answer, you scoundrel! What have you been up to over there?

FIRST RESIDENT. Masha... it's embarrassing, after all, we're in... well, imagine, what if I called you "scoundrel" in court too: see, it's unpleasant, right? Eh?

FEMALE RESIDENT (*screams*). No, you answer me, what are you doing with that wench?

JUDGE. Excuse me, citizen Sapusko! Take the trouble to turn toward me, and no conversations when you are giving testimony to the court. Now why are you so agitated? Is that citizen a relative of yours or something, that you're sewing pants for him?

MOTHER OF THE DEFENDANT. Husband. He's her husband, but last month they made as if they had divorced, so that each would get a room, and not have their space reduced. But he's a husband to her. He was her husband, and he still is her husband.

FEMALE RESIDENT. He's no sort of relative to me at all, and I don't even want to know him! (*Turns to the* FIRST RESIDENT.) Just let him ask me to sew his pants, I'll croak first, but I won't sew them! Go to your wench! (*Indicates* SISTER-IN-LAW OF PLAINTIFF.)

JUDGE. Indeed! Excellent! You are free to go, citizen Sapusko!

(FEMALE RESIDENT *approaches* FIRST RESIDENT *and quarrels with him.*)

Quiet, citizens, quiet!

RESIDENT OF THE BASEMENT (*approaches the bench*). What now, are we just supposed to be flooded then? It's pouring there, from overhead, and from the toilet pipes and the bath.... Two hundred rubles, like kopecks, we laid down—and guess what, it's pouring. It's pouring there, from the bath pipe...

JUDGE. Take your seat! You heard me!

SECOND RESIDENT (*runs in; to the* JUDGE). Sorry, guess I'm late, eh?

(RESIDENT OF THE BASEMENT *walks away.*)

JUDGE. Who are you? Late for what?

SECOND RESIDENT. The Neburchilov-Kharpiliuk case; I'm a witness—Strekach. Here's the documentation, that I'm Strekach, and that I'm a witness.... (*Hands the* JUDGE *two pieces of paper.*)

JUDGE. What, do you live in that same apartment?

SECOND RESIDENT. Absolutely! Here's the documentation, that I am a resident and that I live in the same apartment. (*Takes out two more pieces of paper.*)

JUDGE (*after looking at the papers*). Ahh! What do you do?

SECOND RESIDENT. You see, I'm a curator. Here's the documentation.

JUDGE. What do you curate?

SECOND RESIDENT. A museum. That is, there isn't one yet, but it may turn up, the museum. Here is the certificate that there isn't one, and here, that it may turn up.

JUDGE. How can that be?

SECOND RESIDENT. Well, you see, maybe Pushkin spent a night in the room I occupy. Here is the documentation. But probably not, because maybe bedbugs bit him and he ran away—Pushkin, that is.... Here's a certificate about the bedbugs. Meanwhile, therefore, scholars are investigating the question: Did bedbugs bite Pushkin or not, and I'm curating it, just in case.... (*Points to the documentation previously given to the* JUDGE.) There's the documentation....

JUDGE. Ahh! Well, but do you know anything concerning the entry room?

SECOND RESIDENT. No. Here is the documentation.

JUDGE. Then why are you here?

SECOND RESIDENT. It's Kharpiliuk. He's angry at me. So he says, "You wait," he says, "I'm going to put you down as a witness; you'll suffer through a whole day in court," he says, "then you'll know what's what." Kharpiliuk's mad, so he played a dirty trick on me.

JUDGE. So-o-o! And how much space does your museum occupy?

SECOND RESIDENT. Not much. Compared to the Tretiakov Gallery or the Rumiantsev Museum—it's just a trifle. Fifty square feet. Here's the certificate.

JUDGE. That's enough. It's all clear to the court. You are free to go.

(*The court recesses for deliberation. All rise. The* JUDGE *and* JURY *leave; those remaining onstage divide into groups and buzz.*)

WIFE OF PLAINTIFF. You just wait, the court will show you!

MOTHER OF THE DEFENDANT. Ugh, you're shameless! The Judge didn't even want to talk with you.

DEFENDANT. Mama, leave them to their ignorance!

PLAINTIFF. You just wait, we'll put the billiard table there, and you'll be running around it!

CHAIRMAN OF THE RESIDENTS' ASSOCIATION. Pursuant to your having spoken, it would seem, about the two hundred rubles, so just you wait, I'll expressly give you the floods, and for real, yes.

RESIDENT OF THE BASEMENT. You say that in vain, Nikolai Epifanych. Because there's no place left for any more: It's pouring on us there, from overhead, and from the bath, and from the toilet pipes....

FIRST RESIDENT. Masha, don't hit! Where's the good in that: in the face, eh? My face or someone else's, it makes no difference—it's ugly.

FEMALE RESIDENT. I'll give it to you, you dirty so-and-so, I'll smash your mug! I'll teach you to mess around with wenches!

SECOND RESIDENT (*to the* DEFENDANT). Well, are you pleased with yourself? I didn't waste any time at all in court. I came at the very end of the case. So, are you pleased with yourself?

(*The* JUDGE *and the* PEOPLE'S JURY *return.*)

JUDGE. Please rise! "In the name of the Russian Socialist Republic, the People's Court of the Nikolsky Region, composed of Judge Prostorov and People's Jurors Krylov and Sarynin, having examined the suit of citizen Neburchilov against citizen Kharpiliuk regarding the use of the entry room in apartment number 3 on Zigzag Street, has *resolved:*

"1. To deny the suit.

"2. To bring a case against citizens Neburchilov and Kharpiliuk on the charge of lack of sanitation in the residences occupied by them: against citizen Neburchilov for storing an automobile in the hallway, and against citizen Kharpiliuk for keeping unhealthy animals in the apartment.

"3. To propose that the Residents' Association clear the entry room that was the subject of the suit, and moreover to open the main entry, in accordance with which the chairman of the Residents' Association, citizen Kashkin, will remove from the main entrance livestock belonging to him.

"4. To bring a case against the aforementioned citizen Kashkin on the charges of illegal occupation of the main entrance and the receipt of bribes from the merchant Lepekhin for the basement room assigned to him, Lepekhin.

"5. That citizen Lepekhin, who is illegally lodged, be required to vacate the residence he occupies no later than two weeks from now. Moreover he shall be brought to court on the charge of giving bribes to the afore-mentioned citizen Kashkin.

"6. That citizen Morepanov and citizen Sapusko lodge in one of the rooms occupied by them at present, and that the second room be vacated. To bring a case against citizen Morepanov and citizen Sapusko for the fictitious divorce they used for personal gain.

"7. That citizen Strekach be relocated to a smaller room, in accordance with current residential norms, and that the residence now occupied by him as a nonexistent museum be vacated."

The verdict may be appealed in the next two weeks.

(*The* JUDGE *and the* PEOPLE'S JURY *leave. The others form a dumb scene. A pause.*)

PLAINTIFF. There, that'll teach you, of course!
DEFENDANT. What a dimwit and ignoramus you are!
WIFE OF PLAINTIFF. What scum you are! How spiteful!

(*All four of them leave. The women continue to curse; behind them walks the* SISTER-IN-LAW OF PLAINTIFF *with a stony face.*)

CHAIRMAN OF THE RESIDENTS' ASSOCIATION. Pursuant to which, it would seem, at the present moment.... Yes!
RESIDENT OF THE BASEMENT. It's pouring from overhead, and from the bath and the toilet pipes, and now the Judge has doused us.... Ahh!...
SECOND RESIDENT. I'll go get the documentation that they're evicting me, and that the museum will be vacated.
FEMALE RESIDENT (*to* FIRST RESIDENT). Slime. (*She smacks him one in the face.*)

(*All leave after their remarks.*)

FIRST RESIDENT (*to the audience*). Well, citizens, what's so funny, eh?

(*Curtain.*)

Squaring the Circle

A Vaudeville in Three Acts

Valentin Kataev 1928

Vasya

Lyudmila

Tonya

Abram

Emelian Chernozemny

Sasha

Flavii

Guests

The action takes place in the 1920s.

ACT 1

A large, desolate, neglected room in a nationalized apartment in Moscow. Two doors. In the far left (or right) corner, by way of a bed, is a broken-down striped spring mattress set on four bricks. The pillow on the bed looks appalling, with stains in the fabric and no pillowcase. A chair stands nearby. An old pair of pants hangs on the wall. In the far right (or left) corner is a pile of books, newspapers, and pamphlets. From the center of the ceiling hangs a solitary, bright lightbulb, without shade or cover, right in the socket. Under the lightbulb, on cast iron legs, stands a green park bench with initials and a big pierced heart carved into it. On the bench, an enormous tome, Political Economy, *apparently serving as a pillow. The bench has evidently been brought here to enable a person to read while lying down. On the windowsill a homemade cone for a loudspeaker and a little box with a cathode ray tube. In the same spot is some sort of crock. There is nothing else in the room. The stage is dark when the curtain rises; only the tinselly light of the streetlamp penetrates the frosty blue window, flickering, and looking like a Christmas tree ornament hanging among the branches of the icy pattern.*

SCENE 1

V ASYA *enters; behind him,* LYUDMILA.

VASYA. This way, Lyudmilochka, this way! Don't get lost in the hallway.
LYUDMILA. Ugh! I caught my skirt on something.
VASYA. That's the bicycle. Hold my hand.
LYUDMILA. Tsk, for shame, pussycat! The hallway's two miles long, and not a single light.
VASYA. It burned out last week.
LYUDMILA. You make ninety rubles a month—couldn't you buy a new one?
VASYA. Didn't occur to me. Don't smash into the cupboard. I just didn't have the time. I work during the day and study at night. Come on in.
LYUDMILA. Up 'til now there hasn't been anyone to shape you up. You just wait, my dear spouse, now I'll whip you into shape.

VASYA. Right you are. Whip me into shape. Put me to work. That's why we signed the marriage papers. Here, I'll turn on the light. The room's just right, only there's not much furniture.

LYUDMILA. I'm anxious to see how you live.

VASYA. Shoot, I can't find the light! Abram, are you home? He's not here.

LYUDMILA. What, you don't live alone?

VASYA. I forgot to warn you. Abram is one of the guys.... But don't you worry about that, Lyudmilochka.

LYUDMILA. So, you live together with your comrade? How do you like that! Is your comrade married, by chance?

VASYA. Who? Abram, married? He's a confirmed bachelor.

LYUDMILA. So does he know that we're married?

VASYA. Hang on. He doesn't know.... But that doesn't matter. He'll be happy. Honest! You'll see. He'll dance with joy.

LYUDMILA. Ugh, Vaska!

VASYA. No, really.... He'll come along any minute now, and I'll just lay it out plain: blah, blah, blah, got married... no big deal. Don't you worry, Lyudmilochka, that's the main thing. Then, too, he's gone for days at a time.... Where *is* that darn switch? He just sleeps here. Nothing to worry about; we'll make it work one way or another. There it is. (*Turns on the light.*) Of course, you wouldn't call it posh. See, the main thing is, there's not a whole lot of furniture.... So what do you think, Lyudmilochka?

LYUDMILA. Clean as a pigsty. And it's chilly.

VASYA. That's because the windows aren't caulked. But, hey, Lyudmilochka, don't get, uh, panicked. That's the main thing. We'll get it all together. Just you wait, we'll get it set up a little better. We'll caulk the windows, buy a light for the hall, sweep up the floor—everything'll be swell.

LYUDMILA. So you and your comrade live here together, in this barn?

VASYA. Uh-huh.

LYUDMILA. What do you sleep on?

VASYA. I sleep on that there... on the ottoman. And he sleeps on the bench.... It's a really comfortable bench, if you can believe that. From the park at Clear Pond. I don't want you to get bored, Lyudmilochka. Maybe I should turn on the speaker for you—do you want me to? Homemade. It runs off the electrical grid. You can get Berlin on it; how 'bout that! Lyudmilochka... uh... how come you're so quiet? Don't feel like talking?

LYUDMILA. Go ahead and talk to your radio. I'm not your loudspeaker. Seriously, on ninety rubles a month you'd think you could have bought a few things. Where's your blanket?

VASYA. Don't have one.

LYUDMILA. Then what do you cover up with?

VASYA. I cover up with my coat. I think it's quilted.

LYUDMILA. Your head is quilted! I wish I'd never laid eyes on this place! "Lyudmilochka, Lyudmilochka!" he says—but there's just one pillow for the both of us. Some pillow, too—you'd be afraid to touch it. How do you and your comrade sleep?

VASYA. We just do. We take turns. One night I get the pillow, and he gets *Political Economy*. Next time we switch.

LYUDMILA. And it's filthy, everywhere, filthy! A regular sty! You probably haven't swept the room in a year. And so much trash! It must be embarrassing if people ever come by. Do you have a stove?

VASYA. Nope.

LYUDMILA. Boy, am I glad to hear that! Well, you just wait, my dear husband! (*Walks around the room.*) The bed goes there. A chair here and a chair here. Okay. A rug there, and a little shelf over there.

VASYA. That's right! There's a real homemaker for you! A life companion. Just the thing.

LYUDMILA. Plates here, and a curtain here.

VASYA. Well, a curtain... maybe that's a little much. Petty throughout, really.

LYUDMILA. What? If it's petty bourgeois, then you shouldn't have married me. Put a lid on it! Cupboard goes here. Okay. Hmm. Hang on, I'm going to run over to my sister's and bring back a few odds and ends; there's no way I'm sleeping in this barn the way it is now. Do you have a broom?

VASYA. No.

LYUDMILA. Get one! Understand? While I'm gone, I want everything swept up!

VASYA. Yes.

LYUDMILA. Pussycat, do you love me?

VASYA. One hundred percent!

LYUDMILA. Then kiss me on the nose!

VASYA. Lyudmilochka! (*Grabs and hugs her.*)

LYUDMILA. Tss! You're crazy! Let me go!

VASYA. Lyudmilochka... just wait.... How come...

LYUDMILA. Because. I want that floor squeaky clean. Farewell, my spouse! (*She leaves.*)

SCENE 2

VASYA. Spouse! Get a load of that! It's really something, being married, I'll be damned! (*Pounds on the wall.*) Ni-ka-nor-ov!... You wouldn't have a broom? Are you home? A br-oo-oo-m?... Too bad.

SCENE 3

Enter TONYA *with two bundles of books.*

TONYA (*at the door*). Abram, are you home?

VASYA. He's not back yet. Kuznetsova? Long time no see!...

TONYA. Vasya? Hi!

VASYA. Tonya.... (*Somewhat agitated.*) You're here to see Abram?

TONYA. That's right. Abram. He didn't say anything to you?

VASYA. Nope. I haven't seen him since yesterday. Well, let me take a look at you, see how you've changed.

TONYA. What do you mean, how I've changed? I'm just the same as before, pretty much ordinary. And what are you doing here?

VASYA. What am I doing here? Not much; I just live here.

TONYA. You live here? In this room?

VASYA. This very room.

TONYA. With Abram?

VASYA. Yeah, yeah, with Abram... but now...

TONYA. He never told me anything about this.

VASYA. Otherwise you would have dropped by a long time ago, right?

TONYA. Yes. I mean, not exactly.... Hmm.... Is that Abram's corner? (*Points at the corner with the books.*)

VASYA. That's his alright.

TONYA. I see. So, you have a fair amount of space here. What does Abram sleep on?

VASYA. On the bench. That's his half. And that's mine.... Yeah.... That's pretty much the size of it, Tonechka.

TONYA. I'll sit here for now.

VASYA. Yes, yes. You sit here for now. Abram should be here any moment now. He always comes around this time. I also need to have a talk with him... sort of a ticklish subject.... (*Sticks his head out into the hallway.*) Hey, folks, do you have a broom? No? That's really too bad. Who has one? Apartment Nine? Okay. (*To Tonya.*) You see, I've got to sweep up a little around here, 'cause otherwise it's not especially.... And no one has a broom.... But look here... I haven't seen you in ages.... Don't you go anywhere....

TONYA. I don't plan to.

VASYA. I'll be right back! (*Runs out purposefully.*)

SCENE 4

TONYA (*alone*). Nothing to be done for it. Fair enough.

SCENE 5

Enter ABRAM, *lugging a sawhorse on his shoulders and a book under his arm.*

ABRAM. Kuznetsova, you're here already? Did you get the Plotnikov book?

TONYA. We only have it 'til Tuesday. I gave my word.

ABRAM. We'll have to read together. Look, I acquired an outstanding sawhorse. By the way, on account of that blasted marriage registration office I was late to the Komsomol meeting. Were you late? I ask you, is this really necessary? As if we couldn't get along without registering our marriage. Who would we be hurting?

TONYA. A concession to the petty bourgeoisie.

ABRAM. Aha. Where should I put the sawhorse?

TONYA. Under the light, I think, so we can read. Let me help you. There. Thank you. (*Lies down on the sawhorse.*) Oh, yeah, by the way, it seems there's another comrade living in the apartment? You didn't tell me anything about that.

ABRAM. Akh! It completely slipped my mind. What can you say?... But don't you worry, Kuznetsova, it's nothing. He's a great guy, Vasya.

TONYA. He's not married, I hope?

ABRAM. Who? Vasya, married? He's a confirmed bachelor.

TONYA. Yes, I know him.

ABRAM. Is he back already?

TONYA. He went to get a broom. He'll be back any minute now.

ABRAM. Listen, Kuznetsova.... Did you inform him that we got married?

TONYA. No. But he kept looking at me in a way that made me think he'd figured it out.

ABRAM. You think he's figured it out? Ugh, how unfortunate! By the way, have you had lunch yet today?

(TONYA *shakes her head.*)

I really want to chow down. Maybe Vasya has something to eat? (*Searches.*) Sausage. Kuznetsova, what do you think, if I take a little bit of his sausage, would that be ethical or unethical?

TONYA. Unethical.

ABRAM. But he's one of the guys.

TONYA. Yeah? And I thought I detected the opposite—evidence of unhealthy acquisitions: a striped tie, Nepman boots—all in all, he looks like a newlywed fop.

ABRAM. Does he really look like a newlywed? To tell the truth, I've been noticing Vasya's acquisitions for a long time, too. By the way, we need to come to some sort of understanding with him on the issue of our marriage. I think he can only welcome it. So, I won't take Vasinka's sausage? Or maybe I should? Well, Kuznetsova, what do you think? Or would it be unethical?

TONYA. We can go in on four hundred grams of sausage. Do you have any money?

ABRAM. After the sawhorse, I have twelve kopecks left plus eight for the streetcar tomorrow.

TONYA. I have something here, too.... Hang on.... Five, ten.... Here's some more.... Thirty-nine kopecks. Give me your money. I think there's a stand around the corner. I'll run down there now.

ABRAM. How come you're the one going, and not me? I'm your husband, after all.

TONYA. Husband? Abram, please, cut the petty bourgeois nonsense. You bought the sawhorse and dragged it here, so I'll go get the food.

ABRAM. Mutual understanding, division of labor, and proletarian solidarity?

TONYA. Exactly.

ABRAM. In that case, I won't object.

(TONYA *exits.*)

SCENE 6

ABRAM (*alone*). What do you need for a stable marriage? Compatible personalities, mutual understanding, class consciousness, a shared political orientation, and proletarian solidarity. Do we have compatible personalities? Yes. Mutual understanding? Hardly need to say a word. Class consciousness? Yes, we do. Shared political orientation? Of course! Proletarian solidarity? And then some! So what's left? Maybe love? A social prejudice, a daydream, sickly sweet, rotten idealism... by the way.... (*Sniffs the air.*) Oof! The whole room smells like sausage... or would it be unethical? Eh?

SCENE 7

Enter VASYA, *with a broom.*

VASYA (*sees Abram; embarrassed*). Ah! You're back already. (*Starts to sweep up; extraordinarily embarrassed. To himself.*) I'll have to tell him right away.

ABRAM (*to himself*). I'll have to inform him. (*To Vasya.*) Hi!

VASYA. Hi! Listen, Abram. (*To himself.*) How awkward! (*To Abram.*) Here's the thing, Abram.... Oh, by the way, Kuznetsova was waiting for you here. Did you see her?

ABRAM (*anxiously*). Well, what does that have to do with anything? So, she waited and waited, so what?

VASYA. Nothing, nothing, I just mentioned it in passing.

ABRAM. In passing?

VASYA. In passing... Abram...

ABRAM. Well? She didn't say anything to you?

VASYA. Nothing. How come?

ABRAM. Oh, nothing. I just asked in passing.

VASYA. In passing?... Uh, huh... Abram... I see you bought yourself a sawhorse.

ABRAM. Well, no big deal. What does the sawhorse have to do with anything? (*To himself.*) I have to inform him. (*To Vasya.*) By the way, about the sawhorse... I have a philosophical question for you.

VASYA. Well? (*To himself.*) I bet he knows.

ABRAM (*with despair and grim determination*). Vaska! Do you suppose this room can house three people?

VASYA (*in despair*). What's your point?

ABRAM. I'm asking you: Would it be ethical or unethical?

VASYA. Of course, it's ethical. Where else is there to go? You're one of the guys, right? You understand the situation.

ABRAM (*overjoyed*). Exactly, Vaska! That's why I like you so much. Thanks a lot, buddy. I knew you wouldn't let me down. I give you my Komsomol word that I'll try not to crowd you.

VASYA (*weeping with emotion*). Thank you, my friend! Thank you, Abram! I always said you were one of the guys. I just hope I don't crowd you.

ABRAM. Nonsense! *You* crowd *me*? I just hope *I* don't...

VASYA. Well, all the same... there'll be curtains and whatnot, canaries in cages... this that and the other.... We both know she's a good gal.

ABRAM. Put 'er there, comrade! I'm so glad you like her!

VASYA. Thank you, thank you! I was sure you'd be really happy.

ABRAM. Well, I guess you can say that again, my man! You can say that again! You can say that again!

VASYA. Now, she does like to dance and flirt a little... sort of a bit petty bourgeois....

ABRAM. Who's petty bourgeois?

VASYA. She is.

ABRAM. Kuznetsova?

VASYA. What does Kuznetsova have to do with it?

ABRAM (*losing his resolve*). What do you mean, what do you mean? Absolutely nothing to do with it. I just mentioned her name in passing. Please don't give it another thought. It's just that Kuznetsova went out to the stand to get some sausage. But there's nothing whatsoever....

VASYA. For sausage? Kuznetsova?

ABRAM. Well, yeah. And why shouldn't she go out to get some sausage, when it comes down to it? But here's Kuznetsova now; ask her yourself.

SCENE 8

Enter TONYA.

ABRAM. We were just talking about you. Vaska says that you weren't out getting sausage, and I said you were out getting sausage. Hee-hee!... Just a little misunderstanding. (*Winks desperately at* TONYA.) By the way, do you know Vaska?

TONYA. I do.

VASYA (*sweeping a little too vigorously*). We've met.

TONYA (*quietly, to* ABRAM). Have you informed him?

ABRAM (*also quietly*). I can't get it out. My tongue just won't move. Kuznetsova, you inform him, I'm begging you.

TONYA. Me?

ABRAM. Well, yeah. Otherwise I'll get embarrassed.

TONYA. I don't understand these feudal sensitivities. It's very simple. Nothing scary. Just go right up to him and explain everything.

ABRAM. That's easy for you to say: Explain! Go and explain yourself.

TONYA. Why? You're the husband, aren't you?

ABRAM. Kuznetsova, cut the petty bourgeois nonsense.

TONYA. But after all, I went out for the sausage, so you have to inform him.

ABRAM. Division of labor?

TONYA. Exactly.

ABRAM. So, go right up to him and explain?

TONYA. Go right up and explain.

ABRAM. Or would it be unethical?

TONYA. It's ethical.

ABRAM. Oof! Go right up and explain. Oof! (*Walks toward* VASYA.) Listen, buddy... Here's the thing... I have to have a serious talk with you... Hmm... By the way, how come you're so dressed up today? You look like a newlywed or something!

VASYA. Me—a newlywed? Where'd you get that idea?

ABRAM. Come on, now, I was just kidding. I know that you're a confirmed bachelor.... By the way, speaking of bachelors... I mean, by the way, speaking of newlyweds.... I mean, by the way, speaking of marriage in general...

VASYA (*extremely embarrassed and sullen*). What marriage could you possibly have in mind?

ABRAM. Hang on, hang on, buddy! Don't get upset, that's the main thing. Let's have a serious talk. Oof!... Well, the two of us were living together, and now there'll be three of us. You think that's some kind of tragedy! If I were you, I'd be downright happy.

VASYA. Happy?

ABRAM. Why not? It'll be a lot more fun.

VASYA. Abram! Seriously?

ABRAM. Very seriously.

VASYA. Put 'er there, comrade!

(*A firm handshake.*)

ABRAM. Seriously, and for a long time, you could say. Even registered at the marriage bureau.

VASYA. That's right, that's right. Everything by the book. Then there was that strange guy who runs the marriage desk sitting there with this mustache, see.... He made some speech.

ABRAM. Exactly, exactly. Gave a speech. Hold on... how do you know?

VASYA. What do you mean, how do I know? Just who do you think it was that got married if not me?

ABRAM. You got married? Hold on.... I'm the one who got married.

VASYA. You? You got married also?

ABRAM. What do you mean, I did also? Not also, but first and foremost.

VASYA. Abram! Then... that means that today we both got m—

ABRAM. —arried.... Kuznetsova, there's been a disaster! Did you hear?

(TONYA *has long been standing with an implacable expression on her face, absorbed in her book.*)

TONYA (*completely occupied with her book*). Yes.... No.... What's that? Did you inform him?

ABRAM. I sure did inform him.

TONYA. Does he object?

ABRAM. Object! If only he just objected. It's worse! He doesn't object. More than that; he is in complete and total solidarity with us, a hundred and twenty percent's worth.

TONYA. Then I don't understand what you're bawling about. He's in solidarity; that's terrific. If there are going to be three of us, then three it is. Fantastic!

ABRAM (*almost shouting*). Three? Three, she says! Kuznetsova!

TONYA. What's going on? Perhaps you're opposed to the three of us living together?

ABRAM. The three of us living together.... Kuznetsova, put down your book and try to grasp what's going on here.

TONYA. I don't understand a thing.

ABRAM. She doesn't understand! Tonya, understand this....

TONYA. Well?

ABRAM. He...

TONYA. Yes.

ABRAM. My tongue won't move.... Give me my half of the sausage. I want to chow down, Kuznetsova. Well, do you understand?

TONYA. I don't understand a thing. Let me read in peace, please.

ABRAM. Read, at moment like this, Kuznetsova?

TONYA. Drink a glass of water.

ABRAM. I could drink a whole reservoir! I could drink two reservoirs! (*Utterly exhausted.*)

SCENE 9

From backstage the clank of a bicycle falling.

LYUDMILA (*from the hallway*). Vasya! Vasyuk! We're lost! I've torn my skirt on something.... Come on!

VASYA (*in horror*). Lyudmilochka! Comrades, she'll eat me alive! You can all go to.... (*Yells to her.*) That's the bicycle! (*To Abram, in a harsh whisper.*) You should have thought first, before you got married! (*Yells out the door.*) Coming, Lyudmilochka! (*Runs out. To* ABRAM.) Drop dead! Tss...

SCENE 10

Without VASYA.

TONYA. What's that noise? Who's out there?
ABRAM. It's for Vasya.... A certain official is visiting.

SCENE 11

Enter LYUDMILA, *behind her* VASYA *and a cousin, the Young Pioneer* SASHA. *They are carrying bundles.*

LYUDMILA. I just about ripped up the whole skirt. I want the lamp here by tomorrow! Sasha, don't wreck the lampshade. What's the big idea, stepping on my feet like that? Good Lord, what an insufferable child. Don't break the light.

TONYA (*to* ABRAM). Is that the official?

ABRAM. Well, yes.... I mean, she's not completely official yet.... What are you looking at me for?

TONYA. Why is she carrying those things?

ABRAM. You sure are strange, Kuznetsova! You always have to know why. As if there weren't enough "why's" already! Maybe she's moving out to the country and on the way she stopped off to say goodbye to her comrade....

TONYA. The country? In January?

ABRAM. We both know in two weeks it'll be February. You just read your book and never mind about anyone else.

TONYA (*looks at* LYUDMILA, *shrugs her shoulders*). Pff! Fine.

ABRAM. Total disaster!

LYUDMILA (*to* VASYA). Who are those people?

VASYA. Well, Lyudmilochka, that's Abram. Don't you know him? Abram, come here; I'll introduce you to Lyudmilochka.

ABRAM. Uh, hello. Abram.

(*Handshake.*)

LYUDMILA. And who's that?

ABRAM. That's—

VASYA. Ehem! Lyudmilochka... umm... that's a good friend of Abram's.... You see, she came to visit, have a chat... have a cup of tea. Never mind about her. Isn't that right, Abram? (*Gesticulates desperately.*)

ABRAM. Well, yeah... a good friend... of course.... Don't worry about her.

LYUDMILA. And what's with the sawhorse? Where did that come from?

VASYA. What's with the sawhorse? Abram... what's with the sawhorse? (*Winks desperately.*)

ABRAM. What's with the sawhorse? She brought that sawhorse over from her place. She's so funny! It's January, and she's moving out to the country! Hee hee! She dropped in to say goodbye.

TONYA (*overhearing*). Abram, what is the meaning of this?

ABRAM. Huh? The meaning... Kuznetsova... the meaning is total catastrophe.... (*In a whisper.*) They got married today, too.

TONYA (*somewhat dumbfounded*). Where?

ABRAM. At the marriage bureau.

TONYA (*still not quite getting it*). How come?

ABRAM. A concession to the petty bourgeoisie. Do you think you and I are the only ones smart enough to figure that one out? Kuznetsova, do you understand what's happened here?

(*A bolt from the blue.*)

TONYA. I understand.

LYUDMILA (*to* VASYA). Vasya, what's she doing sprawled out in the middle of the room? I can't set things up with her in the way like that. Tell her.

VASYA. Oh, come on now, Lyudmila, come on! Don't be ridiculous.... Let her sit in peace, and don't you pay any attention to her.

LYUDMILA. What do you mean, don't pay any attention? If we don't pay any attention, she'll probably up and move in. She's taking up the whole floor, the brazen hussy! I'm going to tell her myself—she can come and visit tomorrow.

VASYA. Lyudmilochka, for God's sake....

LYUDMILA. Just watch me!

VASYA. Lyudmilochka! I beg you... I have to tell you... but just don't get angry.... The thing is, Abram also got married today... to her....

LYUDMILA. What? (*Ominously, she drops the bundle and sits down on it.*)

VASYA. So that's how it is.

LYUDMILA. You shameless liar! Don't you dare touch me!

VASYA. Lyudmilochka, my golden...

LYUDMILA. Get out! I hate you!

VASYA. Milochka!

LYUDMILA. Get out, get out, get out, get out!! (*Stamps her feet and sobs.*)

VASYA. Lyudmilochka! Lyudochka! Milochka!... And you can all go to hell! Drop dead, all of you! Milochka, my kitten...

ABRAM. Kuznetsova, what you got here is one regulation catastrophe.

TONYA. Nonsense, we'll manage. No big deal.

ABRAM. The four of us—in one room?

TONYA. I can go.

ABRAM. Where? Where can you go? Where do you have that you can spend the night? It's twenty below outside. I won't let you.

TONYA. I'd like to know how you're going to stop me.

ABRAM. Cut it out! I am your husband, after all.

TONYA. Just drop that petty bourgeois nonsense!

ABRAM. Tonya, I'm begging you! We've got proletarian solidarity, after all. Where am I supposed to find the Plotnikov book?

TONYA. Fine.

VASYA. Honestly, I don't know what to do. Kuznetsova, maybe you can get through to her.

TONYA (*walks up to* LYUDMILA). Comrade, well, what can we do, now that this unfortunate misunderstanding has occurred? Are you a Komsomol member?

VASYA (*in desperation*). She's not a member of the Party... yet.

(TONYA *steps back*.)

ABRAM. I always said that our work among nonmembers wasn't worth a damn.

LYUDMILA (*through tears*). That has nothing to do with it. My grandfather was a Hero of Labor.

ABRAM. All the more reason not to cry.

LYUDMILA. Last night he kept trying to make my head spin with all his talk, comrades, all night long right from when we first met. And, naturally, he ended up taking me in. "We'll live together, Lyudmilochka," he says, "like a family. You move over to my place," he says. "I have plenty of space," he says, "and a homemade loudspeaker, and a gas stove. I have this, that, and the other," he says. And I listened to him and then, fool that I am, ran off to get married. And now—hell-lo! Turns out we have to share the room with this comrade, and *he's* married, and there's no light in the hallway, and as for the gas stove, nobody's even heard of it.

VASYA. We'll get a stove.

LYUDMILA. Get out!

VASYA. Come on, Lyudmilochka, let's make up....

LYUDMILA. Get out, get out! Let go of me, I'm leaving! I'm leaving this minute!

VASYA. Lyudmilochka... I *am* your husband, after all....

LYUDMILA. Husband? Woe is me....

VASYA. So you're staying?

LYUDMILA. Where else can I go? My sister has four people living in her room. Of course, I'm staying. Just don't you dare lay eyes on me!

(*Pause*.)

ABRAM. So she...

VASYA. Ehem, ehem, ehem!

ABRAM. Looks like we're going to have to live together. Four's company, as they say. We'll have to think of a way to make it work.

LYUDMILA. We're going to have to divide the room in half. Right from the door.

VASYA. That's it, Lyudmilochka! Great idea!

ABRAM. Absolutely! I second. Kuznetsova, you hear?

TONYA (*wrapped up in her book*). What?

VASYA. A resolution has been offered to divide the room in half.

TONYA. I don't object.

ABRAM. The measure is adopted unanimously.

LYUDMILA. For now we can use chalk. Vasya, is there any chalk around?

VASYA. Yeah, there is.

LYUDMILA. Start marking. Take it from here right over to here, and you move over just a little bit. (*This is directed to* TONYA.)

VASYA. Right away. Drafting was the first thing they taught us at school. Like so, and so, and so! (*Draws.*)

ABRAM. An unusual experiment: building a household in one room.

VASYA. Get a load of this! It's working out just perfect!

ABRAM. Beautiful! Five minutes and you've got a two-room apartment. Yankee ingenuity!

LYUDMILA. Look, Vasyuk.... We're going to have a lovely apartment, aren't we?

VASYA. And nothing to gripe about at all.

LYUDMILA. Comrade neighbors, this is our half, and that's yours. Vasya, move the bench into their room. There. Now come here. The bed will be here, the chair here, and two chairs over there. Do you like it, pussycat?

VASYA. Very nice. And do you like it?

LYUDMILA. I love it. (*Whispers.*) And do you love me? I really, really love you. Do you love me?

VASYA. Yeah. I love you, too.

LYUDMILA. Then give your wife a little kiss on the nose. (*Whispers.*) They can't see.

(VASYA *kisses her.*)

Hey, Sashka, time for you to leave.

VOICE COMING OVER THE RADIO. Hello, hello, hello! This is Moscow speaking. Comintern radio station, broadcasting at fourteen fifty on your dial. The opera *Eugene Onegin* is coming to you from the Bolshoi Academic Theater. Professor Packoff has given an introductory speech. The overture is about to begin. Hello! Hello! I give you the concert hall.

(*The sound of the orchestra tuning and the noise of people shuffling around are heard. Everyone quiets down.*)

It hasn't started yet. It will start in five or ten minutes. Don't leave your radio. Write down your comments and send them to the Radio Broadcasting Service. For now, I'm signing off.

(SASHA *listens, spellbound.*)

LYUDMILA. Get going, get going! Tell Mama not to worry, everything's fine.

(SASHA *leaves, all bundled up like a doll.*)

SCENE 12

LYUDMILA. What an unpleasant light! Here, I'll take care of it. (*She covers the light with a colorful scarf.*) That's better, isn't it, honey? (*Whispers.*) Do you love me? They can't see....
TONYA. No, comrades, please uncover our side. I can't read like this.
LYUDMILA. I apologize. (*Uncovers their side.*) There, can you see?
TONYA. Yes I can. Great. Thank you. (*Continues to read.*)

(ABRAM *reads.*)

LYUDMILA. Vasya, she's pretty; she just doesn't dress well.
VASYA. Hmm...
LYUDMILA. Have you known her for a long time?
VASYA. Umm... uhh... couple years.
LYUDMILA. Were you ever in love with her?
VASYA. Umm... uhh...

LYUDMILA. Say "meow" to your kitty-cat.

VASYA. Meow!

LYUDMILA. Kiss me. They're not looking.

ABRAM. I'm starving. Vaska! You wouldn't have anything I could scarf down, would you?

VASYA. Got some sausage.

ABRAM. Fork it over!

LYUDMILA. Hold on, comrades. That's not the way it's done. I brought a couple of things over from my sister's. There are some rolls here. We can have some tea. Would you like some tea?

ABRAM. Aha! Kuznetsova, you hear that? There's a resolution on the table to have some tea and rolls.

TONYA. Well, I really don't know....

LYUDMILA. Please don't be shy.

TONYA. Thanks, I'm sure. It's just that we don't have any... you know... cups, spoons, forks....

LYUDMILA. Oh, come now! While you're getting set up you can use ours. Isn't that right, pussycat? You don't mind if they use ours?

VASYA. Of course not.

ABRAM. Resolution adopted.

LYUDMILA (*takes out a kerosene stove*). Where is your kitchen?

VASYA. Here, I'll set it up.

ABRAM. Comrades! This is a breech of protocol. Perhaps I also wish to take part in the labor. Give me the stove. Division of labor. (*Takes the stove. To* LYUDMILA.) Now you instruct me how to operate it. Kuznetsova, you pitch in, too.

LYUDMILA. You're so funny! You're holding it upside down. Don't hold it like that; do it like this.

ABRAM. But how do I light it?

LYUDMILA. You light it like this. You see that tray? Pump out some kerosene onto it. Now, you see that little screw? Unscrew it. Then you take a needle and clean off the top. Got it?

ABRAM. Got it. Take the pump. Clean off the tray. Buy some kerosene....

LYUDMILA. Ugh! You don't understand a thing. Come on, I'll show you. (*To* VASYA.) Pussycat, you won't get jealous? (*To* TONYA.) Maybe you could get the dishes ready in the meantime.

TONYA. Sure. But I don't know where and how.

LYUDMILA. Vasya, help her. (*To* ABRAM.) Let's go. Where is your kitchen? I'll hold on to you because of that bike.

ABRAM (*shakes the stove*). Hold tight. You pump... the pump... the screw... in short, super-industrialization.

(*They leave.*)

SCENE 13

VOICE COMING OVER THE RADIO. Hello, hello! I give you the auditorium.

(*The radio begins to broadcast the overture from the opera* Eugene Onegin.)

TONYA. Well, show me where your stuff is.

VASYA. Take this basket. There are the glasses. Bring them out. Careful!

TONYA. Don't worry.

VASYA. So here we are, Tonechka Kuznetsova. It's been ages!

TONYA. About a year. Where do the rolls go?

VASYA. About... you can put the rolls on the plate. It was a good winter....

TONYA. What should I do with the teapot?

VASYA. Pour tea into it. Do you ever go to Patriarchs' Pond?

TONYA. No—never even thought about it.

VASYA. Never thought about it? Hold on, what are you doing? You've poured out all the tea. Let me do it. Here, like so.... And do you remember, Tonya, how we nearly wiped out on that toboggan riding down Sparrow Hill?

TONYA. What are you looking at me like that for?

VASYA. A year. Just a year. I have a wife, you have a husband. Do you truly love Abram?

TONYA. I think that's my business. Where shall I put the sugar?

VASYA. How come you're blushing?

TONYA. I'm asking you, where shall I put the sugar?

VASYA. Put it... somewhere.

TONYA. Stop looking at me.

VASYA. Such is life, Tonechka. Do you remember that tree on Patriarchs' Pond? The tenth one from the end, counting from the warming house. The whole night afterwards I was.... You know.... And the next day I wandered all over Moscow like a lunatic. I remember the snow was still falling.... My whole chest was covered with it... and my eyelashes were like little needles, you know.... Ugh.... A whole year... that's no joke.... And you—you're just the same as you were.... Yes, yes, hold still. The hair by your ear poking out from under your kerchief.

(TONYA *quickly puts her hair back under her kerchief.*)

Where'd you disappear to?

TONYA. I was working in the country....

VASYA. What a lovely lock of hair....

TONYA. Cut it out. I'm asking you, where shall I put the sugar?

VASYA. To hell with the sugar! Wherever you want. It's over and done with, Tonechka.... But it was something, wasn't it?

TONYA. I'm putting it in this little bowl.

SCENE 14

LYUDMILA *and* ABRAM *with the kerosene stove and a teapot.*

ABRAM. It was hard work, but we got it to boil. She taught me so well, comrades, that now I could light up a whole factory of stoves, never mind just one.

LYUDMILA. Oh, I can't stand it! (*Laughs.*) He's so funny, that Abramchik.... You could die laughing with a guy like that.... I'm going to split my sides....

TONYA (*to* VASYA). I put it in the little bowl.

LYUDMILA. So how are things here? Everything done?

VASYA. Everything. Except we can't tell where to put the sugar.

LYUDMILA. You haven't gotten anything done at all. Is that the way to serve tea? You haven't cut the sausage. You haven't unpacked the rolls. You haven't taken out the bread. You two are worthless. Here, let me set things up. Comrade Abram, sit down here; you've earned it.

ABRAM. After the labor of the righteous.

LYUDMILA. And you, comrade Tonya, sit next to your spouse. And I'll sit right next to mine. There we go. Now let's have some tea....

SCENE 15

Enter EMELIAN CHERNOZEMNY, *poet and athlete.*

EMELIAN. Hey guys, can I stay here tonight? (*Notices the whole group.*) Oho, I see you've got yourselves a regular banquet, with girls and everything. (*Goes up to* LYUDMILA, *then to* TONYA, *peering at them.*) Not bad at all; they'll do the trick. Allow me the privilege of introducing myself. (*To* TONYA.) Ever heard of Demian Bedny?

TONYA. I have.

EMELIAN. Heard of Sergey Esenin?

TONYA. I have.

EMELIAN. Heard of Emelian Chernozemny?

TONYA. I... uh... I haven't.

EMELIAN (*proudly*) Well, Emelian Chernozemny... that's me. Get it? When it comes to poetry, I can whip the pants off anyone you like. Have you heard my latest poem? Listen, everyone! It's called "The Cabby." "Ugh, the city has beaten me down. Nevermore will I see my hometown. I'll just make sure my collar is loose, so there's plenty of room for a noose. Oh, I used to be wild and loud, with my head always held high and proud, whereas now, sir, I'm ready to die, because Moscow has sucked me dry." Mmmmm. Aaaah. Hey, want to see my muscles? Go ahead, feel, don't be afraid, go ahead and feel! How 'bout that!

(LYUDMILA *feels.*)

And check out this chest! I can out-muscle anyone you like. What? You think I'm kidding?

ABRAM. There he goes!

EMELIAN. So how 'bout it, can I stay here tonight?

VASYA. You don't get it, pal. See, the thing is—we're married.

EMELIAN. Who-o-o?

VASYA. We are. Abram and I. So you see, citizen, there's no room.

EMELIAN. No, seriously?

ABRAM. It's a fact.

EMELIAN. Since when?

VASYA. Today. I married her, Lyudmila, and Abram married Kuznetsova there. So...

EMELIAN. Hold on, folks! Here's an impromptu poem. Listen up. Hmm.... "These guys got married in a wink, and everyone is tickled pink. Now Emelian, the well-known bard, is by himself... hmm... hmm... ain't life hard." Heh-heh.

ABRAM. Not much of a poem.

EMELIAN. Then you write a better one, genius. Well, catch you later.

VASYA. Where are you going? Have some tea.

EMELIAN. You kidding? I'm off on official business. (*Leaves in a hurry.*)

SCENE 16

The same people, but without EMELIAN.

ABRAM. Did you see that maniac? He ran off to make a phone call. He'll phone everyone now. Well, let the meeting resume.

TONYA. An overt decadent.

(*Pause.*)

LYUDMILA. That radio sure plays well!

(*Pause.*)

ABRAM. Peaceful family bliss.

(*Pause.*)

(*Curtain.*)

ACT 2

SCENE 1

LYUDMILA *and* VASYA *are on the left.* LYUDMILA *finishes setting up the room. She is bustling around, applying various finishing touches, and admiring the results. She puts up portraits of her grandfather and grandmother.* VASYA *strums his guitar. Yet somehow both of them are bored.*

VASYA. Who's that?

LYUDMILA. That's my grandma—she's a homemaker.

VASYA. Your grandma?

LYUDMILA. My grandma.

VASYA. Grandma?

LYUDMILA. Grandma. And that's my grandpa, a Hero of Labor, and a vanguard worker.

VASYA. Vanguard worker?

LYUDMILA. Vanguard worker, pussycat. What are your dirty boots doing up on that clean blanket! You should be ashamed of yourself! Move your feet.

VASYA (*moves his feet*). Grandma and grandpa.

LYUDMILA. Pussycat, do you love me?

VASYA. Do *you* love *me?*

LYUDMILA. I do. And you?

VASYA. I love you, too.

LYUDMILA. A lot?

VASYA. A lot.

LYUDMILA. A whole lot?

VASYA. A whole lot.

LYUDMILA. A whole, whole lot?

VASYA (*somewhat irritated*). A whole, whole, whole lot.

LYUDMILA. So show me, how much do you love me? This much? (*She indicates with her hands.*)

VASYA. This much. (*Indicates in the same way.*)

LYUDMILA. Well, I love you this much. (*Indicates.*) Do you love me that much?

VASYA (*nearly choking back a growl*). I love you this much.

LYUDMILA. Well, then kiss me on the nosey-wosey.

(VASYA *kisses her.*)

And now I'll kiss you on the nosey-wosey. (*Kisses him.*) Want some warm milk?

VASYA. No, I don't.

LYUDMILA. But you should really have some. You'll be my chubby-wubby hubby.

VASYA. I don't want to be your chubby-wubby hubby.

LYUDMILA. Hmpf! If you don't, you'll be skinny-winny. Come on, just drink the milk. I'm begging you.

VASYA. Hmm... hmm... hmm...

LYUDMILA. Drink it up, pussycat.

VASYA. Hmm...

LYUDMILA. Drink it up.

VASYA. I don't want any milk.

LYUDMILA. Well, I want you to drink some.

VASYA. Well, I don't want to.

LYUDMILA. Well, I want you to.

VASYA. Definitely not.

LYUDMILA. Definitely so.

VASYA. I definitely won't drink it.

LYUDMILA. Then you don't love me.

VASYA. I love you.

LYUDMILA. You definitely don't love me.

VASYA. I definitely do love you.

LYUDMILA. That's not how you love someone.

VASYA (*growling*). Then how do you love someone?

LYUDMILA. Well, not like that, anyway.

VASYA (*almost shouting*). Then how? Well, come on, how?

LYUDMILA. Don't you tell me to come on! I'm not your horse. Calm down. Now let's make up. Give me a kiss on the nosey-wosey. Don't want to? Hmpf! Well, then let me give you a kiss on the nosey-wosey. Pussycat, tell your little kitty "meow."

VASYA (*in a disgusted tone of voice*). Aowmya!

LYUDMILA. Aagh!

VASYA. There's more where that came from. Amu! (*Flies into a rage.*) Come here, pussycat, I'm going to bite off your nosey-wosey! Meow! Drink some milk! I don't want any milk. Meow! Enough! I can't live another minute with your grandma-homemaker and your grandpa-vanguard worker. Meow! I'm allergic to them. I'm starting to rot. And whose fault is it? It's your fault.

LYUDMILA. Why me?

VASYA. Whose grandpa is it? Your grandpa. Whose grandma? Your grandma.

LYUDMILA. Well, how do you like that!

VASYA. Shut up. Whose curtains? Your curtains. Whose milk? Your milk. And who's drowning in a petty bourgeois swamp? Me... I'm drowning in a swamp.

LYUDMILA. Well how do you like that, he's drowning in a petty bourgeois swamp! And I'm not? Who was it that talked such a big game: "Lyudmilochka, we'll build a new life together, Lyudmilochka, I'll read books to you, Lyudmilochka, I'll take you out to clubs, Lyudmilochka, you'll be my guiding light, my mate for life" and so forth and so on? And where is all of it?

VASYA. Well, how do you like that!

LYUDMILA. Shut up! Where is all this stuff you were talking about, I ask you? Nowhere. Forget it. (*Mimics him.*) "Lyudmilochka, could you sew on a button for pussycat? Lyudmilochka, give pussycat some milk. Pussycat wants to go bye-bye. Meow! Pussycat wants a yummy-yum. Kiss pussycat on the nosey-wosey.... Meow...." But you never teach me anything good.

VASYA (*rips his coat off the hanger*). Ugh, so that's how it is....

LYUDMILA. Where are you going, pussycat?

VASYA (*leaving*). I wasn't asking for your permission.

LYUDMILA. Pussycat, wait! Come on, let's make up. (*Runs after him.*) Pussycat! Come on, kiss me on the nosey-wosey!

VASYA. Like hell I will! Get your grandpa, the vanguard worker, to kiss your nosey-wosey. (*Leaves, slamming the door.*)

SCENE 2

LYUDMILA (*alone*). Well, what do you know, he doesn't like my grandpa! Just what I need! Good riddance! (*Suddenly cries.*) So why am I so unhappy? (*Retreats to the far corner, miserable.*)

SCENE 3

The clank of a falling bicycle is heard offstage. ABRAM *and* TONYA *enter with books.*

ABRAM. Ugh, damned bike! Get a load of this hole, Tonya. Wouldn't hurt to regulate it a little bit. Do you have a needle and thread?

TONYA. No.

ABRAM. Some wife you are!

TONYA. Abram, I asked you to drop that petty bourgeois nonsense.

ABRAM. My last pair of pants in shreds—you call that petty bourgeois? Some theory you've got there. Well then, should we mend them?

TONYA. Sure.

ABRAM. Give me...

TONYA. Abram, are you hungry?

ABRAM. Are you?

TONYA. You know what, I am.

ABRAM. You know what, I am, too. What gets me is, how come? Only yesterday morning we scarfed down a pound of sausage, and now I'm hungry again. How about that.... Well, let's read.

TONYA. Let's.

ABRAM. Let's.

TONYA. Abram, do you think maybe we still have some sausage left from yesterday?

ABRAM. There's an idea. We should check. (*Searches.*)

TONYA. Well, anything left?

ABRAM. What's left is two pages of a trashy novel. (*Shows her a sheet of paper.*) Nice snack we'll get out of that. (*Grins bitterly.*) Ha!

TONYA. Some husband you are!

ABRAM. Kuznetsova, drop the petty bourgeois nonsense!

TONYA. What does petty bourgeois have to do with anything? Maybe I should ask, what do I have to do with anything? But let's not get hung up on details. Read. Where were we? (*Searches in the book.*)

ABRAM. We were just at the part where we're hungry.

TONYA (*strictly*). Abram! Don't forget we only have the book until Tuesday. Read.

ABRAM. I don't want to.

TONYA. What's gotten into you, Abram? Read.

ABRAM. But I don't want to.

TONYA. But I want you to read.

ABRAM. Definitely not.

TONYA. Definitely so.

ABRAM. I'm definitely not going to read.

TONYA. Then you don't... respect me... and you don't love me, I mean, we don't have proletarian solidarity.

ABRAM. We do too have proletarian solidarity.

TONYA. We definitely don't have proletarian solidarity

ABRAM. We definitely do have proletarian solidarity.

TONYA. Proletarians in solidarity don't act like that.

ABRAM. How do they act?

TONYA. Well, not like that, anyway.

ABRAM (*ferociously*). Then how? Well, come on, how?

TONYA. Abram! Don't forget I'm not your servant, but an autonomous companion in life and comrade in work.

ABRAM. Tell me something I don't already know.

TONYA. Alright then, let's stop this discussion and keep reading. Where were we? (*Reads.*) "The economic epochs of history. Our understanding of the structure of human economic development is to date far from complete...." I think...

ABRAM (*to the side, with a sigh*). Man, I could eat a horse!

TONYA. What?

ABRAM. Nothing.

TONYA (*continuing*). "We will not pause to consider earlier schemas, but will skip to one of the more recent, that of the German economist Karl Buecher....."

ABRAM. Kuznetsova!... Enough! I don't want any more Karl Buecher. I want a big piece of bread and a bigger piece of meat. I want a huge omelet with at least six or seven eggs. I want bacon, I want cucumbers.... You *are* my wife, after all, so I'm gong to put it to you straight: I want to chow down....

TONYA. Abram, don't yell! You have a feudal conception of marriage.

ABRAM. Feudal conception? Now she's giving me a lesson in elementary politics....

TONYA. Tshsh! What will the neighbors think?

ABRAM. Neighbors? Isn't that a feudal conception? And when a husband has a tear in his last pair of pants and no one to sew them up, isn't that a feudal conception? And when there's nothing to eat, isn't that a feudal conception?

TONYA. So that's what it's come to? (*Rips her coat off the peg and puts it on.*) Nagging?

ABRAM. Where are you going, Kuznetsova?

TONYA. I'm not obliged to report all my actions to you! (*Starts to leave.*)

ABRAM. Tonya... Tonechka.... Okay, okay, let's read, let's...

TONYA. Leave me alone. Let me go cool off. (*Leaves.*)

SCENE 4

ABRAM. No getting around it, this is a one hundred percent, honest-to-goodness feudal family squabble. What gets me is, how come? All the prerequisites have clearly been met. Compatible personalities? We got it. Proletarian solidarity? We got it. Common political orientation? We got it. All the same, there's this awful lack of understanding, and to top it off, I'm starving. (*Sniffs the air.*) Hey! Vasya's half smells great. Hmm.... (*Sniffs. Racked with indecision.*) Cutlets. Possibly cutlets, but I'd say more likely an omelet with onions.... (*Cautiously knocks at the screen. In a barely audible voice, almost a whisper.*) May I?... Nobody.... (*Sniffs.*) Downright feudal smell. Or maybe it wouldn't be ethical?

(*He tiptoes into* VASYA*'s half, not noticing* LYUDMILA, *who is in the far corner, her nose buried in a trunk.*)

Now that's a first-class life! Or maybe it would be ethical? Hmm? Or not? Most likely cutlets.... Or maybe? Or could I just feel it with my hands?...

(*Gets up on a stool and rifles through the shelves—the dishes come crashing down.* ABRAM *is covered in flour.*)

Oof!

(LYUDMILA *looks on, petrified.*)

SCENE 5

ABRAM *and* LYUDMILA.

LYUDMILA (*laughing loudly*). Oh, I can't stand it!... Oh, I can't stand it!...
ABRAM. I apologize, but there's been a colossal misunderstanding.
LYUDMILA. Misunderstanding? Oh, I can't stand it!... Just look at you....
Divine punishment.
ABRAM. Divine? That's a strictly feudal conception.
LYUDMILA. And rifling through other people's shelves—isn't that fee...
fuu.... Oh, I can't even spit it out.... Isn't that strictly feudal?
ABRAM (*still standing on the stool, covered with flour, melancholy*). Who
cares about private property, anyway?
LYUDMILA. You poor thing! Take a look at yourself in the mirror. Oh, I
can't stand it! All covered in flour! Hungry, a torn pant leg.... What is
your wife thinking, I'd like to know.
ABRAM. Unfortunately, my spouse is thinking exclusively about Plotnikov's *History of Social Forms.*
LYUDMILA. Oh, poor little Abramchik! What an unlucky little thing you
are! What are you doing standing up on that stool like a statue? Come
on, I'll fix you up.
ABRAM. Aha! Kuznetsova! You hear? Nonparty comrades are starting to
fix your husband up.
LYUDMILA. Stand still.
ABRAM. What's going on?

LYUDMILA. I'm about to sew up your pants.

ABRAM. At your service.

LYUDMILA (*sews*). There. Don't jabber like a sailor or I'll prick you. There. Now that's a hole! Like a bunch of dogs tore it up.

ABRAM. It's that feudal bicycle, damned thing.

LYUDMILA. So, and so…. Hold still or I'll prick you, I'm serious. There. There. (*She sews.*)

ABRAM. Who's that up on the wall?

LYUDMILA. That's my grandma; she's a homemaker.

ABRAM. An exceptional lady. And that?

LYUDMILA. That's my grandpa.

ABRAM. He's a first-class guy, too.

LYUDMILA. A vanguard worker and Hero of Labor.

ABRAM. Who would have thought it? So young and already a Hero of Labor! It must be wonderful having such an exceptional grandmother and such a distinguished grandfather!

LYUDMILA. Stop mocking me.

ABRAM. How could I be mocking, when I'm prepared to go right up and give your splendid ancestors a great big hug! (*Makes a motion, pricks himself on the needle.*) Ow!

LYUDMILA (*laughing*). I told you not to move, now you've gone and pricked yourself. Stand still. (*Bites off the thread.*) Done.

ABRAM. There was a hole, and now there's none. Downright astonishing! The wonders of science and technology!

LYUDMILA. Well?

ABRAM. Well?

LYUDMILA. Well?

ABRAM. Well? Well what?

LYUDMILA. Well, now what do you do?

ABRAM. I don't know.

LYUDMILA (*mockingly*). Gee, I wonder. Now you're supposed to thank me, get it?

ABRAM. Thank you very much.

LYUDMILA. Who ever heard of thanking a lady like that? That's not it at all. Pshew, some knight in shining armor you are!

ABRAM. Perhaps I should say "merci"? Alright, "merci."

LYUDMILA. Nope. (*Insistently stretches out her hand.*) Well?

ABRAM. What?

LYUDMILA. You're supposed to kiss my hand, get it?

ABRAM. Kiss..... your hand?...

LYUDMILA. Why so bashful? Well? Hurry up!

ABRAM (*in a daze, kisses her hand*). Oo! (*Runs headlong into his half of the room and starts digging furiously through some books.*)

LYUDMILA (*laughs loudly*). Oh, I can't stand it! Oh, I'm going to die! Oh, How ridiculous! Where'd you go off to? Abramchik! Hold on. (*Runs after him.*) What about the other hand? You've got to get the other hand.

ABRAM. Just wait. (*Rapidly sifts through the books.*)

LYUDMILA. What are you looking for in there?

ABRAM. I'm looking for a book on ethics. Just wait, there's been a disaster. Someone swiped it.

LYUDMILA. Well, so what?

ABRAM. Now how am I supposed to find out whether it's ethical or unethical for a Komsomol member to kiss a nonparty comrade!

LYUDMILA. A nonparty comrade? You're a gas! That's what I call funny! Hurry up, now, and kiss me!

ABRAM. You think it would be ethical?

LYUDMILA. Kiss me!

ABRAM. Or maybe it wouldn't be ethical?

LYUDMILA. For crying out loud! So it's ethical for the hand to sew up your pants, but not for you to kiss the hand, is that it? Come on, kiss it!

ABRAM. Or maybe it would be ethical? Eh? Or maybe it wouldn't be? Or not? Eh?

LYUDMILA. Kiss...

ABRAM (*kisses her hand*). Or maybe it would be?

LYUDMILA. Now this one.

(ABRAM *kisses it.*)

Now this one again. Now this one.

ABRAM. Now this one again, right? (*Kisses it.*)

LYUDMILA. You sly dog! Enough, enough! (*Laughs, pulls back her hand.*) That'll do.

ABRAM. Entirely ethical.

LYUDMILA. What did I tell you? Oh, you poor dear, and no one to feel sorry for you. You sure are skinny! You need to drink some milk. Would you like a little milk?

ABRAM. Now you're talking! And some bread.

LYUDMILA. Drink up, Abramchik, drink up. (*Pours him some milk.*) Would you like me to get you a cutlet?

ABRAM. I'd love a cutlet.

LYUDMILA. Good boy! Eat up. Put some meat on your bones.

ABRAM. At your service.

LYUDMILA. Enjoy. We'll make you chubby-wubby.

ABRAM (*with a full mouth*). Won't bother me a bit if I get chubby-wubby. You know, for some reason I have a really healthy appetite today.

LYUDMILA. More power to you, Abramchik, now don't be shy. You know, Abramchik, I dreamed about you all last night. It was awfully funny. You and I were skating down the railroad. The night was dark and scary all around, and all of a sudden a kerosene stove comes up behind us on the rails, like a locomotive with its headlights... choo-choo-choo... it's gaining on us... choo-oo-oo...

ABRAM. Big trouble on the railway.

LYUDMILA. And all of a sudden you hug me....

ABRAM. Really now!...

LYUDMILA. Honest to God. And then I hug you.

(*They hug instinctively.*)

And suddenly we...

(*They kiss.*)

ABRAM. Now you're talking.

LYUDMILA. Yeah! And then we wake up.... I mean I wake up.

ABRAM. Don't I wake up?

LYUDMILA. You... wake up... too.

ABRAM. That's a good one. And what about kissing?

LYUDMILA. What about it?

ABRAM. Kissing your comrade's wife—is that ethical or unethical?

LYUDMILA. Well, that was in a dream.

ABRAM. In a dream?

LYUDMILA. In a dream.

ABRAM. Well, if it was in a dream, then I'd say it was probably more ethical than unethical.

LYUDMILA (*with a sigh*). Abramchik, I'm so ashamed, honest to God. I don't know what "ethical" and "unethical" are.

ABRAM. She doesn't know what "ethical" is! What is your esteemed husband thinking, I'd like to know. He's supposed to look after your intellectual development.

LYUDMILA. He just looks after my looks.

ABRAM. What a jerk!

LYUDMILA. So there's no one to fix me up, and no one to help me develop. (*Cries.*) And no one to read a book with. And no one to take me to the zoo....

ABRAM. Oh, you poor thing! Why haven't you said a thing all this time? Let me be the one to fix you up, let me be the one to develop you. Let me be the one to read books to you. (*Runs to get a book.*) The only thing is, please don't cry. There's something horribly feudal about a woman crying. Well, let's read. We can start with the simplest one. (*Reads.*) "The electromagnetic theory of light. The age in which we live is an epoch of profound changes, revolutionary upheavals in all walks of life. It remains for the future historian of our epoch to lay bare the immutable link that unites under one historical law the sociopolitical changes we are undergoing and those profound changes which...."

LYUDMILA. Abramchik! Take me to the zoo.

ABRAM. At your service! Do you have any change?

LYUDMILA. My knight in shining armor! I do, I do.

ABRAM. So what's to stop us?

LYUDMILA. And Vasya? What will Vasya think?

ABRAM. And Tonya? What will Tonya say?

LYUDMILA. Oh, but this is interesting! Be a good knight in shining armor and help me put on my coat. Well, let's go. (*Leaves.*)

ABRAM. Coming, Lyudmila, coming. (*Stays back, takes* VASYA's *tie, combs his hair.*) Coming, coming.... Couldn't hurt to put on a measly little tie.

Should I take this one—Vasya's? Would that be ethical or unethical? But what is a tie, anyway? And what are ethics, anyway? Ethics are a feudal conception. That's all there is to it.

LYUDMILA'S VOICE. Abram!

ABRAM. Coming. I'm just freshening up a bit. Do you have any tooth powder? Let me have some tooth powder. And then my hair, I'll just.... Coming, coming.... That's it.... (*Looks in the mirror.*) Ethical, eh? Yeah, now that's what I call ethical! Here I come....

(*Bumps into* TONYA, *who is entering.*)

SCENE 6

TONYA. Abram! What is the meaning of this?

ABRAM. A concession to the petty bourgeoisie and the wealthy peasantry. Adieu!

TONYA. Where are you going, Abram?

ABRAM (*proudly*). I'm not obliged to give you an accounting of my actions.

TONYA. Abram!

ABRAM. Leave me alone. Let me go cool off. (*Leaves quickly.*)

SCENE 7

TONYA (*alone*). Ugh, so that's how it is? Pl-lease! (*Takes up a book and reads.*) "Crude pragmatism, the abetting... the abetting...." (*Her head falls onto the book; she cries silently.*)

SCENE 8

VASYA *enters rapidly, looking irritable.*

VASYA. Lyudmila, are you home? Her fur coat's not here. She's gone. All the better. Enough! Things can't go on like this. The tie? To hell with the tie! Hairdo? To hell with the hairdo! Kuznetsova, you home?

TONYA (*quickly raises her head, fixes her hair and scarf*). Vasya? Is it you?

VASYA. May I?

TONYA. Sure. Just a minute. (*Feverishly gets herself together and pretends to be engrossed in a book.*) Hold on. Okay.

VASYA (*enters ABRAM's half*). Abram's gone? You by yourself?

TONYA. By myself.

VASYA. That's good. I need to have a serious talk with you....

(*A brief pause.*)

Tonya...

TONYA. Yes?

VASYA. What's wrong with you? Have you been crying?

TONYA. Nonsense!

VASYA. Tonya...

TONYA. Yes.

VASYA. Have you eaten anything today? Would you like some milk?

(TONYA *shakes her head.*)

Kuznetsova, I'm begging you, please have some milk.

TONYA. Thanks, I don't feel like... milk....

VASYA. Kuznetsova, you should be ashamed! Standing on petty bourgeois ceremony like that! I know very well you haven't had a thing to eat all day long. Have some, I'm begging you. (*Goes to get the milk.*) We've got a whole jug here. (*Notices with surprise that there's no milk in the pitcher.*) Empty. Hmm.... Who slurped it up, I'd like to know?... Tonya, turns out there's no milk. I'll get you a cutlet; we had about six of them here. (*Notices that the cutlets are gone.*) Hmm.... Gone.... Disappeared. Very strange.... I bet I know whose work this is. Well, not to worry. Can there really be nothing left? Aha, there's a little bit of sausage... and half a roll.... There. (*Walks toward TONYA.*) Eat this sausage, I'm begging you.

TONYA (*takes the food and eats it*). Thank you.

VASYA. That's it. Good job! You'll be chubby-wubby... Tonya...

(*A brief pause.*)

TONYA (*with her mouth stuffed*). Yes?

VASYA. Tonya! Things can't go on like this. Look into my eyes.

TONYA. Why should I do that?

VASYA. Look. Honestly.

TONYA. Well?

VASYA. Do you love Abram?

TONYA. That doesn't concern you.

VASYA. Yes it does concern me. Do you love him or don't you? Just tell me the truth.

TONYA. I don't understand—what an ideological way of putting it: "Do you love him or don't you?" You've got to be kidding!

VASYA. Tonya.... This is very important to me.... Do you love him or don't you?

TONYA. Well, really, I don't understand.... I respect Abram deeply.... Abram respects me, too.... Abram and I have proletarian solidarity.... We have compatible interests... a common political orientation.... It seems to me that, for the purposes of contemporary life...

VASYA. Hold it! Not another word. You don't love him! You really, truly don't love him.... You don't love him.... Kuznetsova.... How come you're blushing? Hurray! Tonya! I can't live without you, do you understand?

TONYA. Have you gone mad?

VASYA. That's right! I have gone mad! And I don't give a damn! Tonya... Tonechka.... Do you love me? Do you?

TONYA. Hang on, just wait!

VASYA. You love me! Honest to God, you love me! I can see it in your eyes. Hurrrray! Now everything will be different, everything will be happy. Tonya, we'll read together, work together, love together, walk together.

TONYA. You maniac!

VASYA. Hurrrray!

TONYA (*strictly*). Just wait, Vasya. Hang on, sit down. We'll have an objective discussion of the present situation. Fair enough, let's suppose you leave comrade Lyudmila, and I leave comrade Abram, and you and I come together on the basis of.... (*Indecisively.*) Will that be good from the point of view of the new family morality?

VASYA. Definitely good.

TONYA. Definitely bad. Married today, divorced tomorrow, married to someone else the next day.... What kind of example are we giving the members of our organization, not to mention the most active segments of nonparty youth and the impoverished peasantry?

VASYA. Perhaps the impoverished peasantry won't notice.

TONYA. Pure opportunism! Besides, we can't build our own individual well-being and, if you like, happiness on top of the unhappiness of other comrades. I mean comrades Lyudmila and Abram. I don't have any data regarding Lyudmila, but as far as comrade Abram is concerned, his life would definitely be shattered.

VASYA. Lyudmila's life would be shattered, too.

TONYA. If I may express myself in obsolete ideological terminology, comrade Abram is madly in love with me. He wouldn't survive this.

VASYA. Neither would Lyudmilka. She's head over heels in love. It's an undeniable fact. Talks about her grandma and grandpa all day long and forces me to slurp milk.

TONYA. See!

VASYA. Then what are we to do, Tonya?

TONYA. We'll have to forgo our individual interests in favor of the common interest.

VASYA. What a drag....

TONYA. Be brave, Vasya. You see, it's... it's going to be hard for me, too. We'll be friends.... Let's shake on it like friends. (*Extends her hand.*)

VASYA (*squeezes her hand, but then doesn't release it from his own*). What a drag!... Besides, I dreamed about you all last night. You and I were setting the table. But the dishes kept breaking and breaking. And all around us the night was... the wind was howling.... And the dishes kept breaking.... Whoo-sh-sh...

TONYA. An ideologically undisciplined dream.

VASYA. And all of a sudden you hug me....

TONYA. Really now.

VASYA. Honest to God. And all of a sudden I hug you.

(*They hug instinctively.*)

And suddenly we... Tonechka...

(*They kiss.*)

TONYA. Just wait, my precious pussycat.... What are we doing?

VASYA. And we both do it again....

(*They kiss.*)

SCENE 9

FLAVII *enters during a lengthy kiss.*

FLAVII. Go ahead and kiss, guys, don't mind me!

TONYA. Ugh!

VASYA. Ugh!

TONYA. Comrade Flavii!

VASYA. Flavii!

FLAVII. Don't sweat it, stay put, stay put, don't mind me.

VASYA. Fine cutlet this is!

TONYA. Comrade Flavii.... Who knows what you might think.... Honestly....
It's purely a misunderstanding....

FLAVII. Ho-ho! Vaska, how do you like that? She calls a Soviet marriage a
pure misunderstanding. As her husband, aren't you going to protest?

TONYA. I give you my word... that he... that I...

FLAVII. No, guys, all joking aside, how did all this happen so quickly? Double time, you might say. Our famous poet Emelian Chernozemny runs
up—and pow! Without any kind of warning, then and there, "Comrades! The latest news: Vaska's married. Abramchik's married. They're
all sitting together drinking tea and eating rolls—in other words, total
disintegration." Wait! Who's married? Married to whom? Why did they
get married? Do you think you can get a straight story out of that clod?
"I'm running out on official business," he says, "to throw a party, get all
the guys together—and that's that." That was the last I saw of him. So
you have guests coming, guys; get the tea ready, fire up the stove.

TONYA. The stove.... (*Sits down, exhausted.*)

FLAVII. No, guys, all joking aside, congratulations. Live happily ever after, guys, don't quarrel, work together.... But what really surprised me was our little Abramchik. Who would have thought it? Abram got married! Ho-ho! That would make a good subject for Demian Bedny. By the way, where is Abramchik?

TONYA. Yes, where is he, I'd like to know.

VASYA. Abramchik is umm... out uhh....

TONYA. On a walk with his wife....

VASYA. The weather is lovely,... snowing a little....

TONYA. Yes, it's snowing a little bit.... They'll probably be back soon.

FLAVII. Who did Abramchik marry?

VASYA. Yeah, who did he marry, I'd like to know. That is, I mean, he married that... uh... Kuznetsova, who's Abramchik married to?

TONYA. Abram? He's married to comrade Lyudmila....

VASYA. To Lyudmila? That's a good one. That is, I mean, that's right, he's married to comrade Lyudmilochka.... You know, on the whole she's pretty likable....

TONYA. I don't see anything especially likable about her—she's petty bourgeois, with the ideology typical of her class,.... Ehem, but let's not talk about that.

FLAVII. Well, well, guys, show me your territory, demonstrate your technical accomplishments. Just where do you live, exactly?

VASYA. We... basically... just... you know...

FLAVII. And Abramchik and his family?

TONYA. Abram... also... lives.... Basically.

VASYA. Here... you see... it's like this....

FLAVII. Aha.... Hmm.... Very nice, very nice.... And who is that? (*Points at the picture of Grandma.*)

TONYA. That? That's uh... an elderly intellectual....

VASYA. Grandma.

FLAVII. Whose grandma?

VASYA. Her grandmother... Homemaker... And that's Grandpa, my grandpa.... Hero of Labor... vanguard worker...

FLAVII. Good for you, guys! And I take it that's your technical equipment. (*Looks around at their dishes and appliances.*) A stove. Oho! A good stove. Pots and pans. How about that—four glasses.... A mirror.... Well, well, well, guys, you're surrounded with stuff.

TONYA (*taking advantage of the fact that* FLAVII *is busy looking around*). Vasya.... Well?

VASYA. Total disaster!

TONYA. How shameful! What a disgrace! I can't take part in this petty farce any longer. We have to nip this despicable lie in the bud.

VASYA. What do you want to do?

TONYA. I'm going to go right up to Flavii and tell him it was a joke.

VASYA. Tonya, you've gotta be crazy! He saw us kissing.

TONYA. I don't care.

VASYA. Kuznetsova!

SCENE 10

Enter GUYS *and* GIRLS.

FLAVII. Enter the guests.

FIRST MALE GUEST. Hey! Flavii's already here. Hi, Flavii!

SECOND MALE GUEST. First on the scene.

FIRST FEMALE GUEST. That's what I call an organizer—the real thing!

SECOND FEMALE GUEST. He's not just a man; he's more like an ambulance.

FLAVII. That's right. I race out at the first call....

FIRST MALE GUEST. But hey, who are the real stars, the victims of reckless love? Let's have a look at you.

FIRST FEMALE GUEST. Vaska! Just look at him. Hey, thanks a lot!

SECOND MALE GUEST. Tonya Kuznetsova! You gave in—couldn't hold out.

FIRST MALE GUEST. Comrades, please, a little more organization! Don't everyone go all at once. Ready! One, two, three!

ALL TOGETHER. Long live the Red Spouses!

VASYA (*to the side*). Disaster, disaster!

TONYA (*to the side*). I can't bear the shame!

SECOND MALE GUEST. Well, so where's Abram and his spouse? I don't see Abram.

FLAVII. Abramchik will be here.

FIRST MALE GUEST. And I don't see anything to eat or drink. That's worse....

FIRST FEMALE GUEST. Well, then, you two, the family unit, show off your household operation.

SECOND FEMALE GUEST. Yes, yes, a little tea wouldn't hurt at all. Kuznetsova, why are you so quiet? You invite guests over, and then you go and hide in the corner.

SECOND MALE GUEST. This is an outrage! We want some tea! Comrades, voice your protest!

FIRST MALE GUEST. Ready! One, two, three!

ALL TOGETHER. We de-mand tea! We want to eat!

SECOND FEMALE GUEST. Honestly, this is scandalous! Where's the famous party we've been hearing so much about?

FLAVII. Guys! How about some peace and quiet! Don't embarrass the young spouses. All in good time.

FIRST FEMALE GUEST. Look how neatly they've divided up the room.

SECOND MALE GUEST. Fantastic!

FIRST MALE GUEST. Come on now, comrades, down with petty bourgeois fences! Or else we won't have anywhere to party. Hit it!

(*They pull back the screens, the curtains, and the cupboard.*)

VOICES. Here, bring 'er this way, here! Just drag the screens! There we go! Much more room. Ugh, like so, and then like so! Girls, lean into it!

(*They move things out of the way.*)

TONYA. Vasya.... What's going to happen? What will Abram think?

VASYA. Abram? What will Lyudmila think?

TONYA. This is horrible.... He'll never survive this.

VASYA. She won't survive it either.

TONYA. What will we do?

FLAVII. Hey guys, heads up! Abram and his spouse are coming.

VASYA. Death! Darkness! Cutlets!

VOICES. Hide, hide! What are you standing there for? Come here, behind the books.

SECOND FEMALE GUEST. Vaska, hurry up and hide! Over here....

FLAVII. Absolute silence. I can just imagine Abram in the role of husband....

VASYA. Hey guys!

TONYA. Comrades! There's been a mistake.... We...

FIRST MALE GUEST. Psst! Not a sound.... Shshsh...

(*The sound of* LYUDMILA*'s loud laughing can be heard from backstage.*)

SCENE 11

Enter LYUDMILA *and* ABRAM.

LYUDMILA (*runs in, laughing loudly*). Pussycat, give me a kiss on the nose!

TONYA. What a slime!

ABRAM. But would that be ethical? (*Kisses her.*) Or maybe unethical? (*Kisses her.*)

VASYA. Filthy renegade! And what's worse—he's wearing my tie.

LYUDMILA. Pussycat, say "meow."

FLAVII. Look, now Abramchik's a pussycat!

LYUDMILA. Well?

ABRAM. Meow!

VASYA (*threateningly*). Meow!

(*Everyone jumps out.*)

ALL TOGETHER. Meow!

LYUDMILA. Ugh, Vasya!

ABRAM. Oof, Kuznetsova! An unbelievable disaster! We're in for it now!

ALL TOGETHER. Long live the Red Spouses!

TONYA (*rushes into* VASYA*'s embrace*). I can't stand this any longer. Get me out of here!

ABRAM. Lyudmila, catch me, I'm fainting. (*Falls into her embrace.*)

FLAVII. Let's see a kiss, guys, let's see a kiss!

SCENE 12

The clank of a falling bicycle. Enter CHERNOZEMNY.

EMELIAN. Hey you, to hell with you and your damned bourgeois bicycle! Just about tore my pants to shreds.

FLAVII. Emelian! Just what we needed to make the celebration complete.

EMELIAN. Hi guys! (*Freezes suddenly, seeing* ABRAM *in* LYUDMILA'*s embrace and* TONYA *in* VASYA'*s*.) Hold on! What do we have here? Vaska and Tonya... Abramchik and Lyudmilka.... Amazing, astounding! Wow! Here's an impromptu poem. "A marriage like the one we see is not the way it ought to be. Don't try to guess, not on your life, which end is up, and who's whose wife."

FLAVII. Well, how do you like that! Seems pretty clear to me who is whose wife. Lyudmila is Abramchik's, and Kuznetsova is Vaska's. Why, you were the first one to break the news. Are you drunk or something?

EMELIAN. Oh no, guys, just hang on... maybe someone's drunk, but it sure isn't me. I saw with my own eyes who is whose wife.

VASYA (*in a desperate whisper*). Psst! Be quiet!

ABRAM (*also in a whisper, with a gesture*). Be quiet... that's unethical.

FLAVII. Comrades, do you understand any of this? A marriage in a madhouse!

EMELIAN. You're the ones from the madhouse. But I, thank God, being of sound mind and firm memory, can outdo anyone. Have you heard my poem "The Cabby"? Listen. "U-u-ugh, the city has beaten me down...."

FLAVII. Drop it, genius! I'm sick and tired of your "Cabby." Can't stand the sound of it.

EMELIAN. And as for these firecrackers... (*Points at the pairs; they gesture to him.*) Enough already! As for them, I saw with my own eyes that Vaska's married to Lyudmila, and they're just pulling your leg, you fools.

ABRAM. Well, yeah. That's right. Of course, we're pulling your leg. Lyudmila, tell them.

VASYA (*with a forced laugh*). Well, yeah, we were pulling your leg.... And what did you think? He-he.... Flavii, we really put one over on you, didn't we? Tonya, tell him.

TONYA. Comrades, it was all a joke. Comrade Lyudmila can tell you, too.

LYUDMILA. Oh, how ridiculous you guys are, you didn't even get the joke! Ha! (*Despondently takes* VASYA's *hand.*) This is my lawful, wedded spouse. We can even show you the certificate from the marriage bureau.

ABRAM (*walks despondently over to* TONYA). This is my lawful, wedded companion for life. Right, Kuznetsova? Proletarian solidarity? We got it. Compatible interests? We got 'em. Political platform? We got it.

TONYA (*mournfully*). We have.

ABRAM. So what's the problem?

EMELIAN. Got it! Four lines. Listen. Impromptu poem. "They led everyone around like sheep, except for Emelian, you see, 'cause Chernozemny is the smartest—he's no sheep."

FIRST FEMALE GUEST. Pretty bad.

EMELIAN. Then let's hear you come up with a better one, you fool.

FLAVII. What can you say? Sure put one over on us! But the one who really surprised me was our little Tonechka Kuznetsova. Who would have thought that such a serious young woman, with such sound a sociopolitical record, would be capable of such foolishness? Eh? What do you say, guys? Good for you, Kuznetsova, I'm really happy to see this. You don't only go around spitting bullets; you know how to have a good time, too. Isn't that so?

FIRST MALE GUEST. So what are we waiting for? Comrades, let the congregation resume. Break out the food.

(*The guests take out what they've brought.*)

SECOND MALE GUEST. A pound of sausage.

FIRST FEMALE GUEST. Four rolls. Four eggs.

FIRST MALE GUEST. Sturgeon.

SECOND FEMALE GUEST. Half a pound of butter. Two herrings.

EMELIAN (*brings out three bottles of beer*). "U-ugh, the city has beaten me down!"

TONYA. Comrades, I categorically object to the consumption of alcohol among Komsomol members.

EMELIAN. What are you talking about, alcohol... it's just a lousy beer. Flavii, it's up to you. Can we have three bottles of beer?

FLAVII. On an occasion like this? Three bottles? Go right ahead!
EMELIAN. Alright! (*Opens the beer.*)
FIRST MALE GUEST. Comrades, ready. All together now!

(*They sing.*)

ABRAM. Farewell, Lyudmilochka.
VASYA. Farewell, Tonya.
LYUDMILA. Farewell, Abramchik.
TONYA. Farewell, Vasya....

(*Curtain.*)

ACT 3

The same room, but in a somewhat chaotic state.

SCENE 1

ABRAM *and* LYUDMILA, *on their respective halves of the room. For a while they listen and look around until they're sure no one sees them. Then they run toward each other and in the middle of the stage they embrace each other passionately and impetuously. They pause for a bit.*

LYUDMILA. What are we doing?

ABRAM. How am I supposed to know what we're doing?

LYUDMILA. No, no, don't kiss me anymore! I have a husband.

ABRAM. That's easy for you to say—husband! Easy for you to say—don't kiss me!

LYUDMILA. Don't kiss me, pussycat. Don't torture me. I'll go crazy! No, no!

ABRAM. It's either that or put a muzzle on me.

LYUDMILA. I can't live without you!

ABRAM. You think I can live without you?

LYUDMILA. What will come of this?

ABRAM. To the marriage bureau!

LYUDMILA. This is madness!

ABRAM. Or would it be unethical? Eh?

LYUDMILA. What about Vaska?

ABRAM. Don't talk to me about Vaska. When I hear Vasya's name, I want to rip his head off. What about Vaska?

LYUDMILA. He'll never survive it. He'll take his life in an instant. No question.

ABRAM. He loves you?

LYUDMILA. Oh, Abramchik, woe is me, he loves me so much—he simply adores me. It's just impossible.

ABRAM. All the same, it's one or the other: either me or Vaska. To the marriage bureau? Eh? Lyudmilochka, be a politically conscious comrade. Well?

LYUDMILA. Come on, now, pussycat. Married today, split up tomorrow, married again the next day, but to someone else. That won't do. What will people say?

ABRAM. Lyudmila! Drop that petty bourgeois nonsense. What do people have to do with it, when we can't live without each other? I just don't see what the problem is. Do we have compatible personalities? Yes. Mutual understanding? Got it. Do we have proletarian solidarity? You bet. Lyudmila!... Well? So what's the problem?

LYUDMILA. You're making my head spin.

ABRAM. Lyudmila, decide— here and now.

LYUDMILA. This is madness....

ABRAM. What a life we'll have, what a life!

LYUDMILA. Well then, what the hell. (*Throws herself into his embrace.*) My love!

(*They kiss.*)

Let's go....

ABRAM. Let's go!

LYUDMILA. My sunshine! (*Grabs his hand.*) My dearest spouse! And you really don't feel a bit sorry for Tonya.

ABRAM. Hold it! I really hadn't thought of Tonya.... There's a fine thing to do: Tonya comes home after a day at the Komsomol bureau, all tired out, and all of a sudden she finds out that her husband isn't her husband anymore, but someone else's husband. Is that ethical or unethical?

LYUDMILA. Let's go, pussycat, let's go....

ABRAM. But what about Tonya?

LYUDMILA. What about Tonya?

ABRAM. She'll never survive it.

LYUDMILA. She loves you?

ABRAM. You bet! She just adores me.

LYUDMILA. All the same, it's one or the other: either me or Tonya. Hurry up and put on your jacket, or else the marriage bureau will close. Come on, be a politically conscious comrade!

ABRAM. Married today... split up tomorrow... married again the day after. What will the guys at the Regional Committee think? What will Flavii say?

LYUDMILA. F... la... vii.... (*Sobs quietly.*) Would it be unethical?

ABRAM. Definitely.

LYUDMILA (*sobbing*). My sunshine.... Or... maybe... could it be eth-i-cal?

ABRAM. There's no question about it. It is categorically incorrect to build one's own domestic happiness on the basis of the domestic unhappiness of other comrades.

LYUDMILA. So... we... mustn't.

ABRAM. We mustn't.

LYUDMILA. But I thought... but I... Abramchik.... But I... just.... (*Sobs.*)

ABRAM. Lyudmilochka... I also.... Look, I pulled myself together. You pull yourself together, too. Be a man.

LYUDMILA. Well then, farewell, Abram!

ABRAM. Farewell, Lyudmila!

LYUDMILA. Alright.... Now I know.... (*Choking up.*) Farewell, pussycat.

(*They embrace, crying.*)

Say... "amu" to your kitty....

ABRAM. Amu! (*Nearly sobbing.*)

(*They part.*)

LYUDMILA. Abramchik!

ABRAM. Yes.

LYUDMILA. Farewell, farewell!

(*They embrace.*)

ABRAM. Farewell!

(*They embrace. They part.*)

I just don't get how it turns out to be unethical, when it's all so ethical!

(*They have gone into their respective halves of the room.* ABRAM *dejectedly sticks his nose into a book. The right side of the curtain is drawn.*)

LYUDMILA (*alone on her half of the room*). Alright.... Now I know... I can't.... (*Decisively starts gathering her things. Suddenly drops to the floor, exhausted, and buries her head in the pile of things.*) I... can't... I... can't....

SCENE 2

The clank of the falling bicycle. VASYA *enters decisively.*

VASYA. Damn that blasted bicycle! Family bliss my foot—to hell with it! There. Got that off my chest.... Lyudmila... I need to have a serious talk with you. Things can't go on like this.... The thing is, I.... The thing is, we.... The thing is, our relationship... is radically.... But don't get mad, that's the main thing, just try to understand me. How can I explain this?... You can see that I want to be completely fair with you. Maybe this will be unpleasant for you, maybe even painful. But it's best to be frank and honest.... Sew up these pants for me. (*To the side.*) I mean... what am I saying?

LYUDMILA. Drop that petty bourgeois nonsense.

VASYA. What? What?

LYUDMILA. The petty bourgeois nonsense. It's unethical.

VASYA. How about that! (*Looks at* LYUDMILA *for some time in amazement, whistling. After a bit of a pause, heatedly.*) No, no, Lyudmilochka! You're wrong to say that this is unethical. Now if I were deceiving you, or lying, or faking... do you understand? Then, of course, that would be rotten and unethical. But you see, I want to talk frankly and honestly to you, comrade to comrade.

LYUDMILA. I'm not your slave, but an autonomous companion. You ripped your pants; sew them up yourself.

VASYA. What do my pants have to do with anything? This isn't about my pants.

LYUDMILA. Then what is this about?

VASYA (*irritated*). Not about that. You see.... (*To the side.*) I just can't bring myself to say it... she'll never survive this; she'll take her own life, for sure. But.... (*With exaggerated brusqueness.*) It's about you and... well, of course... well, and about Abram.... About your...

LYUDMILA. Oh my God! He knows everything. This is madness....

VASYA. Don't interrupt me. I'm talking... about your... I mean about... have a drink. Do you understand me?

LYUDMILA. Oh, pussycat! I don't understand a thing. Cross my heart, I don't understand a thing. (*To herself.*) He'll never survive it, that's for sure; he'll end his life. His eyes are wild.... (*To him.*) I don't know anything, pussycat, I don't understand a thing.... I just beg you one thing, pussycat, don't get upset... don't torture me. As it is.... (*Drops her head on the bundle.*)

VASYA. Here's the thing, Lyudmila.... (*Turns away from her toward the cupboard in despair.*) I just can't bring myself to say it. She'll never survive it; she'll end her life.... For sure. She adores me so much, it's just awful. (*Throws up his hands.*) What's the use? (*Collapses against the cupboard.*)

LYUDMILA (*lifts up her head and sees* VASYA's *dispirited figure*). Poor thing! He's suffering so much.... (*Decisively.*) But who cares.... Let him. (*Once again starts picking up the bundles.*) It doesn't matter, it doesn't matter....

VASYA. What are you doing?

LYUDMILA. Don't ask me, Vasya.

VASYA. What, are you leaving?

LYUDMILA. Yes, I'm leaving.

VASYA (*with poorly concealed joy*). How come?

LYUDMILA. I'm leaving. Don't ask!

VASYA (*hypocritically*). But, really, now... Lyudmila...

LYUDMILA. No, no! Do you remember how we agreed it would be? Don't say anything to me... don't ask. Don't try to hold me back; let me go....

VASYA (*hypocritically*). What are you talking about, Lyudmilochka? How could I not let you go, kitty-cat? Don't be ridiculous.... We don't have some sort of feudal marriage.... For God's sake.... Please... I only... I was just curious. Of course, you can't force love.

LYUDMILA. Well, then... so.... (*Lifts the bundles.*) I'm going. Farewell.

VASYA. Well.... (*Goes up to see her off, not sure how to behave.*)

LYUDMILA (*wanting to avoid a difficult scene*). No, no, don't worry, I'll be back.... There are a few things left here.... Farewell, Vasya.

VASYA. Farewell, Lyudmilochka....

(*She leaves. Barely able to contain his joy at the fact that everything has worked out so well, he walks behind her, mumbling.*)

But still, maybe.... Somehow.... You could stay.... I promise.... Honestly, Lyudmilochka.... Watch out, don't bump into the bicycle. (*Walks to the door and starts to do a little dance.*) She's gone, she's gone! And it was all so easy. She's gone.... He-he!... Ho-ho!... Without any melodrama.... Oh, thank you! Tonya, my Tonechka, Tonya... my Tonechka... Tonya, my little peach.... (*Starts dancing and laughing loudly. The left half of the curtain closes on him as he is dancing.*)

SCENE 3

The right side of the curtain opens. ABRAM *is by himself.*

ABRAM (*sitting, bent over*). Compatible personalities? We got it. Mutual understanding? We got it. Class affiliation? We got it. Proletarian workers' solidarity? We got it. We've got everything—but all the same there's this spectacular disaster. What's the problem? I don't understand.... Compatible personalities? We got it. Proletarian workers' solidarity? We got it. We've got everything, but everything's still down in the dumps. Or should I go right up to Tonya and tell her everything? Or would that be unethical? Huh? No, she'll never survive it. Or would it be ethical? Huh? Or not? A guy could go crazy!

SCENE 4

Enter EMELIAN.

EMELIAN. Hi, buddy!
ABRAM. Hi.
EMELIAN. Dance.
ABRAM. Why should I dance?

EMELIAN. Because you're supposed to. Dance.

ABRAM. How do you like that!

EMELIAN. Dance, I said.

ABRAM. What, are you drunk or something?

EMELIAN. Dance, dance! Well? "Why are you so down? Because you've got a frown...." Come on! (*Sings a dance tune and stomps his foot.*)

ABRAM. Ever see a loony bird? That's one there.

EMELIAN. Takes one to know one. Dance!

ABRAM. Why should I dance?

EMELIAN. Because you don't know the rules and regs. We have a rule: If someone gets a letter, he's duty-bound to dance. (*Takes out a letter.*) There it is. A letter. So dance! (*Sings.*)

ABRAM. Who's the letter for?

EMELIAN. For you, for you! Dance!

ABRAM. A letter for me? That's a rare historical event. I haven't received a letter since 1917. I even forgot what you're supposed to do. Let me have it.

EMELIAN. Dance!

ABRAM. Seriously, let me have it.

(EMELIAN *holds the letter above his head and won't give it up.*)

Quit fooling around!

EMELIAN. Dance, or else you-know-what. (*Shows his muscles.*) Ha! Feel!

ABRAM. Get a load of that maniac! Who's it from?

EMELIAN. From your life's companion, from your spouse.

ABRAM. What spouse?

EMELIAN. Uh, yours. Tonya.

ABRAM. Kuznetsova? Something happen to her?

EMELIAN. Nothing happened to her. I ran into her in the administration building. She asked me to give the letter to you. Dance!

ABRAM. Gimme a break. Let me have it.

EMELIAN. Fat chance. Dance!

ABRAM. Oh lord! Get a load of that fool. I've got a family crisis staring me in the face, and he's trying to get me to dance! I don't know how to dance; I have no idea. Well, come on, let me have it!

EMELIAN. Dance!

ABRAM. But I don't know how.... Aw, damn you! (*Awkwardly dances to* EMELIAN'*s hand-clapping and musical accompaniment.*) Well, let me have it!

EMELIAN. You know, you're about as much of a dancer as a bull in a china shop. Comic dancer. Here you go.

ABRAM. Ugh, I can just taste it, here comes the feudal part. (*He's so upset he can't tear open the envelope.*)

EMELIAN. Hang on, give me the letter. Your hands are shaking. (*Opens the envelope.*)

ABRAM (*reads*). "Comrade Abram, I have thought for a long time and have come to the conclusion that things can't go on like this. Under the current objective circumstances...."

EMELIAN. I told you so. Remember, on the way to the sauna....

ABRAM (*annoyed*). Hold it, Emelian, this is no laughing matter. (*Keeps reading.*) "Under the current objective circumstances our shared domestic life is unacceptable. Of course, you understand what I'm referring to." Total disaster.... (*Reads.*) "I consider it imperative to take official action in this regard...." Oh no, she's probably about to poison herself....

EMELIAN. No, she'll drown herself, my dear, she'll drown herself.... (*Strokes his head.*)

ABRAM (*in a rage*). Back off, Emelian. (*Reads.*) "I have to leave. Gather your courage and don't try to hold me back.... This is how it must be...." Total catastrophe!

EMELIAN. Terrible! Terrible!

ABRAM (*reading*). "By the time you read this letter, I will most likely be...." Just not in the crematorium, just not in the crematorium....

EMELIAN. No, in the Moscow River. It's cooler there....

ABRAM (*jumps up in a rage*). Emelian!

(EMELIAN *quiets down.* ABRAM *keeps reading.*)

"I will be riding..."

EMELIAN (*correcting him*). "Writhing...."

ABRAM (*yielding in fright*). "... Writhing a train out...."

EMELIAN (*reading over his shoulder*). "Writhing a train out to the countryside...." No, somehow that doesn't sound quite right.

ABRAM (*joyfully*). "Riding a train out to the countryside, where the administration has sent me at my personal request. Try to forget about me and give the books back to Sonya Ogurtsova. With my Komsomol regards. A. Kuznetsova." Oh, Tonya! Good job! And I thought there would be something horribly feudal. Ha! No melodrama! Lyudmilka, you hear? "With my Komsomol regards. Kuznetsova!" (*Starts dancing wildly.*)

(*From the left side of the stage, behind the curtain, dance music: a guitar and the stomping and shrill singing of* VASYA *are heard.*)

EMELIAN. Get a load of that! Look what's gotten into him! And he was just whining that he had no idea how to dance. Oho!

ABRAM (*dancing*). She's gone! She's gone! She's gone!

(*The left half of the curtain draws open and reveals* VASYA, *playing the guitar and dancing joyfully.*)

SCENE 5

VASYA *is dancing on the left,* ABRAM *on the right.* EMELIAN *looks on in quiet bewilderment. While they are dancing,* VASYA *and* ABRAM *move toward each other in the middle of the stage, stare, and wink at each other.*

VASYA (*sings and dances*). She's gone, she's gone, she's gone, she's gone!

ABRAM (*sings and dances*). She's gone, she's gone, she's gone, she's gone!

EMELIAN. What a bunch of fools!

VASYA (*stops, looks at* ABRAM). She's gone! Ha-ha! She's gone....

ABRAM (*stops, looks at* VASYA). She's gone! That's a fact!

VASYA (*laughing loudly, winking*). She's gone....

ABRAM (*laughing loudly, winking*). She's gone!

VASYA. Just wait! Who's gone?

EMELIAN. Just wait! Who's gone?

ABRAM. Yeah, who is gone?

EMELIAN. Yeah, who is gone?

VASYA. Lyudmilka, of course.

EMELIAN. Lyudmilka, of course.

ABRAM. What... Lyudmila's gone?... Are you crazy? Kuznetsova's gone!

EMELIAN. Are you crazy? Kuznetsova's gone.

VASYA. What? Are you crazy? Tonya... gone? Are you joking?

EMELIAN. Are you joking?

ABRAM. Just wait! (*Dumbfounded.*)

VASYA. Just wait! (*Dumbfounded.*)

EMELIAN. Just wait all you want, folks, but it's very simple: Both chicks have split. Clear as day.

VASYA. Just wait... she's... really... gone?

ABRAM. She's really gone.

EMELIAN. Really gone?

ABRAM. Really. So?

EMELIAN. Really. So?

VASYA. Where to?

EMELIAN. Where to?

ABRAM. She went to work out in the country. So?

EMELIAN. She went out to the country. So?

VASYA. To the country.... How can that be? Just wait....

EMELIAN. How can that be? Just wait....

ABRAM. Just wait! Lyudmila... really?

EMELIAN. Really?

VASYA. Really. So?

EMELIAN. So?

ABRAM. Where to? Where to? Tell me!

VASYA. Pretty much... not really sure.... So?

ABRAM (*in despair*). What were you thinking?

EMELIAN. What were you thinking?

VASYA. What do you mean, me? What were you thinking? How could you let her go?

EMELIAN. No, really, how could you let her go?

ABRAM. No, really, what were you thinking?

EMELIAN. No, really, what were you thinking?

VASYA. What was I thinking? Just wait! What does this have to do with you, anyway?

EMELIAN. What does this have to do with you?

ABRAM (*in a fit*). What does this have to do with who? What does this have to do with you, more like.

EMELIAN. What does this have to do with him?

VASYA. Shut up! You drove that girl to the point where she'd go out to the middle of nowhere rather than look at your stupid face. Where is she? Where can I find her now?

EMELIAN. Where can he find her now?

ABRAM. I drove her? What about you? What were you sitting there doing? What did you drive Lyudmilochka to do? (*Mimicking.*) "Pussycat, give me a kiss on the nose! Pussycat, say 'meow!'"

VASYA. What business is that of yours?

EMELIAN. What business is it of yours?

ABRAM. What business is it of yours?

VASYA. Ugh! I can't stand the sight of you! Lousy bourgeois so-and-so!

ABRAM. Well, you're a renegade!

VASYA. Who are you calling a renegade? Me, a renegade?

ABRAM. Renegade and opportunist!

EMELIAN (*delighted*). That's right, guys, get it on, just watch out for the musical instrument.

VASYA. Who's a renegade?

EMELIAN. Who are you calling a renegade?

ABRAM. Put that guitar down! (*Steps out the door.*)

EMELIAN (*looking out the door*). That's right, you tell him! Ho-ho! A regular impromptu performance!

VASYA'S VOICE. Who are you calling a renegade?

(*The clank of the bicycle falling.*)

EMELIAN (*speaking out the door*). Guys, that's not the way to do it, you'll wreck the guitar. Fight by the rules, like they do in the novels. On the second floor, in apartment eighteen, Volodya Sinitsyn has a couple sabers from the Civil War. Have at it!

(*Noise.*)

Go for it! Just make sure everything's by the book. No ifs, ands, or buts!

ABRAM'S VOICE. Put that guitar down!

VASYA'S VOICE. Who are you calling a renegade?

ABRAM'S VOICE. Put that guitar down, or I won't answer for my actions. Let go of it!

VASYA'S VOICE. Stop right there!

EMELIAN (*speaking out the door*). Go get the sabers! Ho-ho! Fight it out, guys!

(*The noise in the hallway dies down.*)

SCENE 6

EMELIAN (*returns, wiping his brow, as if after a fierce battle*). Now that's what I call a dance! What fun! I'm a little hot myself. Well, now that the chicks have split for good, I'll even be able to stay overnight, praise be. And check out the grub! (*Lies down.*) I'm going to write a new poem. (*Eats, kicks back, and writes.*) I just need to set up a decent work space. (*Moves all the furniture around.*) Well, okay, let's start with that jingle I'm supposed to do for mineral water. "Here's our water, try a box; it'll make you strong as an ox." Somehow that doesn't quite work....

SCENE 7

Enter FLAVII. *Looks around in bewilderment at the havoc-stricken room and at* EMELIAN, *who is sprawled out impressively.*

FLAVII. Emelian, is that you?

EMELIAN. We are here.... Hi, Flavii! You hungry?

FLAVII Hi! What are you doing, setting up shop in someone else's home?

EMELIAN. Yes, it was someone else's home, but they've all left.

FLAVII (*taking in the devastation*). What's going on here?

EMELIAN. A six-act drama. The chicks have split, and the guys ran up to apartment eighteen to get some swords.

FLAVII. Are you drunk or something? Talk sense.

EMELIAN. I am talking sense. Tonya, that weirdo, got the hots for Vasya. Lyudmilka fell for Abram. Vaska, ass that he is, has a crush on Tonya. Abramchik's got a thing for Lyudmilka. And they're all so uptight about it that it just came to a head today. Tonya couldn't take it, so she split. Lyudmilka couldn't take it, so she split. Vaska and Abramchik ran up to apartment eighteen to cut each other up with swords. And I figured in the meantime I'd move in here.

FLAVII. A duel?

EMELIAN. By the book, just like the old authors would say: A sword to the head, and that's all she wrote. They're really steamed—it's kind of scary. He-he!

FLAVII. Then what are you doing sitting around here laughing, you dimwit? Two numbskulls have run off to fight an idiotic duel, bring shame on the organization, and a third numbskull is kicked back with his feet on someone else's bed—and all he can say is he-he.... Well! Up and at 'em! Let's see you use those muscles! Bring the duelists here! Dead or alive! On the double!

EMELIAN. U-ugh! (*Leaves.*)

SCENE 8

FLAVII. Bring scandal on the whole region. (*Whistles significantly.*) Nice work.

(*Pause.*)

Soviet Hussars, eh? Pshaw!

SCENE 9

Enter TONYA, *gasping for breath between sobs. She gathers her things and means to leave.*

FLAVII (*walks across the stage to* ABRAM's *half; sees* TONYA). Where are you headed?

TONYA. I'm going, Flavii.

FLAVII. Where are you going?

TONYA. To work. Out in the country.

FLAVII. Well how do you like that! All of a sudden takes it into her head to go work out in the country. How come?

TONYA. Don't ask, Flavii. This is very difficult for me. It's just the way it has to be. Farewell, Flavii.

FLAVII. Oh, no, you don't! Hang on. You just tell me all about it. Something happen?

TONYA. Yes.... No.... Nothing happened. Well... farewell.

FLAVII. Kuznetsova! Don't try to fast-talk me. Tell me straight: What has happened here?

TONYA. Nothing.

FLAVII. Hmm... nothing?

TONYA. Nothing. I don't know.

(*Pause.*)

SCENE 10

During the pause, LYUDMILA, *in tears, enters her half of the room with a bundle.*

LYUDMILA (*holding back sobs and blowing her nose*). I forgot Grandma and Grandpa....

(*Climbs up to get the pictures, takes them, and on the way down starts listening to the voices of* FLAVII *and* TONYA, *which are growing louder. Goes up to the partition.*)

FLAVII. You don't know? Well, then I know. Do you love Vaska? Come on, look me in the eyes.

TONYA. I do.

FLAVII. Does Vaska love you? Look me in the eyes.

TONYA. He does.

FLAVII. So why are you trying to keep me in the dark? What's with the psychological melodrama? You love each other—what's the big deal? Just hop down to the marriage bureau, no reason to go out to the country.

TONYA. What about Abram?

FLAVII. You should have thought of that before you...

TONYA. I thought.... We thought.... Compatible personalities.... Proletarian solidarity.... Common... political platform. (*Sobs.*) And here... and here.... (*Through her tears.*) No, no, comrade Abram would never survive it. Comrade Lyudmila would never survive it. You see, Flavii, we must not build our own happiness on the misery of other comrades....

(*Sobs.* LYUDMILA *stares into the room and suddenly drops the pictures of her grandma and grandpa on the floor, stands there holding the bundle in her hands, howls, and wants to run.*)

FLAVII (*to her*). Where are you headed?

(LYUDMILA *stops, hesitates, then runs to* TONYA, *who is crying over her own bundle, and hugs her. Speaks through her tears.*)

LYUDMILA. Oh, Tonechka, oh, my little darling...

TONYA. Comrade Lyudmila...

LYUDMILA. My little kitten, I heard everything.... There's no need to cry, honest.... You take Vaska, but for God's sake, just don't get upset, because I don't mind. But without Abram... life's not worth living....

(*They both shed tears of joy over the bundles.*)

TONYA. My darling, my little baby, my sister...

FLAVII (*comforting them*). Here it comes, now they're really going to cry. Ugh, chickadees! But, then again, sometimes it helps.... Go ahead and cry!

(*Backstage shouting, clanking, cacophony, the sound of the bicycle falling, general uproar.*)

TONYA. What's going on?

LYUDMILA. Wha-a.... What is it? Fire?

FLAVII. Calm down, girls. No big deal. It's our two roosters, the white one and the black one, settling a little domestic score.

SCENE 11

VASYA *and* ABRAM *stumble into the room, fighting.* VASYA *is bandying his sword about, while* ABRAM *is still trying to draw his from the sheath. Behind them, and louder than either, is* EMELIAN.

EMELIAN (*clumsily running around the fencers*). Where are you going? Where are you going? Hold it! Easy, easy! Honestly, you guys are crazy! You're going to wreck a musical instrument.... Vaska... Abramchik...

VASYA. Where's Tonya, I said!

ABRAM. What have you done with Lyudmilka?

VASYA. What business is it of yours?

ABRAM. What business is it of yours?

VASYA. Petty bourgeois scum!

ABRAM. Let me go! I'm going to rip his head off!

(*He pulls his sword out of the sheath. Turns out the blade is broken, with only a little bit sticking out of the hilt.* VASYA *steps back and knocks the screen over. Behind the screen are* TONYA, LYUDMILA, *and* FLAVII. *General confusion. Everyone is dumbfounded.*)

VASYA. Tonya! Lyudmilka!

ABRAM. Lyudmilka! Tonya!

(*They don't know what to do or how to act.*)

VASYA. Flavii!

ABRAM. Flavii!

FLAVII. Beautiful! Tonya, Lyudmilka, what do you say to this? Two damn fools are dueling with musical instruments. A picture worthy of Ayva-zovsky's brush.

ABRAM (*faking happiness*). Kuznetsova, you're not out in the country yet?

(*He's about to run to her.* TONYA *stops him with a grandiosely righteous gesture and points to* LYUDMILA.)

VASYA (*faking*). Lyudmilochka, you're back? I'm awfully happy!

(LYUDMILA *copies* TONYA*'s gesture with respect to* VASYA *and* TONYA.)

ABRAM. What's wrong, Tonechka?

FLAVII. Guys! Drop this foolishness! Don't hem and haw—Everything's clear, everybody knows, it's all out in the open.

EMELIAN. And it all checks out.

FLAVII. Tonya, do you love Vaska?

TONYA. I do.

FLAVII. Lyudmilochka, do you love Abramchik?

LYUDMILA. I do.

ABRAM. Comrades, this is unethical. Isn't it? Or is it ethical?

FLAVII. Abramchik, don't try to be a smarty-pants. Guys, what are you standing around for?

(*Everyone understands everything. Pause.*)

You guys rushed headlong into marriage without stopping to think, and then the whole thing turns into some kind of melodrama, and I'm left picking up the pieces. Comrades, I do have other responsibilities! Well, I never!

(LYUDMILA *runs to* ABRAM, *and* TONYA *to* VASYA.)

TONYA. Vasyuk!

LYUDMILA. Abramchik, my darling!

VASYA. Tonya!

ABRAM. Lyudmilochka!

(*Hugs.*)

FLAVII (*to* EMELIAN). Better pull up stakes, brother. As you can see, you're not spending the night here. Get going!

EMELIAN. Maybe I could do an impromptu poem? Want me to?

FLAVII. Get going, get going! Beat it....

EMELIAN. "U-ugh! the city has beaten me down. Nevermore will I see my hometown. I'll just make sure my collar is loose. So there's plenty of room for a noose...." U-ugh! The self-taught genius expires in front of everyone. I'm going to go spend the night in apartment eighteen. (*Leaves.*)

FLAVII. Fair enough. Perhaps he won't expire. (*Picks up the pictures of Grandma and Grandpa off the floor and gives one of them to one couple, the other to the other couple.*) Well then, in accordance with the laws governing matrimony you'll split up the property. You take Grandpa. You take Grandma.

(*They take them.*)

So.... I guess everything is in order, then.

VASYA (*to* ABRAM, *humorously*). Pussycat, say "meow" to your kitty.

ABRAM (*cheerfully*). Meow!

FLAVII. It's okay, guys. Love one another, and no more monkey business.

VOICE FROM THE RADIO (*interrupts* FLAVII). Hello! Hello! The performance is over; we now turn to the next part of our program. I give you the auditorium.

(*The lights are raised in the auditorium. A song from onstage.*)

ALL.

O, comrades, life's a bumpy ride,
You love, you suffer, and you play;
So laugh, and take it all in stride
When something funny comes your way.

TONYA *and* VASYA.

> Now who's the groom and who's the bride
> Is often difficult to say.
> But laugh, and take it all in stride
> When something funny comes your way.

FLAVII.

> When someone loses all his pride
> And smokes and drinks wine night and day
> Well then, don't grin or take his side
> For laughter here is not okay.

LYUDMILA *and* ABRAM.

> But if he's at his sweetheart's side
> With kisses driving cares away
> Then laugh, and take it all in stride
> When something funny comes your way.

EMELIAN (*suddenly rides out onstage on the bicycle*).

> Although all day I've tried and tried,
> I'm stuck without a place to stay.
> I'm begging you, please don't be snide;
> This is no joke, say what you may.

ALL.

> O, comrades, life's a bumpy ride,
> You love, you suffer, and you play;
> So laugh, and take it all in stride
> When something funny comes your way.

(*Curtain.*)

Elizaveta Bam

Daniil Kharms 1927

A small, shallow, simple room.

1. REALISTIC MELODRAMA

ELIZAVETA BAM. Right now, at any moment, the door will open and they
will come in.... They are sure to come in, to catch me and wipe me off
the face of the earth. (*Softly.*) What have I done! What have I done! If
only I had known.... Escape. But where to? This door opens onto the
stairs, and I'll run into them on the stairs. Through the window? (*She
looks out the window.*) Ooh! It's high up.... I can't jump it. Well, what can
I do.... Eh, someone's footsteps. It's them. I'll lock the door and I won't
open it. Let them knock as much as they want.

(*A knock at the door, then a voice offstage, threateningly.*)

VOICE. Elizaveta Bam, open up. (*Pause.*) Elizaveta Bam, open up.
A VOICE FROM THE DISTANCE. Well, what is she up to? Why won't she
open the door?
A VOICE BEHIND THE DOOR. She'll open it. Elizaveta Bam, open up.

(ELIZAVETA BAM *flings herself onto the bed and covers her ears. Voices
are heard from behind the door.*)

FIRST VOICE. Elizaveta Bam, I order you to open this door at once.
SECOND VOICE (*softly*). You tell her we'll break down the door otherwise.
Here, let me try.
FIRST VOICE (*loudly*). We'll break the door down ourselves if you don't
open it this instant.
SECOND VOICE (*softly*). Maybe she isn't here.
FIRST VOICE (*softly*). She's here. Where else could she be? She ran right
up the stairs. There's only one door here. Where else could she get to?
(*Loudly.*) Elizaveta Bam, I'm telling you for the last time—

(ELIZAVETA BAM *lifts up her head.*)

—open the door. (*Pause.*) Break it down.

(*With an alliterative sound, they try to break down the door.* ELIZAVETA BAM *runs to the middle of the stage and listens.*)

SECOND VOICE. You don't happen to have a knife, do you?

(*A crash.* ELIZAVETA BAM *listens, with a shoulder pushed forward.*)

FIRST VOICE. No. Use your shoulder.
SECOND VOICE. It won't give. Just hold on, I'll try it again.

(*A cracking sound, but the door doesn't break.*)

ELIZAVETA BAM. I won't open the door for you until you tell me what you are going to do with me.

(*The banging dies down.*)

FIRST VOICE. You know yourself what you're facing.
ELIZAVETA BAM. No, I don't know. You want to kill me?
FIRST VOICE (*speaking together with* SECOND VOICE). You are subject to dire punishment!
SECOND VOICE. No matter what, you won't get away from us!
ELIZAVETA BAM. Maybe you could tell me what I'm guilty of.
FIRST VOICE. You know yourself.
ELIZAVETA BAM. No, I don't know. (*Stamps her foot.*)
FIRST VOICE. Forgive us if we don't believe you.
SECOND VOICE. You are a criminal.
ELIZAVETA BAM. Ha, ha, ha, ha. And if you kill me, do you think your conscience will be clear? (*Runs to another spot.*)
FIRST VOICE. We'll do it in consultation with our consciences.
ELIZAVETA BAM. In that case, alas, you have no conscience.

2. REALISTIC COMEDY GENRE

SECOND VOICE. What do you mean, no conscience? Pyotr Nikolayevich, she says we have no conscience.

ELIZAVETA BAM. You have no conscience at all, Ivan Ivanovich. You're just a crook. (*Stands with her hands on her thighs, head straining toward the door.*)

SECOND VOICE. Who's a crook? Me? Me? I'm a crook?

FIRST VOICE. Now wait a minute, Ivan Ivanovich. Elizaveta Bam, I order you...

SECOND VOICE. No, Pyotr Nikolayevich—so I'm a crook? Bobchinsky.[1]

FIRST VOICE. Hold on, don't get offended. Elizaveta Bam, I ord...

SECOND VOICE. No, *you* hold on, Pyotr Nikolayevich. Tell me, am I a crook?

FIRST VOICE. Just drop it.

SECOND VOICE. So, in your opinion, I'm a crook, am I?

FIRST VOICE. Yes, you're a crook!!!

SECOND VOICE. Ah, so, in your opinion I'm a crook! Is that what you said?

(ELIZAVETA BAM *runs around the stage.*)

FIRST VOICE. Get the hell outta here! What a clown!! And he goes out on a big case. Somebody says one word to you and you're climbing the walls. And what does that make you? A simple idiot!

SECOND VOICE. And you're a fraud.

FIRST VOICE. Get the hell outta here!

ELIZAVETA BAM. Ivan Ivanovich is a crook.

SECOND VOICE. I'll never forgive you for this.

FIRST VOICE. I'm going to chuck you down these stairs right now.

(ELIZAVETA BAM *opens the doors.* IVAN IVANOVICH *is standing on crutches, while* PYOTR NIKOLAYEVICH *sits on a chair with a bandaged cheek.*)

IVAN IVANOVICH. You just go ahead and try.

PYOTR NIKOLAYEVICH. I'll chuck you. I will, I will!

ELIZAVETA BAM. You're not up to it.

PYOTR NIKOLAYEVICH. What? *I'm* not up to it?

ELIZAVETA BAM (*speaking together with* IVAN IVANOVICH). That's right.

IVAN IVANOVICH. Yeah, you! You! Tell him, you mean him, right? (*Points to* PYOTR NIKOLAYEVICH.)

ELIZAVETA BAM. Him.

PYOTR NIKOLAYEVICH. Elizaveta Bam, how dare you speak like that?

ELIZAVETA BAM. Why?

PYOTR NIKOLAYEVICH. Because you've been deprived of any voice. You have committed a vile crime. You can't say insolent things to me. You are a criminal.

ELIZAVETA BAM. Why?

PYOTR NIKOLAYEVICH. What do you mean, why?

ELIZAVETA BAM. Why am I a criminal?

PYOTR NIKOLAYEVICH. Because you've been deprived of any voice.

IVAN IVANOVICH. Deprived of any voice.

ELIZAVETA BAM. I am not deprived! You can check it with your watch.

(*The backdrop is pulled away, giving* IVAN IVANOVICH *and* PYOTR NIKOLAYEVICH *access through the door.*)

3. COMICALLY ABSURD NAIVE GENRE

PYOTR NIKOLAYEVICH. It'll never come to that. I've stationed guards at the doors and, at the slightest push, Ivan Ivanovich will hiccup to one side.

ELIZAVETA BAM. Show me. Please, show me!

PYOTR NIKOLAYEVICH. Now watch. Please turn around.

(PYOTR NIKOLAYEVICH *goes downstage.* IVAN IVANOVICH *follows after him. One. Two. Three. He taps on a pedestal.* IVAN IVANOVICH *hiccups loudly and upends the pedestal.*)

ELIZAVETA BAM. Once more. Please.

(*They repeat the action.* PYOTR NIKOLAYEVICH *taps the pedestal again while* IVAN IVANOVICH *hiccups again.*)

How do you do that?

PYOTR NIKOLAYEVICH. It's very simple. Ivan Ivanovich, show her!

IVAN IVANOVICH. With pleasure. (*He gets down on all fours and kicks up one of his legs.*)

ELIZAVETA BAM. Why this is just incredibly good! (*She shouts.*) Mommy! Come here. Some magicians have come. Mommy is coming any minute now.... May I introduce Pyotr Nikolayevich, Ivan Ivanovich.... Will you show us something?

IVAN IVANOVICH. With pleasure.

PYOTR NIKOLAYEVICH. Alley-oop!

(IVAN IVANOVICH *tries to stand on his head, but fails.*)

Here we go! Here we go!

(MOMMY *and* DADDY *enter. They sit down and watch.*)

IVAN IVANOVICH (*sitting on the floor*). There's nothing to lean on here.

ELIZAVETA BAM (*flirtatiously*). Perhaps you'd like a towel?

IVAN IVANOVICH. What for?

ELIZAVETA BAM. Just because. (*Giggles.*)

IVAN IVANOVICH. You're extremely attractive.

ELIZAVETA BAM. Oh, really? Why?

IVAN IVANOVICH. Uhhhhh, because you are a forget-me-not. (*Hiccups loudly.*)

ELIZAVETA BAM. I'm a forget-me-not? Really? And you are a tulip. (*She pronounces "tulip" through her nose.*)

IVAN IVANOVICH. What was that?

ELIZAVETA BAM. A tulip.

IVAN IVANOVICH (*perplexed*). Pleased, I'm sure.

ELIZAVETA BAM (*through her nose*). Allow me to pluck you.

FATHER (*in a bass voice*). Elizaveta, stop this nonsense.

ELIZAVETA (*to* FATHER). I will stop right now, Daddy. (*Squats and props herself up on a root. To* IVAN IVANOVICH, *through her nose.*) Get on your hands and knees.

(PYOTR NIKOLAYEVICH *approaches* DADDY *and* MOMMY. MOMMY *is displeased by something. She goes downstage.*)

IVAN IVANOVICH. If you'll allow me, Elizaveta Cockroachson, I'd better be going home. My wife is waiting for me at home. She has many kids, Elizaveta Cockroachson. Pardon me for boring you so. Don't forget me. I am the kind of person that everyone kicks out. For what, I wonder. Have I stolen something? But no, Elizaveta Edwardson, I am an honest man. I have a wife at home. My wife's got a lot of kids. Great kids. Each one holds a matchbox between his teeth. So you must excuse me. I, Elizaveta Michaelson, am going home.

(IVAN IVANOVICH *puts on a winter coat and exits.* ELIZAVETA BAM *ties a cord to one of* MOMMY*'s legs, and she ties the other end of the cord to a chair. Everyone is silent.*)

MOMMY (*sings to music*).
Look, the morning has burst into flame.
The water reddens,
A seagull flies swiftly over the lake....

(MOMMY *finishes singing. She goes to her place, dragging the chair behind her.*)

PYOTR NIKOLAYEVICH. Well, there we are.
DADDY. God be praised. (*Exits.*)

4. REALISTIC GENRE, A COMEDY OF DAILY LIFE

ELIZAVETA BAM. And you, Mommy, aren't you going out for a walk?
MOMMY. Why? Would you like to?
ELIZAVETA BAM. Terribly!

MOMMY. No, I won't go.
ELIZAVETA BAM. Can't we go? Ple-ea-ease.
MOMMY. Well, alright, let's go.

(*They exit. The stage is empty.*)

5. RHYTHMIC (RADIX), AUTHOR'S RHYTHM

IVAN IVANOVICH *and* PYOTR NIKOLAYEVICH *run in.*

IVAN IVANOVICH *and* PYOTR NIKOLAYEVICH.
  Where, where, where,
  Elizaveta Bam
  Elizaveta Bam
  Elizaveta Bam.
PYOTR NIKOLAYEVICH. Here, here, here.
IVAN IVANOVICH There, there, there.

(PYOTR NIKOLAYEVICH *and* IVAN IVANOVICH, *accentual verse.*)

PYOTR NIKOLAYEVICH. Iván Ivanovích, whére are wé?
IVAN IVANOVICH. Pyótr Nikoláevich, we're únder lóck and kéy.
PYOTR NIKOLAYEVICH. Mán alíve! I bég you to stop shóving me.
IVAN IVANOVICH. Wéll Í'll bé! Thát's enóugh. It's fíve to five.

(PYOTR NIKOLAYEVICH *and* IVAN IVANOVICH, *singsong.*)

PYOTR NIKOLAYEVICH. Where's Elizaveta Bam?
IVAN IVANOVICH. Why do you need her?
PYOTR NIKOLAYEVICH. So I can kill her.
IVAN IVANOVICH.
  Hmm. Elizaveta Bam
  Is sitting on a bench down there.
PYOTR NIKOLAYEVICH. Then let's go. Scram!

(Both of them run in place. A log is carried to front stage, and while PYOTR NIKOLAYEVICH *and* IVAN IVANOVICH *run, the log is sawed up.)*

PYOTR NIKOLAYEVICH *and* IVAN IVANOVICH.
Hop, hop, with your feet,
The sun's behind the hills.
Like rosy clouds
downy, downy,
like locomotives
hoots an owl
hoot, hoot
The log is sawed.

6. THE DAILY GRIND, RADIX

The sidewing moves away, revealing ELIZAVETA BAM, *seated.*

ELIZAVETA BAM. Are you looking for me?
PYOTR NIKOLAYEVICH. Yes, you! Vanka, there she is!
IVAN IVANOVICH. Where, where? Where!
PYOTR NIKOLAYEVICH. Here, under the thingamajig.

(A BEGGAR *enters.)*

IVAN IVANOVICH. Drag her out.
PYOTR NIKOLAYEVICH. She won't drag.
BEGGAR *(to* ELIZAVETA BAM*).* Comrade, help me.
IVAN IVANOVICH *(stammering).* Next time I'll have more experience. As a matter of fact, I've been paying close attention.
ELIZAVETA BAM *(to the* BEGGAR*).* I have nothing.
BEGGAR. Even a penny would do.
ELIZAVETA BAM. Here, ask that nice man over there. (*Points to* PYOTR NIKOLAYEVICH.)

(*A table comes riding out.* ELIZAVETA BAM *moves the chair toward the table and sits down.*)

PYOTR NIKOLAYEVICH (*to* IVAN IVANOVICH, *stammering*). Watch what you're doing.
IVAN IVANOVICH. I'm digging roots up.
BEGGAR. Help me, comrades.
PYOTR NIKOLAYEVICH (*to* BEGGAR). Come on. Climb in there.
IVAN IVANOVICH. Prop your hands on the pebbles.

(BEGGAR *crawls under the wing.*)

PYOTR NIKOLAYEVICH. Don't worry, he knows how.
ELIZAVETA BAM. Why don't you sit down, too. Don't stand on ceremony.

(*Pause.*)

IVAN IVANOVICH. I thank you.
PYOTR NIKOLAYEVICH. Let's sit down.

(*They sit. They eat soup in silence.*)

ELIZAVETA BAM. For some reason, my husband isn't here. Where could he have gotten to?
PYOTR NIKOLAYEVICH. He'll come. (*Jumps up and runs around the stage.*) Abracadabra.
IVAN IVANOVICH. Ha, ha, ha. (*Runs directly toward* PYOTR NIKOLAYEVICH.) Where's base?
ELIZAVETA BAM. Right here, past that line.
PYOTR NIKOLAYEVICH (*taps* IVAN IVANOVICH). You're it!

(DADDY *comes onstage with a quill in his hand.*)

ELIZAVETA BAM. Ivan Ivanovich, run here.
IVAN IVANOVICH. Ha, ha, ha! I have no legs.

PYOTR NIKOLAYEVICH. Then come on all fours.

DADDY (*to the audience*). She about whom it was written.

ELIZAVETA BAM. Who's it?

IVAN IVANOVICH. Me, ha, ha, ha, the one wearing pants.

PYOTR NIKOLAYEVICH *and* ELIZAVETA BAM. Ha! Ha! Ha! Ha!

DADDY. Copernicus was a very great scientist.

IVAN IVANOVICH (*collapses on the floor*). I have hair on my head.

PYOTR NIKOLAYEVICH *and* ELIZAVETA BAM. Ha! Ha! Ha! Ha! Ha! Ha! Ha!

IVAN IVANOVICH. I'm lying right on the floor.

(MOMMY *enters.*)

PYOTR NIKOLAYEVICH *and* ELIZAVETA BAM. Ha! Ha! Ha! Ha!

ELIZAVETA BAM. Stop. Stop. I can't stand it!

DADDY. When you buy a bird, check to see whether it has teeth. If it has teeth then it's not a bird. (*Exits.*)

7. SOLEMN MELODRAMA EMPHASIZED BY THE RADIX

PYOTR NIKOLAYEVICH (*raising his hand*). I beg you to listen carefully to my words. I want to prove to you that every misfortune comes unexpectedly. When I was still quite a young man I lived in a small house with a squeaky door. I lived alone in that little house. Besides me there were only mice and cockroaches. Cockroaches crop up everywhere. When night fell I would lock the door and turn off the lamp. I slept, fearing nothing.

OFFSTAGE VOICE. Nothing.

MOMMY. Nothing.

WIND INSTRUMENT OFFSTAGE. I—I.[2]

IVAN IVANOVICH. Nothing.

PIANO. I—I.

PYOTR NIKOLAYEVICH. Nothing! (*Pauses.*) I had nothing to fear. Honest to goodness. Burglars could have come and searched the house. What would they have found? Nothing.

WIND INSTRUMENT OFFSTAGE. I—I.

(*Pause.*)

PYOTR NIKOLAYEVICH. And who else could have broken in at night? After all, there was no one else, right?
OFFSTAGE VOICE. After all, there was no one else.
PYOTR NIKOLAYEVICH. Right? But one time I wake up—

(*They hide one another.*)[3]

IVAN IVANOVICH.—and I see: the door's open and there's a woman standing in the door. I stare straight at her. She stands there. It was already fairly light. It must have been toward morning. In any case, I had a good look at her face. And that's who it was. (*Points at* ELIZAVETA BAM.) At that time she looked like...
EVERYONE. Like me!
IVAN IVANOVICH. I speak in order to exist.
ELIZAVETA BAM. What are you saying?
IVAN IVANOVICH. I speak in order to exist. Because I think that soon it will be too late. She listens to me.

(*Everyone leaves, except for* ELIZAVETA BAM *and* IVAN IVANOVICH.)

I asked her why she did it. She said they fought it out with swords. They fought fair and square, and it was not her fault that she killed him. Listen, why did you kill Pyotr Nikolayevich?
ELIZAVETA BAM. Hooray, I didn't kill anyone.
IVAN IVANOVICH. To up and butcher a man. How underhanded that is; hooray, you did do it, but why?

8. A SHIFTING OF LEVELS

ELIZAVETA BAM (*moves to one side*). OO-OO-OO-OO-OO-OO-OO
IVAN IVANOVICH. The she-wolf.

ELIZAVETA BAM. oo-oo-oo-oo-oo-oo-oo

IVAN IVANOVICH. Woo-oo-oo-oolf.

ELIZAVETA BAM (*trembling*). oo-oo-oo-oo-oo prunes.

IVAN IVANOVICH. Gr-rr-rr-reat-grandmother. Arm.

ELIZAVETA BAM. Exaltation!

IVAN IVANOVICH. She is ruined forever. Finger.

ELIZAVETA BAM. A black stallion, and on the stallion, a soldier.

IVAN IVANOVICH (*lighting a match*). Elizaveta, my dear. (IVAN IVAN-
OVICH's *hands tremble.*)

ELIZAVETA BAM. My shoulders are like the rising sun. (*She climbs up on a
chair.*)

IVAN IVANOVICH (*squatting*). My legs are like cucumbers.

ELIZAVETA BAM (*climbs higher*). Hooray! I said nothing.

IVAN IVANOVICH (*lying down on the floor*). No, no, nothing, nothing. G.
G. Psh. Psh.

ELIZAVETA BAM (*raising her hand*). Koo-nee-ma-ga-nee-lee-va-nee-bau.

IVAN IVANOVICH (*lying on the floor*).

Hickory, dickory, dock,

the mouse ran up the clock.

The clock struck nine,

the mouse fell down,

Hickory, dickory, dock.

ELIZAVETA BAM (*shouts*). Two wicker gates, a shirt. A rope.

IVAN IVANOVICH (*raising himself slightly*). Two carpenters come running
up and ask what's going on.

ELIZAVETA BAM. Hamburgers! Varvara Semyona!

IVAN IVANOVICH (*shouts through clenched teeth*). A high-wire dancer-r-r.

ELIZAVETA BAM (*jumping down from the chair*). I am glittering all over.

IVAN IVANOVICH (*running upstage*). We don't know the cubic measure-
ments of this room.

(*The set revolves from a room to a country setting. The wings serve up*
MOMMY *and* DADDY.)

ELIZAVETA BAM (*runs to the other side of the stage*). It's all in the family.
We'll work it out ourselves.

9. BUCOLIC LANDSCAPE

IVAN IVANOVICH (*jumping up on a chair*). The well-being of a Pennsylvania shepherd and shepher-r-r.

ELIZAVETA BAM (*jumping up on another chair*). Ivan Iva-a-a!

DADDY (*holding up a little box*). This box is made of woo-oo-oo!

IVAN IVANOVICH (*from his chair*). Show i-i-i-i-i!

DADDY. Take a loo-oo-oo!

MOMMY. Haloo-oo-oo.

ELIZAVETA BAM. I found a brown mushroo-oo-oo!

IVAN IVANOVICH. Let's go to the lake!

DADDY. Haloo-oo-oo!

ELIZAVETA BAM. Haloo-oo-oo!

IVAN IVANOVICH. I met Nicky yesterday!

MOMMY. No, really-y-y?!

IVAN IVANOVICH. Yes, yes, I met him, I did. I'm looking and here comes Nicky carrying apples. "Did ya buy 'em?" I says. "Yes," he says, "I bought 'em." Then he ups and walks away.

DADDY. You don't sa a ay!

IVAN IVANOVICH. Yes, indeed. I says to him, "Did you buy them apples or steal 'em?" And he says, "What do you mean, steal 'em? I bought 'em." And off he went.

MOMMY. Where'd he go?

IVAN IVANOVICH. Don't know. He just said, "I bought 'em; I didn't steal them," and off he went.

10. MONOLOGUE, ASIDE, A TWO-LEVEL PIECE

DADDY. With this not exactly cordial greeting, her sister led her to a more open place where golden tables and armchairs were piled up pell-mell. And fifteen or so young beauties gaily chatted among themselves, sitting on whatever was available. All of the maidens were in great need of a hot iron, and they all were distinguished by a strange manner of rolling their eyes without stopping their chatter for a moment.

(*A MAID enters. She brings out a tablecloth and a basket of groceries.*)

11. A SPEECH

IVAN IVANOVICH. Friends, we are all gathered here today. Hooray!

ELIZAVETA BAM. Hooray!

MOMMY *and* DADDY. Hooray!

IVAN IVANOVICH (*trembling and striking a match*). I want to tell you that thirty-eight years have passed since I was born.

DADDY *and* MOMMY. Hooray!

IVAN IVANOVICH. Comrades. I have a home. At home is my wife. She has many kids. I've counted them—there are ten.

MOMMY (*shuffling in place*). Darya, Maria, Feodor, Pelagaya, Nina, Alexander, and four others.

DADDY. Are they all boys?

12. CHINAR PIECE[4]

ELIZAVETA BAM (*runs around the stage*).

I've broken loose from everywhere.

I've broken loose and started running.

Broken loose and off I went.

MOMMY (*runs after* ELIZAVETA BAM). Do you eat bread?

ELIZAVETA BAM. Do you eat soup?

DADDY. Do you eat meat? (*Runs.*)

MOMMY. Do you eat flour?

ENTR'ACTE-CATARACT[5]

IVAN IVANOVICH. Do you eat rutabagas? (*He starts running.*)

ELIZAVETA BAM. Do you eat mutton?

DADDY. Do you eat burgers?

MOMMY. Oh, my legs are tired.

IVAN IVANOVICH. Oh, my arms are tired.

ELIZAVETA BAM. Oh, my scissors are tired.

DADDY. Oh, my springs are tired.

(*Offstage the* CHORUS *sings the theme of the overture.*)

MOMMY. The door to the balcony is open.

IVAN IVANOVICH. I'd like to jump up to the fourth floor.

ELIZAVETA BAM.

I've broken loose and started running.

I've broken loose and started running.

(*Music is heard.*)

DADDY. Hey, my right hand and nose are the same kind of objects as my left hand and ear!

(*One after another, everyone runs offstage.*)

CHORUS (*sings to the tune of the overture*).[6]

Well, goodbye now, do svidania

II—I.

II—I.

Up above, he says, there's a pine

And around, he says, it is dark.

On the pine, he says, is a bed,

And in bed there lies a spouse.

Well goodbye now, do svidania.

II—I.

II—I.

One time we ran

To an endless house,

And in the window up above,

A young old man looked through his glasses.

Well goodbye now, do svidania.

II—I

II—I

As the gate was swinging wide,

There appeared some I—I.

(*Overture. Lights go out.*)

13. RADIX

Only PYOTR NIKOLAYEVICH *is spotlighted.*

PYOTR NIKOLAYEVICH.
  You're all broken.
  Your chair is broken.
VIOLIN. Pa-pa-pí-pa. Pa-pa-pí-pa.
PYOTR NIKOLAYEVICH.
  Stand up like Berlin.
  Put on your pelerine.
VIOLIN. Pa-pa-pí-pa. Pa-pa-pí-pa.
PYOTR NIKOLAYEVICH.
  Eight minutes
  Will pass unnoticed.
VIOLIN. Pa-pa-pí-pa-pa. Pa-pa-pí.
PYOTR NIKOLAYEVICH.
  You've been given your orders
  wake the workers
  the platoon or the regiment
  to haul the machine gun.

  (DRUM *taps out a march.*)

  Week after week
  The fur was flying.
SIRENS *and* DRUMS. Viya-a-boom, boom
  viya-a-boom.

  (*The lights begin to get brighter.*)

PYOTR NIKOLAYEVICH
  The bride, *insouciant,* did not notice
  The stimy captain-noise.
SIREN. Viya-viya-viya.

PYOTR NIKOLAYEVICH.

Help me, help me this instant.
Over me there is salad and slush.

(*Full light.*)

VIOLIN. Pa-pa-pí-pa. Pa-pa-pí-pa.

(*The wings serve up* IVAN IVANOVICH.)

14. CLASSICAL PATHOS

IVAN IVANOVICH.

Please tell me, Pyotr Nikolayevich,
You've really been on yonder mount!
PYOTR NIKOLAYEVICH.

I've only just returned.
It's beautiful up there. (*Recitativo.*)
The trees are rustling and the flowers grow.
There stands a hut, a little wooden cottage
And in the hut there glows a little flame.
Around that flame the blackflies hover
And night's mosquitos bang against the window.
From time to time beneath the roof
An aged robber magpie flits and darts.
There barks a dog into the void before it
And with its chain it agitates the air.
And in reply unprepossessing dragonflies
Mumble incantations in every key.
IVAN IVANOVICH.

And in the little house, the one that's made of wood,
The one that has been called a hut,
The one in which a flamelet glows and dances,
Who lives inside that little house?

PYOTR NIKOLAYEVICH.

Inside it no one lives
And no one opens up the door.
There are just some mice in it who grind flour in their palms
There's just a lamp inside which glows like rosemary,
And all day long, upon the stove, a hermit cockroach sits.

IVAN IVANOVICH.

Who lights the lamp, then?

PYOTR NIKOLAYEVICH.

No one; it burns all by itself.

IVAN IVANOVICH.

But that just never happens!

PYOTR NIKOLAYEVICH.

Stupid empty words!
There is never-ending motion,
Respiration of the lightest particles.
The planets whiz, the earth is turning,
Wild exchange of night and day,
Deaf nature's combinations,
The strength and rage of swarming beasts,
And human conquest of the
Laws of light and wave.

IVAN IVANOVICH (*lighting a match*).

I've got it, got it, got it now
I'll curtsy and say thank you.
As usual I'm interested—
What time is it, pray tell?

PYOTR NIKOLAYEVICH.

It's four. Oh, time to dine!
Ivan Ivanovich, let's go,
But don't forget, tomorrow night
Elizaveta Bam will die.

DADDY (*entering*).

That is, Elizaveta Bam
Who is my daughter?
Whom you would like tomorrow night

To slaughter,
To string her up
Upon the highest tree,
The slender one,
For all the land
And all the beasts to see?
But by my mighty hand
I give to you this command:
Despite the laws of the land,
Forget Elizaveta Bam.

PYOTR NIKOLAYEVICH.

Just try and stop me,
I'll crush you in a minute.
With crimson lashes
I'll beat your joints,
And hack you, and blow you up high,
And set you on fire, and light up the sky.

IVAN IVANOVICH.

He knows it all, across the board,
He is a friend, though he's my lord.
He flicks his wing
And moves the seas.
He swings his ax but once
And fells the woods and mountains.
With but a single breath of air
Invisible, he's everywhere.

DADDY.

Let's fight it out, enchanter,
I with fists and you with words.
A minute passes, then an hour,
A second and a third.
And you will perish, so will I
And all will be at peace.
But let Elizaveta Bam, my child,
Let her rejoice at least.

15. BALLADIC PATHOS: THE COMBAT
OF TWO EPIC HEROES

Two tables are brought onstage.

IVAN IVANOVICH.

The combat of two epic heroes!
Scenario—Emanuel Krisditerik.
Music—by Heliopagus (A shepherd from the Netherlands).
Cybernetics—by an unknown traveler.
Church bells will announce the commencement of hostilities!

VOICES FROM VARIOUS PARTS OF THE HALL.

The combat of two epic heroes!
Scenario—Emanuel Krisditerik.
Music—by Heliopagus (The shepherd from the Netherlands).
Cybernetics—by an unknown traveler.
Church bells will announce the commencement of hostilities!
The combat of two epic heroes!

(*Et cetera.*)

BELL. Boom, boom, boom, boom, boom.

PYOTR NIKOLAYEVICH.

Kurabir, doramur
Dintsiri,
Slakatir, pakaradagu,
Da ki chiri, kiri, kiri
Zandudila, khabakula
Wha-a-a-a-h
Wanchu ana kudi
Stum chi na lakudi
Para vi na litena
Wha-a-a-a-h
Chapu, achapali
Chapatali mar,
Nabalóchíná,
Wha-a-a-a-h.

(Raises one hand.)

DADDY.

    Let winged parrot fly
    Up to the sun.
    Let day be wide
    And golden when it's done.
    Let hoofbeats' clop and clunk
    Through forests penetrate.
    And let foundation's trunk,
    Derailing, stridulate.
    A knight behind a table sits,
    With sword at hand
    A chalice lifts
    And cries aloud, to all the land
    "To my enthusiastic lips
    I will this chalice take.
    To Lizzy Bam, the best of all,
    A toast I now will make.
    Her hands are white and fresh
    My vest they've oft caressed...
    Hooray, long live Elizabeth
    Ten thousand years 'til death."

PYOTR NIKOLAYEVICH.

    Well, alright, let's begin.
    I beg you follow carefully
    The oscillation of our blades
    Whence that which sharpened saber throws
    And what direction which assumes.

IVAN IVANOVICH.

    Thus, I score an attack to the left.

DADDY *(attacking)*.

    I swipe to the right, to the flank I swing,
    Each man is on his own.
    The leafy grove is shivering
    The gardens round have grown.

PYOTR NIKOLAYEVICH.

    Don't let your focus wander,
    Observe instead the iron center's motion
    And deadly forces' concentration.

DADDY (*lifts his rapier and beats time as he recites*).

    My praise to iron—carborundum.
    It strengthens up the roadways and,
    Glowing electrically,
    It lacerates our foes to death.
    I praise the sword! A battle song!
    It agitates the brigand
    Transforms the infant to a youth
    And lacerates our foes to death.
    O battle song! I praise the quills!
    About the atmosphere they fly.
    They cloud the eyes of infidels
    And lacerate our foes to death.
    O praise to quills and wisdom to the rock!
    It lies beneath the solemn pine
    And under it the water flows
    To meet the slaughtered foes.

PYOTR NIKOLAYEVICH (*falls*).

    I've fallen wounded to the ground
    Elizaveta Bam, goodbye.
    Up to my mountain cabin go
    And once you're there, collapse.
    And all along your arms
    And over you will run
    Deaf mice, and then
    A hermit cockroach.

    (*A bell chimes.*)

    You hear above the rooftops
    A bell rings ding and dong.

Forgive me and excuse me
Elizaveta Bam.

IVAN IVANOVICH.

The combat of two epic heroes
Is concluded.

(PYOTR NIKOLAYEVICH *is carried offstage.*)

16. CHIMES

ELIZAVETA BAM (*entering*).

Ah, Daddy, you're here. I'm very glad.

I've just come back from the cooperative.

I was just buying sweets.

I wanted to buy a cake to have with tea.

DADDY (*unbuttoning his collar*). Whew, am I exhausted.

ELIZAVETA BAM. And what were you doing?

DADDY. Hmm... I was chopping firewood. And I'm terribly exhausted.

ELIZAVETA BAM. Ivan Ivanovich, go over to the Halfmoon Saloon and
bring us back a bottle of beer and some peas.

IVAN IVANOVICH.

Aha. Peas and half a bottle of beer.

Go to the saloon and from there to here.

ELIZAVETA BAM.

Not a half-bottle; a bottle of beer.

And not to the saloon, but go to the pea-patch.

IVAN IVANOVICH.

Now I will hide my coat in the Halfmoon Saloon,

And I will wear half a pea on my head.

ELIZAVETA BAM.

Ah, don't bother, but just hurry,

Because my father is tired from chopping wood.

FATHER.

Oh, these here women have almost no idea.

In their ideas they have emptiness.

17. PHYSIOLOGICAL PATHOS

MOMMY (*enters*). Comrades. This here villainess has bumped off mah son.
VOICES. Which one? Which villainess?

(TWO HEADS *stick out from the wings.*)

MOMMY. This one here, with those there lips.
ELIZAVETA BAM. Mommy, Mommy, what are you saying?

(IVAN IVANOVICH *strikes a match.*)

MOMMY. It's all because of you that his life ended in a draw.
ELIZAVETA BAM. Can't you at least tell me what you're talking about?
MOMMY (*with a stony face*). Eek! Eek! Eek!
ELIZAVETA BAM. She's lost her mind!

(DADDY *gets out his handkerchief and dances in place.*)

MOMMY. I'm a clumsy cuttlefish.

(*The scenery starts to revolve, changing from the landscape into a room. The wings swallow up* MOMMY *and* DADDY.)

ELIZAVETA BAM. They are coming now. What have I done?
MOMMY. Three times twenty-seven equals eighty-one.

18. REALISTICALLY DRY AND OFFICIAL

The scene is the same as at the beginning.

ELIZAVETA BAM. They're sure to come to catch me and wipe me off the face of the earth. Escape. I must escape. But where to? This door opens onto the stairs, and I'll run into them on the stairs. Through the window? (*She looks out the window.*) O-ooh, I can't jump it. It's real high. But what can I do? Eh, someone's footsteps. It's them. I'll lock the door, and I won't open it. Let them knock as much as they want. (*She locks the door.*)

(*A knock at the door.*)

VOICES. Elizaveta Bam, I order you to open the door in the name of the law.

(*Silence.*)

FIRST VOICE. I order you to open the door.

(*Silence.*)

SECOND VOICE (*softly*). Let's break the door down.
FIRST VOICE. Elizaveta Bam, open up, otherwise we'll break down the door.
ELIZAVETA BAM. What are you going to do with me?
FIRST VOICE. You are subject to dire punishment.
ELIZAVETA BAM. What for? Why won't you tell me what it is I've done?
FIRST VOICE. You are accused of the murder of Pyotr Nikolayevich Krupernak.
SECOND VOICE. And you'll answer for it.
ELIZAVETA BAM. But I didn't kill anyone.
FIRST VOICE. The court will decide that.
ELIZAVETA BAM. I am in your power.

(ELIZAVETA BAM *opens the door.* PYOTR NIKOLAYEVICH *and* IVAN IVANOVICH *enter dressed as firemen.*)

PYOTR NIKOLAYEVICH. In the name of the law, you are under arrest.
IVAN IVANOVICH (*striking a match*). Come with us.

19. OPERATIC FINALE

ELIZAVETA BAM (*shouting*). You may tie me up! You may pull me by the hair! You may drag me through the gutter. I didn't kill anyone! I couldn't kill anyone!

PYOTR NIKOLAYEVICH. Elizaveta Bam, calm down.

IVAN IVANOVICH. Look ahead of you into the distance. (*Hiccups loudly.*)

ELIZAVETA BAM. And in the cottage, the one that's on the mountain, a flame is already burning. The mice are wiggling, wiggling their whiskers. And on the stove, Cockroach Cockroachson sits in a shirt with a reddish collar and an ax in his hands.

PYOTR NIKOLAYEVICH. Elizaveta Bam, stretching out your arms and quelling your steady gaze, follow me, maintaining the balance of your joints and the exhalation of your tendons. Follow me.

(*They slowly leave.*)

(*Curtain.*)

Grain

A Play in Five Acts and Nine Scenes

Vladimir Kirshon   1930

Mikhailov
secretary of the Regional Committee of the Party, thirty-five to forty years old

Olga [Olka, Olenka]
his wife, twenty-five to twenty-seven years old

Rayevsky
thirty to thirty-five years old, a delegate who has arrived at the Regional Committee

Kosyakov
director of the Regional Collectivization Department

Laryonov
assistant manager of the railroad

Zhukov
director of the Organizational Section of the Regional Committee

Perevoznikov
editor of the regional newspaper

Dasha
Mikhailov's Secretary

Kononov
a local Party worker

Gromov
a local administrator

Messenger
an elderly man

Kvasov
a kulak, fifty-five to sixty years old

Pasha
his daughter, twenty to twenty-five years old

Dyedov
chairman of the village council

Loktev
secretary of the local branch of the Communist Party; thirty years old

Zotova
secretary of the local branch of the Komsomol, eighteen years old

Mokrina
a nun

Grunkin
a poor peasant

Mikhail [Mishka, Mikhailo]
his son

Kotikhin, Zubov, Proshkin
kulaks

Olkha, Korytko, Shilov
peasants

Katerina
a peasant

Romanov
a former partisan, thirty-five to forty years old

Sotin
a farmhand and Party member

Mishka Afanasyev
a Komsomol member

Peasants

Komsomol members

ACT 1

An office with two doors. Bookshelves. A table. Reports. A telephone. MIKHAILOV *works at the table. One of his feet is bandaged.* OLGA *stands at the bookshelf, sorting through books. She throws several on the couch.*

MIKHAILOV. Why are you throwing those books around? You could pick them out calmly, you know.

OLGA. I'm tired of being calm.

MIKHAILOV. You're brooding again, Olka.

OLGA. I'm sick of this little town, with its age-old gloomy ignorance and only three hundred and eleven streetlamps to light it.

MIKHAILOV. How do you know that?

OLGA. I read it in your reports.

MIKHAILOV. If you had read to the end, you would have found out that we are putting up five hundred and nineteen more within the year.

OLGA. I want to move to a big city.

MIKHAILOV. In five years we'll have a hundred thousand people living here.

OLGA. I'm really bored, Mikhailov.

MIKHAILOV. I just can't understand that.

OLGA (*sighs*). No, that you cannot understand.

(*The doorbell rings abruptly; for a second there is a pause.*)

MIKHAILOV (*takes his cane and rises*). I'll get it, Olka. It's the plumbers.

OLGA. Stay there, please. (*Exits.*)

(*Voices offstage.* RAYEVSKY *runs into the room. He is wearing a good-looking coat and a hat and is carrying a flashy yellow suitcase, which he flings to the side. He grabs* MIKHAILOV, *shakes him, kisses and smothers him, slapping him on the back.* OLGA *enters and stands at the door, a faint smile on her lips.*)

RAYEVSKY. Mitka!

MIKHAILOV (*joyously*). Well, the Devil! Always a surprise. Let me take a look at you.

(*They look each other over.*)

RAYEVSKY. What's wrong with your foot, Mitka?

MIKHAILOV. It's nothing. I fell out of a cart. Our roads, you know.... Well, so I fell out of the cart. But where are you coming from?

RAYEVSKY. I'm going to work for you. Here. (*Takes out his documents.*) I was in Germany, Mitka.

MIKHAILOV (*reads*). Is that right? You're going to work with us? Well, take off your things. But what am I thinking? This is Olka.

(RAYEVSKY *and* OLGA *shake hands.*)

And this, Olka, is Rayevsky, Pavlushka, my commissar.

OLGA. So I gathered.

RAYEVSKY. How did you know?

OLGA. Dmitri told me you were a lunatic.

RAYEVSKY (*removes his hat and bows deeply to* MIKHAILOV). Thank you, Mitya.

(*The telephone rings;* MIKHAILOV *picks up the receiver and listens.*)

OLGA. Have you been back from Germany for a long time?

MIKHAILOV (*into the receiver*). Yes....

RAYEVSKY. About three weeks.... Mitka's gotten scrawny, and he's stooped over. He used to be quite a commander... danced better than anyone in the whole brigade.

MIKHAILOV (*still on the phone*). Yes....

OLGA. He danced? Were you working in the embassy?

MIKHAILOV. Yes....

RAYEVSKY. No, I was with a research team.

OLGA. Then you're a professor? (*Smiles.*)

MIKHAILOV. Yes....

RAYEVSKY. Is that funny?

MIKHAILOV (*still on the phone*). I agree. (*Hangs up the phone.*) What's funny?

RAYEVSKY. Olga—I'll call you Olga, alright? (OLGA *nods.*) Olga is laughing because I'm a professor. I think it's funny myself.

MIKHAILOV. Well, I was always sure that you would be a professor some day. Come on, take your things off.

(RAYEVSKY *takes off his coat. He is wearing the Order of the Red Banner.*)

I suppose you'd like to wash up?

RAYEVSKY. No. I took care of it at the station.... You've gotten thin, Mitka.

MIKHAILOV. Nonsense. How's Europe holding up?

RAYEVSKY. Europe? There's no more Europe. The tip of the Eiffel Tower is still sticking up. And a bit of the Alps. The rest is blocked out by our hats.

MIKHAILOV. You're not offended on account of the old lady?

RAYEVSKY. I'm irritated by our primordial, boorish, sneering attitude toward everything we don't know.

MIKHAILOV. You've become neurotic, you know.

RAYEVSKY. I'm annoyed because you're not the first. They can still teach us a thing or two. Mitka, I could just kill all those vulgarians who see and hear nothing but the foxtrot in Europe....

MIKHAILOV. Were you in Germany?

RAYEVSKY. In Berlin, Hamburg, Dresden.... The whole country works like a gleaming machine. You take a plane from Königsberg, all Germany is spread out before you like the mechanism of a watch. Engines roar incessantly. Dozens of underground railways shake the earth with thunder. That's something worth listening to!

OLGA. Is it bright there at night?

RAYEVSKY. The electric lights are so bright that you can't even read on some of the streets there. Several of the buildings are completely flooded with light. An electric goblet blazes up every night over one of the buildings in the Tauenzenstrasse. A bottle lights up, and, outlined against the dark background of the sky, champagne begins to foam.

(*The telephone rings.* MIKHAILOV *picks up the receiver.*)

MIKHAILOV. Speaking.... Yes, I asked for.... Why the hell aren't you supplying the Ruchevsky District with kerosene? The secretary called me. They had to burn candles in the District Committee last night. Pretty soon you'll have the peasants back to using matchsticks.... That's not true! You received five tanks three days ago.... Watch out, you could end up in hot water.... Alright.... (*Hangs up the phone. To* RAYEVSKY.) Champagne?

OLGA. And is it true there's a sea of automobiles in the streets?

RAYEVSKY. Yes, it's true. If you fly over the city, it seems like the automobiles are just sitting there, squeezed against each other. They take up the whole street. And they stop only at crossings, when a white bar flies up, and the pedestrians can go.

MIKHAILOV. Lovely.

RAYEVSKY. What?

MIKHAILOV. You tell a story in a lovely way. And how is the revolutionary work there? (*The telephone rings.*) Excuse me. (*Picks up the receiver.*) Yes.... Yes, yes. I've read it.... It's very good.... The writing is clear.... Put something about the manure at the end.... Say that it should be collected right away and brought down to the fields.... Let them heap it up in piles. They can spread it later. How many are being printed? Fifty thousand? Sounds good. Have you turned it in yet? When will it be ready? Alright. (*Hangs up the phone.*) Well, what do you say—is there any chance of a revolution in the West?

RAYEVSKY. Are you asking just for the hell of it?

MIKHAILOV. I...

(*The doorbell rings.*)

Olga.... It's the engineers.... Stay there, Pavel, this won't take long. Olga, this should also come in handy for the newspaper.

(OLGA *exits.* MIKHAILOV *searches for a report at the table.* PAVEL *looks through the books that* OLGA *threw on the couch.* OLGA *enters, followed by the assistant manager of the railroad, Engineer* LARYONOV, *and* KOSYAKOV, *Director of the Regional Collectivization Department.*)

KOSYAKOV. Well, here we are. What happened to your foot?

MIKHAILOV. Nothing. A little sprain. We're running late, comrades. We're running fifteen minutes late.

KOSYAKOV. It's not my fault, honest to God, it's not.... This comrade...

LARYONOV. I'm Laryonov, assistant manager of the railroad.

MIKHAILOV. So, you came? Greetings!

(*He points to a chair.* LARYONOV *sits down.*)

Well, now. So you don't want to pay?

LARYONOV. We can't pay.

MIKHAILOV. But you *can* use the water?

LARYONOV. The water is national property.

MIKHAILOV. Everything is national property. We're the ones building the water main, right?

KOSYAKOV. That's right.

MIKHAILOV. Money, comrades, money. The railroad needs water, so pay up.

LARYONOV. We can't. It's your water main.

MIKHAILOV. So you won't pay up?

LARYONOV. We can't.

MIKHAILOV. Fine, we'll get it kopeck by kopeck.

LARYONOV. What do you mean, kopeck by kopeck?

MIKHAILOV. We'll charge you one kopeck per hundred pails of water you use. Here are the figures. (*Picks up a report.*) In two years you will have paid off the first installment; in five the whole cost; and by the tenth year....

LARYONOV. Hold on.... How is that? By what right?

MIKHAILOV. You said yourself, it's our water main.

LARYONOV. No, hold on.... And when the second branch comes along, we'll have to pay for that kopeck by kopeck, too?

MIKHAILOV. That one will be kopeck by kopeck, too.

LARYONOV. Let me get back to you tomorrow. I'll wire the management right away.

MIKHAILOV. As you like. But tell them to hurry with the money. We need it now.

(LARYONOV *stands, makes his farewells, and exits.*)

KOSYAKOV. You think they'll pay up?

MIKHAILOV. What else can they do? That little one-kopeck charge will beat you every time. Have you gotten through the clay yet?

KOSYAKOV. We have four hundred meters left.

MIKHAILOV. Have you given any thought to the bricks?

KOSYAKOV. They're still working on it.

MIKHAILOV. You were supposed to have the estimate done yesterday. Just a moment. (*Reads from a notebook.*) "Kosyakov, the 12th, brick factory estimate."

KOSYAKOV. I couldn't get it done, honest to God—honest, I just couldn't get it done.

MIKHAILOV. So they're still working on it?

KOSYAKOV. Honest to God, I'll bring it tomorrow. Come on, give me a break.

MIKHAILOV. Tomorrow at eleven.

(*He extends his hand to* KOSYAKOV. KOSYAKOV *exits.*)

They'll never learn to be punctual. (*Writes in his notebook.*) We'll stick those railroad guys with that kopeck, like a beetle on a pin. What were you starting to say about the West, Pavel?

RAYEVSKY (*irritably*). Things are a little different in the West. When the proletariat takes to the street there, blood is spilled.

MIKHAILOV. Are you talking about the mass demonstrations?

RAYEVSKY. Every demonstration gets broken up. I went to the Reichstag with a crowd of unemployed workers, and the police beat us with rubber clubs and with the butts of their revolvers. They broke my arm, and I just barely escaped four Schutzmänner.

MIKHAILOV. Totally useless. It wasn't worth it for you to go with them.

RAYEVSKY. So I should have stood on the sidelines and watched the workers being clubbed?

MIKHAILOV. If the Schutzmänner had caught you, the police could have made up some fairy tale about Russians organizing the workers' demonstrations. Believe me, that would have done more harm than your standing on the sidelines.

RAYEVSKY. You're very reasonable. But, you know, there are times when reasonable behavior borders on the criminal.

OLGA. I'm sure Dmitri would never have gone to the Reichstag.

MIKHAILOV. You're right. It seems to me that unreasonable behavior is what's criminal.

RAYEVSKY. Then I'm a criminal. But if everything happened again tomorrow, I would throw myself in front of the Schutzmänner's clubs together with the German workers all over again. You go ahead and watch while we get clubbed.

MIKHAILOV. That sounds great, but from my point of view, pointless heroism and cowardice are just two sides of the same coin.

RAYEVSKY. You wouldn't have said that five years ago.... Ah, but.... (*Jumps up, paces around the room, sits down on the couch, looks at the books.*)

MIKHAILOV. But you must be hungry, Pavel. You're jumping all over people because you're hungry. Olka....

OLGA (*to* RAYEVSKY). Dmitri always has a fine sense of other people's psychological states....

MIKHAILOV. Give him something to eat, Olka....

RAYEVSKY. I don't want anything to eat.

MIKHAILOV. You're ranting, Pavel. (*Remembers something, digs through his papers.*)

RAYEVSKY. Can it really be true that you're through ranting, Mitka? Can it be true that you've settled down?

OLGA. Settled down, did you say?

MIKHAILOV. No.... (*Leafing through his papers.*) So you're not hungry? Perhaps you'd like some vodka? We have some.

RAYEVSKY. No.

(*The telephone rings;* MIKHAILOV *answers.*)

MIKHAILOV. Yes, yes, Mikhailov. Fine. I'll wait. (*Sits down at the table.*) The Regional Committee is calling.

OLGA (*quietly*). Why are you so edgy?

RAYEVSKY (*also quietly*). So much has changed here over the last few years. On the faces of my friends I see the dull, expiring rays of sunset. People used to be on fire, now they are smoldering like... burnt torches.

I look at Mitka... and I want to cry. He used to fly astride a thorough-
bred horse.... He wanted to ride to Berlin on that horse.... But now...

MIKHAILOV. Yes, yes, it's me, comrade Antonov. We delivered everything
in the last five days. Yes, sixty men have left. We kept a hundred thousand for ourselves. Aha, I see. I'll start loading tomorrow. Very well, we'll
gather up what's left. Consider it done. Goodbye. (*Hangs up the phone.*)
We need grain.

(*Curtain.*)

SCENE 2

The same room. MIKHAILOV *is at the table. Nearby is* ZHUKOV.
PEREVOZNIKOV *is at an end of the table working on an article on a steno
pad.* DASHA *is at the typewriter.*

MIKHAILOV (*examines a list; crosses something out*). Chistyakov can go to
hell. He'll mess everything up. Now *these* guys are just fine. Why is there
a question mark after Kononov?

ZHUKOV. He categorically refuses. He's making noise, wants to write to
the Central Committee.

MIKHAILOV. Did you send for him?

ZHUKOV. He's coming here.

MIKHAILOV. Which Lobzikov is this? From the Regional Office?

ZHUKOV. That's the one.

MIKHAILOV. But he stutters.

ZHUKOV. Well, he's not giving a lecture.

MIKHAILOV. We'll cross him out. By the time he gets one word out, any
peasant will have twenty ready for him.... Gromov doesn't want to go, either?

ZHUKOV. I sent for all of them.

(*The telephone rings.*)

MIKHAILOV. Speaking. The chairman? Drop by. Looks like we'll have to travel through the districts tomorrow. Yes. Yes. All right! (*Hangs up the phone. To the editor.*) Have you finished the article?

PEREVOZNIKOV. You know, I can't seem to get anywhere with it.

MIKHAILOV. What's wrong?

PEREVOZNIKOV. You know, it comes out bombastic, somehow.

MIKHAILOV. Get rid of the bombast.

PEREVOZNIKOV. You know, it'll be dry then.

MIKHAILOV. Well, then, write, just write.... Dasha, is the report here?

DASHA. No, it's not.

MIKHAILOV. As usual.

(*The doorbell rings.*)

ZHUKOV (*goes to the door and yells*). It's open!

MIKHAILOV (*on the phone*). Give me one sixteen. Yes, yes, one sixteen... Popov, actually. Popov? Hello. Listen, where is the report? It's ten minutes to one. I'll have you arrested, Popov. I warned you yesterday. What do I care about your messenger? For all I know, he could be a congenital alcoholic. The report is supposed to be here at twelve sharp. It's twelve minutes to one right now... and no report. Better pack yourself a little bag with some biscuits.... Prison food is mediocre at best....

(KONONOV *enters during the conversation and listens with interest to* MIKHAILOV. MIKHAILOV *hangs up the phone. Speaks to* KONONOV.)

MIKHAILOV. Ah, Kononov, hello! So what's going on—I hear you don't want to go to the countryside?

KONONOV. Me? Says who? Not at all. I'd love to go.

ZHUKOV (*surprised*). Love to? Then what were you making such a fuss about?

KONONOV. I was kidding. Just kidding. That's all. But you went and told Mikhailov?

MIKHAILOV. Then why did you come here?

KONONOV. Well, I.... Well, I came to say goodbye.

MIKHAILOV. In that case, have a safe trip, Kononov. Your traveling papers are in the Regional Committee office.

KONONOV. Goodbye, Mikhailov, goodbye. (*Leaves.*)

MIKHAILOV. How about that article?

PEREVOZNIKOV. You know, I can't seem to get anywhere with it.

MIKHAILOV. What are you talking about?

PEREVOZNIKOV. You know, it sounds kind of pathetic.

MIKHAILOV. Get rid of the pathos.

PEREVOZNIKOV. You know, in that case it sounds like a decree.

MIKHAILOV. Well, keep working, keep working.

(GROMOV *enters, goes to the table.*)

GROMOV. I can't go.

MIKHAILOV. Why on earth not?

GROMOV. The Inspection Committee from Moscow is coming, isn't it?

MIKHAILOV. So?

GROMOV. I have to finish the construction project on time, don't I?

MIKHAILOV. You do.

GROMOV. Raw materials have to be stocked for next year, don't they?

MIKHAILOV. They do.

GROMOV. We are thirteen percent behind on the plan. We have to catch up, don't we?

MIKHAILOV. Absolutely.

GROMOV. I have to stay and manage the project, don't I?

MIKHAILOV. No. You, Gromov, have to go to the country. Drop by the Regional Committee office and get your traveling papers.

GROMOV. And who will answer for the work here?

MIKHAILOV. You, Gromov, will answer. If you haven't selected capable assistants, you will answer for it. If your quota isn't fulfilled, you will answer for it. If the construction work isn't finished on time, you will answer for it.

GROMOV. *And* I have to travel?

MIKHAILOV. And you have to travel. These are difficult times, Gromov.... Do you have any other questions?

GROMOV. I have a lot questions. But I'll ask you at the Party Conference.

MIKHAILOV. If you're chosen for the Conference. *If* you're chosen. Seems you haven't been going to the Party office lately?

GROMOV. So you have informers?

MIKHAILOV. Our Party has no informers. Quit wasting your breath.

GROMOV (*insolently*). Our Party has...

(*The door opens with a bang, and, pushing* GROMOV *aside, an elderly messenger rushes in.* GROMOV *exits.*)

MIKHAILOV (*stands, calling after him*). What does our Party have? What does our Party have?

MESSENGER (*panting, trying to catch his breath*). The report... due by twelve.

MIKHAILOV. Give it to me. (*Takes the papers. Looks over the report.*) He's gone to pieces, the jerk....

MESSENGER (*loudly*). Not at all!

MIKHAILOV. What do you mean, not at all?

MESSENGER. Not one little bit. As for being out of breath, that's from running.

MIKHAILOV. I wasn't talking about you. (*Looks over the report.*) And don't run. Tell them to give you the report ten minutes earlier. Otherwise you'll always be behind.

MESSENGER (*quietly*). That's right.

MIKHAILOV (*to the messenger*). You may go. (*To* ZHUKOV.) You go, too. Everybody has to get going tomorrow. Get on the phone, call all the secretaries.

ZHUKOV. Have they called you from the factory yet?

MIKHAILOV. No. Why?

ZHUKOV. There's something going on there. (*Exits with the messenger.*)

(MIKHAILOV *works.* PEREVOZNIKOV *reads his article and gesticulates. He crosses something out. He thinks and then crosses something else out. He writes. Then he crosses something out again. He crumples up the sheet of paper, throws it away, and starts writing on a new one.* OLGA*'s laughter is heard from the hall. She enters together with* RAYEVSKY. *They are both very animated and cheerful.*)

OLGA. He really is a lunatic, this Rayevsky of yours. First he stops to play tag with the kids outside. Then he carries some old woman across a puddle, and just now he almost got run over by a car, right in front of the house.

PEREVOZNIKOV. What?

OLGA. Good morning, comrade editor. We're walking along the street, and this car flies out from behind a corner going full speed. Then all of a sudden he leaves me and jumps out right in front of the car. I screamed so loud, the whole town must have heard me.

MIKHAILOV. Now that was uncalled for.

RAYEVSKY. Don't worry, I have strong legs.

MIKHAILOV. I know. It was uncalled for because the driver feels rotten when something like that happens. He doesn't have time to stop the car, and he won't enjoy running you over if you can't get out of the way. But you think it's all a big joke.

OLGA. Good Lord! How boring!

RAYEVSKY. Perhaps you're right. But you can't go thinking out every move you make, Dmitri! You'll go crazy.

MIKHAILOV. It seems to me you can't go not thinking out every move. We're sending you to the country for grain procurement. That'll be your first job.

OLGA. When?

MIKHAILOV. Tomorrow.

RAYEVSKY. Tomorrow? Are you, Dmitri Mikhailov, suggesting that I go tomorrow, or is this an official order from the Secretary of the Regional Committee?

MIKHAILOV. What's the difference?

RAYEVSKY. If you're giving me an official order, then I'll leave tomorrow.

MIKHAILOV. That's the decision of the Regional Committee. (*To the editor.*) How are you doing with the article?

PEREVOZNIKOV. You know...

MIKHAILOV (*shouts*). To hell with "you know." I'll write the article myself. (*More calmly.*) Dasha, bring the typewriter. Let's go, I'll dictate.

(DASHA *takes the typewriter.* MIKHAILOV, *leaning heavily on his cane, follows her out.* PEREVOZNIKOV, *frightened, also exits.*)

OLGA. You're leaving tomorrow?

RAYEVSKY. I have never yet disobeyed an order of the Party, Olga.

OLGA. But this is crazy. They should use your leadership abilities.

RAYEVSKY. The Party will use what it needs, when it deems it necessary.

OLGA. But people can be motivated by their own personal considerations. You can't hide behind the word "Party." The Party is people.

RAYEVSKY. No.

OLGA. Then what is it?

RAYEVSKY. The Party is a ring. It's an iron belt that holds people together.

OLGA. That may be so. But there are times when this belt pinches. Not everyone is identical, after all. People aren't bushes; you can't level them and trim them up. For example, you're not like...

RAYEVSKY. I've thought of that. Yes, the belt often cuts into my flesh, but I can't live without that belt.

OLGA. I don't understand what you're saying.

RAYEVSKY. It's complex, Olga. I haven't had to talk about this before. Imagine a crowd. A crowd made up of identical, standardized people. They're all wearing the same color necktie. They're all going in the same direction and saying the same measured words. I don't want to be identical. Sometimes I'm terrified at the thought that every day I put on the same colored necktie as everyone else. But there's another feeling that's even more terrifying. Just imagine, Olga, that this crowd is going by without you. And you're left, all alone with your thoughts, with your doubts, while the columns keep passing by. They keep repeating *their* words. They sing *their* songs. Not one of them turns to look at you, and their measured steps are merciless. I can't step out of my column precisely because I myself have different thoughts, different feelings. I can't leave. I need to feel another shoulder next to mine. I need someone to give me orders and discipline me. I need that belt to force together the different sides of my "I."

OLGA. And what if they lead you in the wrong direction?

RAYEVSKY. I'll go and die along with everyone else. I fought for the Party. I'm its soldier.

OLGA. A soldier unsure of victory? Can a soldier like that ever be victorious?

RAYEVSKY. Who says I'm unsure of victory? It's impossible for the proletariat not to be victorious. Victory is inevitable, like death. I'm not sure that we—that Russia—will be victors. Perhaps we are just another Paris Commune which has managed to hold out for twelve years. If so, I shall know how to stand up against the wall of our Père Lachaise.

OLGA. Don't you want to go to the countryside?

RAYEVSKY. I don't like the countryside. I don't like the snowstorms, the rain, the frost. I don't like those dumb elements that man can't control. The countryside—the village—is one of those elements. But I'm leaving tomorrow.

OLGA. You know...

RAYEVSKY. What?

OLGA. No... I'm still not sure.

RAYEVSKY. I'm going to my room. I have some writing to do. (*Exits.*)

OLGA (*paces the room with her hands clasped and her head lowered. She bends downward, looks at the sheets* PEREVOZNIKOV *has thrown down, and reads*). "Peasants! The Party is sounding the trumpet and unfurling its crimson banners. Twelve years...."

(DASHA *and* MIKHAILOV *enter.* DASHA *exits silently.* MIKHAILOV, *leaning heavily on his cane, goes to the table.* OLGA *steps toward him. They stop face-to-face and stand like that for the entire ensuing conversation.*)

Are you sending Pavel to the country because you're jealous?

MIKHAILOV (*is silent, looks at her*). I can't believe you're asking this seriously.

OLGA. Oh, yes! What about the Regional Committee's resolution. He's not the only one who's going, after all. It is the will of the Party. Our country needs grain. Well, say something, say something! You're never at a loss for words, wise words, like the headlines of your articles.... "Peasants! The Party is sounding its trumpet."

MIKHAILOV. Are you ill?

OLGA. Well, of course; just feel my forehead, see if I have a fever. How simple life is, Mikhailov. Olga's sick. Pavel's hungry. The Party's sounding its trumpet.

MIKHAILOV. What trumpet? What does a trumpet have to do with anything? Settle down, Olga.

OLGA. For once, Mikhailov, just once, stop being the Secretary of the Regional Committee for one minute. Look me straight in the eyes and tell me the truth. Are you sending Pavel away out of jealousy? Well, answer me!

MIKHAILOV. This is crazy, what you're asking me.

OLGA. What do you mean, crazy? Why are you hiding, Dmitri? I can tell, you know. I know your hidden thoughts. You want to get rid of him! Honorable people grab each other by the throat in open battle. Honorable people fight with the same weapons. But you—you're the Secretary of the Regional Committee. You can get rid of your friend because that's the "will of the Party." (*Practically screaming.*) Traveling papers for Pavel Rayevsky!

(*Without saying anything, leaning on his cane,* MIKHAILOV *crosses over to the table and sits down.* OLGA *walks the length of the room, stops, and looks at* MIKHAILOV.)

Forgive me. I suspected you of feelings which are not natural to you.

(MIKHAILOV *quickly raises his head.*)

No, not natural, because you have no feelings whatsoever. I forgot that you think in resolutions. I imagined that you might suddenly deviate from the collection of reports you're made out of. You're just one big report. Do you understand? You're just one big report!

MIKHAILOV. Sometimes there are deviations in reports.

OLGA. Then you're not even a report. You never deviate. You overflow with rationality. You're a walking rule of order. You're sickeningly precise. You'd love to write down every hitch that ever occurs in life, together with the answer for each one, like the interpretations of dreams in a dream-book. You've drawn up a schedule of feelings and, just like trains, your desires follow only one set of railway tracks, and only after the second bell has rung. Be quiet!

MIKHAILOV. I'm not interrupting you.

OLGA. I've tried a few times to make you angry. You never lost your composure. I've done everything I could to insult you, but you just can't be insulted. You're entirely wrapped up in your own world of official business and telephone directives. You're a Party automaton. I can't stand it any longer. (*Falls into an armchair and cries.*) You can't even be jealous, Dmitri!

MIKHAILOV. Olka! Olka! You really are ill. I'll bring you some water right away.... (*Gets up.*)

OLGA (*jumps up*). I don't need water. Journalists are needed in the countryside. I'll write sketches. I'm leaving with Rayevsky tomorrow! (*Turns around and starts going.*)

(MIKHAILOV *takes a step after her; cries out.* OLGA *turns around abruptly.*)

What is it, Mitya?

MIKHAILOV. I stepped on my bad foot.

OLGA. Ah....(*Exits.*)

(MIKHAILOV *follows after her for a second with his eyes, then tosses his cane aside, gets out from behind the table, and follows her, limping. The telephone rings abruptly.* MIKHAILOV *stops. Pause. It rings again.* MIKHAILOV *goes to the telephone.*)

MIKHAILOV. Speaking.... Yes. Hello.... A report at the general meeting? But why didn't you tell me about this earlier? Ah, ah... in connection with the departure. Well, you see, it's a little tough for me today.... Yeah, I guess I'm sick.... What's hurting me? How can I put it.... Yes, my heart, too, I guess.... Aspirin? It helps.... I'll definitely take some.... Well, then, I'll just sit right down and get to work. Goodbye. (*Hangs up the phone.*)

(*Curtain.*)

ACT 2

SCENE 3

KVASOV's house. It is spacious. The furnishings are solid and sturdy. On a separate little table there are newspapers and books. There are icons in the house. KVASOV sits behind a table reading a newspaper. PASHA is dealing herself a hand of cards. There is a knock at the window. KVASOV lifts his head. PASHA goes to the window and opens the curtain.

PASHA. It's the chairman of the village council. He's not alone.

DYEDOV (*offstage*). Open up, Ivan Gerasimovich. You have guests.

(KVASOV rises quickly and goes to the door. He can be heard in the hall raising the deadbolt and unlocking the door. RAYEVSKY, OLGA, and DYEDOV enter. DYEDOV is carrying RAYEVSKY's suitcase. RAYEVSKY is wearing the same coat as before, but a cap instead of his fur hat.)

You'll be comfortable here. Ivan Gerasimovich will set a room aside for you. As for the insects,.... (*To* KVASOV.) Comrade Rayevsky, District Delegate. We're here to collect grain, Ivan Gerasimovich.

KVASOV. Well, hello there, welcome. Did I hear you say something about grain, Mikhail Pavlovich? We've already fulfilled our quota.

DYEDOV. The State needs it.

KVASOV. It knows best, of course. Pashka, take the masters to their room.

RAYEVSKY. What masters? I used to dunk masters in the Black Sea.

KVASOV. Beg your pardon, it's our ignorance.

OLGA (*to* PASHA). Don't bother. I'll stay here.

RAYEVSKY. You won't be comfortable here. I'll stay in this room.

OLGA. Don't argue, please. I like it better here. (*To* KVASOV.) But do you have another room? Where are you going to stay?

KVASOV. Thank you kindly; we do have one.

RAYEVSKY. Excellent. Then I'll take that one.

(Picks up the suitcase and carries it out. OLGA walks out after him.)

KVASOV. A hero!

DYEDOV. Order of the Red Banner for distinguished military service.

KVASOV. Now, then, how much are they taking?

DYEDOV. We'll get the orders any time now.

KVASOV. Where are we going to get it, Mikhail Pavlovich?

DYEDOV. If they need it, we'll find it.

KVASOV. Our grain is salty with the sweat of our brows, Mikhail Pavlovich. We've been sending out the Red shipments.

DYEDOV. We'll send more.

KVASOV. Oh, the life of a peasant!

(PASHA *stops in the doorway.* RAYEVSKY *enters.*)

RAYEVSKY. Let's not waste any time, Comrade Dyedov. Have you informed the Secretary?

DYEDOV. I haven't had the chance. I will right away. I'll bring in both Secretaries, the Party Secretary and the Komsomol Secretary.

RAYEVSKY. Good idea. I'll wait.

DYEDOV. Give Comrade Rayevsky something to eat.

KVASOV. Whatever the Good Lord has blessed us with. Pashka!

RAYEVSKY. I'll pay you for everything.

KVASOV. Who's keeping track? All we have is plain old peasant food.

(PASHA *brings sour cream, bread, butter, cottage cheese, and jelly doughnuts.*)

RAYEVSKY (*looks at the food*). It's magnificent food. So what are these, fritters?

PASHA. Jelly doughnuts.

RAYEVSKY (*takes one and eats it*). Marvelous doughnuts. They're rosy, like your cheeks.

PASHA. My cheeks *were* rosy. Now they're getting pale.

RAYEVSKY. What do you mean?

PASHA. Shall I call your missus?

RAYEVSKY. My missus? (*Laughs.*) Yes, call her, call her. (*Shouts.*) Missus! Olga! Missus!

OLGA (*comes in, having changed clothes*). What is it?

RAYEVSKY. Breakfast is served, my little Missus. The jelly doughnuts are blazing red for you, Missus. The milk is steaming. The cottage cheese is nice and crumbly.

OLGA. So you're a poet as well, Rayevsky.

RAYEVSKY. Morning invigorates the spirit, Olga. So does a wonderful trip. The forest does, too. Did you notice how it couldn't hold back a smile as we were passing through.

OLGA (*laughing, quietly*). I notice that our landlord is staring at you as if you were a lunatic.

RAYEVSKY (*also quietly*). He's a terrific old man. And what a terrific girl; just take a look.

OLGA. Sure. Well, let's eat, Pavel. (*They sit down.*)

RAYEVSKY (*to* KVASOV). How come you're not sitting down? And how about Pasha?

KVASOV. Oh, we rise with the roosters. We've already eaten. Thank you kindly.

RAYEVSKY (*eating*). Come on, sit down. Where's the missus?

KVASOV. The missus passed. (*Sits.*) It's almost a year now since she left us....

RAYEVSKY (*not catching everything, surprised*). Where'd she go? Who with?

KVASOV. Where she went no man can ever know.

OLGA. She's dead. Why are you asking such ridiculous questions?

RAYEVSKY. Dead? I didn't understand. I thought.... (*He eats. Pause.*) So, anyway, are you putting together a kolkhoz soon?

KVASOV. We haven't heard anything about that.

RAYEVSKY. What's there to hear! You have to put it together yourselves.

KVASOV. Ourselves? Hmm, yes.... Our country folk are slow to decide. They're a cautious folk.

RAYEVSKY. What is there to be cautious about? So, what then? Live the old way?

KVASOV. You've got a point. The olden days were no picnic, either. But here's what folks say: We like what we know—our grandfathers lived this way, and they passed it on to our fathers. The new ways are like the Heavenly Kingdom: We believe in it, but for now, we'd rather stay where we are.

RAYEVSKY. But shouldn't you at least try the new ways?

KVASOV. Fair enough. It's just that folks live in such darkness. They reason like this: The snipe says to the horse, "Let's head across the swamp. You go ahead and drown, and I'll keep my head above water."

RAYEVSKY. Does everybody reason that way?

KVASOV. Everyone.

OLGA. What about you?

KVASOV. What about us? Whatever direction we're pointed, that's where we'll go. In the meantime, we're staying put.

RAYEVSKY. Just you wait. Don't count your chickens before they're hatched.

KVASOV. That's a true saying. But we don't have many chicks left.

RAYEVSKY. What do you mean, chicks?

KVASOV. You know, baby chickens.

(PASHA *laughs.*)

OLGA. How come you don't have many left?

KVASOV. The city folk ate them. When peasants are low on grain, they sell their poultry to buy more grain.

RAYEVSKY. So you're saying you're low on grain?

KVASOV. Where in God's name are we supposed to get it from? We've paid our tax, we've bought our savings bonds, we've paid the voluntary contribution, and the government's taken all our surplus. How could there be any grain left?

RAYEVSKY. Don't the kulaks have some stored away?

KVASOV. Anything is possible.

(*There is a knock at the window.*)

RAYEVSKY (*jumps up*). They're here.

KVASOV (*to* PASHA). Open the door.

(PASHA *goes and opens the door.* DYEDOV, LOKTEV, *and* ZOTOVA *enter.*)

DYEDOV. This is our whole Council of People's Commissars.

LOKTEV. The full complement. (*Shakes* RAYEVSKY's *hand.*)

ZOTOVA (*to* RAYEVSKY). Secretary of the local Komsomol branch. (*Shakes his hand.*)

RAYEVSKY. Let's get started, comrades. (*Catches* LOKTEV *looking at* OLGA.) This is comrade Belozerova. From the Regional newspaper. Olga, if you please.

(*They all sit around a table.* DYEDOV *makes a sign to* KVASOV. *The latter exits with* PASHA.)

Alright comrades, let's get down to work. You collected four hundred tons for the grain procurement?

DYEDOV. Four hundred twenty tons.

RAYEVSKY. Excellent. Our job now is to get the village to turn in another hundred twenty-five out of the remainder.

DYEDOV. Hundred twenty-five!

ZOTOVA. We can get a hundred twenty-five. The kulaks alone have bought up five hundred fifty.

LOKTEV (*warningly*). Zotova!

ZOTOVA. Well, three hundred fifty.

LOKTEV. Three hundred fifty?

ZOTOVA Well, they've bought up two hundred fifty for sure.

(LOKTEV *shakes his head and looks at her reproachfully.*)

DYEDOV. We don't have a hundred twenty-five. But we'll get it!

LOKTEV. The grain is there, Dyedov, you're wrong about that.

DYEDOV. Maybe it is, maybe it isn't, but I do know one thing. Comes down to it, we'll get it.

RAYEVSKY. We have no choice but to get it. Seems to me we might as well think now about *how* we're going to get it.

DYEDOV. There is nothing to think about. We'll announce a requisition. Period.

LOKTEV. No, that's not going to work.

ZOTOVA. Let's take it from the kulaks. Half of the peasants in this village are kulaks, and everyone follows their lead.

LOKTEV (*reproachfully*). Half?

ZOTOVA. You haven't been here very long. You don't know. The whole village is kulak. You just go out, follow them, listen to what they're saying. We have kulaks of all sorts and colors here. And we've got twenty former tsarist cops, to boot.

DYEDOV. Seven.

ZOTOVA. Well, alright, seven, what's the difference? We have to get that grain; we'll take it at gunpoint.

LOKTEV. You're getting carried away and babbling. But it's all hot air.

RAYEVSKY. And your opinion?

LOKTEV. We'll mostly have to get it from the kulaks. The kulaks will put up a big fight. I think we ought to put on a propaganda campaign for several days.

RAYEVSKY. What do you mean several days? Before we even start?

LOKTEV. Before we do anything else.

RAYEVSKY. And then collect for another several days?

LOKTEV. If we do the groundwork first, then we'll come out ahead. It's dangerous for us to set sail without some preliminary rigging. Stow the extra sails, check the rigging. A strong wind is on the way.

OLGA. And the workers are just supposed to wait? Sit around without any grain while you're rolling up your sails?

DYEDOV. What is there to discuss? We get an order, and we carry it out. We'll call a meeting for tomorrow. Period.

LOKTEV. Whatever you like. But we'll mess it all up, comrades.

RAYEVSKY. You're behind the times, comrade Loktev. We shouldn't be running away from a fight.

LOKTEV. But it never hurts to gather your forces before the fight.

RAYEVSKY. We're going on the attack. The Party is calling us to arms.

LOKTEV. All the same, I would at least get the poor peasants together a couple of times. And I would talk things over with the middling peasants, too. The kulaks will move all their forces.

RAYEVSKY. Your tactics are bad, comrade Loktev. Apparently you've never been to the front.

LOKTEV. Yes, I have. I fought for five years.

RAYEVSKY. Well, you didn't learn anything. You should always take the enemy by surprise. He's at home scratching his head, but we're already making rounds and conducting raids. We show up all of a sudden and attack then and there. Don't give him a chance to collect himself. Your kulak will be asleep, he'll be resting in his featherbed, while we're sounding the alarm. First the meeting, then the collection. And if the kulaks decide to make a fuss, we'll be ready for them; everything will be settled and in place. Tomorrow at eight, then. (*Gets up.*)

ZOTOVA (*to LOKTEV*). Now that's a man!

DYEDOV. Your orders will be carried out.

LOKTEV. Until tomorrow. Only...

RAYEVSKY. Goodbye. Don't be offended that I scolded you a little bit. You'll work all the better.

LOKTEV. Who's offended? Thank you!

ZOTOVA (*to RAYEVSKY*). There's going to be a show at the Club tonight. Why don't you come?

RAYEVSKY. I... we will come. Olga and I. Who's performing?

ZOTOVA. Our own local talent. But our guys do a great job. They can make the whole auditorium burst into tears.

LOKTEV. That's right. They can make the audience cry when it should laugh and laugh when it should cry.

ZOTOVA. You're always laughing at something. We don't get any help from you, no guidance. Only sneers and more sneers. (*Exits.*)

LOKTEV (*shaking hands with RAYEVSKY*). What about weapons, comrade Rayevsky? We ought to have some at the ready. It's safer that way.

RAYEVSKY. I wasn't born yesterday.

(*He shakes hands with LOKTEV. DYEDOV and LOKTEV leave.*)

The Secretary is a coward. Spend several days holding discussions! Heck, I'll be done in three days. I've been assigned four villages. I'll go through ten in that time. I'll collect my whole quota way ahead of time. I'll show these hicks what military tempo is.

OLGA. You did a great job talking to them. You're so intense, so forceful.

RAYEVSKY. I am just a decisive man, Olga.

OLGA. Yes, you're a man. You're the real thing. You know, I'd lost any hope of ever meeting you.

RAYEVSKY. Me?

OLGA. Yes, you. Someone like you.

RAYEVSKY. What am I like?

OLGA. You're... you're.... It's hard to explain.

RAYEVSKY. But we'll stay together, Olga.... Right?

OLGA. What do you mean?

RAYEVSKY. Like this.... (*Grabs* OLGA *suddenly and kisses her.*) Olga! Olga, my dear, we have blood in our veins, not water that you can meter by the kopeck.

(*Grabs and kisses her again.* OLGA *breaks away. He runs around the table after her. He can't catch her, so he jumps up on the table. At that moment the door to the hall opens and* MOKRINA *enters. She is frozen in place with her arms raised over her head so that her face is hidden from* RAYEVSKY.)

What do you want, little Mother?

MOKRINA (*crosses herself*). Amen! Amen! May you rot in Hell!

RAYEVSKY. Amen! (*Jumps off the table.*)

MOKRINA. Come no closer, fiend! (*Makes a large sign of the cross over him.*)

RAYEVSKY. What do you want?

MOKRINA. What do *you* want here, accursed one? What do you, who bear the mark of the Evil One, want here? Why were you flying all over the house? Begone!

(KVASOV *comes in with* PASHA. *Once again* PASHA *remains at the door.*)

KVASOV. You may return to your room, Mother. (*To* RAYEVSKY.) She's a nun. Paying me a visit. Keeps blathering on about God.

(MOKRINA *exits.*)

OLGA. Did you see the spark in her eyes? How old is she? She must be pretty young.

KVASOV. I never thought to ask.

RAYEVSKY. Hell with her! Olenka, let's go for a walk. There are woods on the outskirts of the village. The snow is deep and crisp. Let's go.

OLGA. Come with us, Pashenka.

PASHA. No, thank you.

RAYEVSKY. Really, Pasha, show us the forest.

PASHA. There's the forest. You can find it yourselves. Walking around all day long isn't my idea of a good time.

RAYEVSKY. Why are you such a stick-in-the-mud, Pashenka? You should be having fun, making friends.

PASHA. Having fun won't fill your stomach.

RAYEVSKY. What is it you want, then?

PASHA. Lots of stuff. The ceilings are low here, for instance, but I'd like them to be high.

RAYEVSKY. Tell your father to raise them.

PASHA. Father? He won't do it.

KVASOV. Get to work, Pashka.

OLGA. Do you have chores to do?

KVASOV. Our chores are peasant chores. Did you bring any weapons with you? Forgive me. I don't know your name and patronymic.

RAYEVSKY. I'm comrade Rayevsky.

KVASOV. Comrade Rayevsky, you ought to take a pistol with you.

RAYEVSKY. Why do you keep bringing that up? Is there trouble here or something?

KVASOV. God has spared us from trouble. But considering why you're here, anything could happen.

RAYEVSKY. Don't worry. Let's go, Olyenka. Cheer up, Pasha. (*Waves to her.*)

(*He and* OLGA *exit.* PASHA *remains in the same place.* KVASOV *goes up to the window and watches them leave.*)

PASHA. Why did you want to know if he had a revolver?

KVASOV (*turning around laboriously*). Did you say something?

PASHA. Don't pretend to be deaf. What are you up to, I'm asking.

KVASOV (*quietly*). Just who do you think you're talking to, Pashenka?

PASHA. I'm talking to you, Kvasov, Ivan Gerasimovich. I'm talking to my own father.

KVASOV. Pashka! Our Lord takes no joy in anger. Don't lead me to sin, Pashka.

PASHA. If you try to trip him, if you harm so much as one hair on his head, then you better watch your step, Ivan Gerasimovich. I won't have it! (*Turns and leaves.*)

KVASOV. You won't have it? How about that! Just you ask him, and he'll give you a tall building in the city, but you'll have to walk the streets in front of that building. You'll be a big-city slut.

PASHA (*runs headlong out of her room, screams into* KVASOV'*s face*). What did you say? What?

KVASOV. Now, now, daughter. Now, now! (PASHA *backs away.*) Why would you even bring up something like that. What are we, murderers? Don't we have souls? What we haven't given is not for us to take away. Lord!

(PASHA *throws on a fur jacket and a kerchief.*)

Where are you going?

PASHA. I'm going to Anka's.

KVASOV. Go ahead, Pashenka. Go over to Anka's. But send Mikhail to me. And bang on Grunkin's window. Tell him to come over. Will you send him?

PASHA. I will.

KVASOV (*goes into the hall and bolts the door behind her. His voice can be heard from there*). Some daughter I raised. Seed of the Devil! (*Comes in.*) But my flesh and blood. (*Loudly.*) Mother!

MOKRINA (*enters*). Here I am, Ivan Gerasimovich.

KVASOV. We must defend ourselves, Mother. The city has sent us a present. A red broom that'll sweep our barns clean. They've come to steal our grain.

MOKRINA. The marked one?

KVASOV. Marked with a red seal, Mother. Great powers have been given to him. He'll go to every house.

MOKRINA. That must never be.

KVASOV. We must defend ourselves. Go to all the women. Open their eyes. So that tomorrow, when the meeting is called, they'll know who's calling it and why. Make haste, Mother, make haste.

MOKRINA. Goodbye, Ivan Gerasimovich. We have a long day and night ahead of us. Our Savior will help us.

KVASOV. Glory to Him! (*Follows her and closes the door; looks out of the window.*) Go ahead and walk, comrade, have a nice walk! We have wonderful snow, we have nice woods. Go ahead and walk, while we're tossing and turning on our beds. While we're here scratching our heads. While we're...

(*A knock at the door;* PASHA, MIKHAIL, *and* GRUNKIN *enter.*)

Come on in. (*Greets* GRUNKIN.) Have a seat, have a seat right here.

(*They sit.*)

What are things coming to?

GRUNKIN. Don't I know it.

KVASOV. So you know—that's good. And how will it all end, Nikanor Semyonych?

GRUNKIN. That I don't know.

KVASOV. But I know. We'll all be beggars. They'll squeeze us peasants to death. How much does the State pay you for grain?

GRUNKIN. 'Bout eight rubles.

KVASOV. And how much did I pay you?

GRUNKIN. 'Bout sixty rubles.

KVASOV. The reason I paid you so much, Nikanor Semyonych, is because I know what kind of work we put in. I myself get out into the field before dawn. I've watered our earth with my own sweat and tears. And so have you. See, our earth is salty. But in Moscow the cabdrivers feed their horses baked bread. You think they know the value of our grain?

GRUNKIN. But what can we do? They'll just take it.

KVASOV. Why should they take it? If there is no grain, they can't take any. We have to take a stand, Nikanor Semyonych. One for all, and all for one.

Most of all—we can't let them divide us. We can't let them wreck our families. If one of us falls, we all go down.

GRUNKIN. So what shall I do with your grain, then?

KVASOV. Let it sit there, Nikanor Semyonych. It isn't getting in your way. If they search your house, just tell them it's yours. They have no right to take it away from you.

GRUNKIN. I'll keep it for now. I just hope nothing happens.

KVASOV. Go to the meeting tomorrow. And tell everybody else, too. Those guys think we're just a bunch of stupid hicks. They're wrong.

GRUNKIN. Well, then, goodbye, Ivan Gerasimovich.

KVASOV. God be with you. Don't be a stranger. (*Sees him out, comes back.*) Mishka, we have to play for keeps. They're going to try to make us pay. They'll take about sixty of us and make us pay for the whole village.

MIKHAIL. Do they want much?

KVASOV. A hundred and twenty-five.

MIKHAIL. Whew....

KVASOV. We have to go around to people right now. No sleep for us tonight. We have a big puzzle to solve.

MIKHAIL. What do you think of the newcomer?

KVASOV. All flame. But we can put it out.

MIKHAIL. Can he be bribed?

KVASOV. We'll play the mouse, and the cat will follow.

MIKHAIL. What have you thought up, Papa?

KVASOV. I have a little something in mind. Oh, insult to injury. (*Gets up and walks toward the room where* PASHA *is; quietly.*) I'll whisper it to you. Our cat...

MIKHAIL (*quietly*). What are you saying, Papa?!

KVASOV. Maybe there's nothing to it.... Pasha's growing up. The meeting is tomorrow....

(*Bends toward* MIKHAIL *and whispers. A broad grin gradually spreads over his face, and he nods and leaves.*)

(*Curtain.*)

ACT 3

A meeting on the village square. The church is nearby. The village town hall and a cooperative store can also be seen. Men and women peasants stand. The old men sit on logs. KVASOV *and* ZUBOV *sit a ways off to one side. On a bench at the foot of the platform sit* OLGA, LOKTEV, ZOTOVA, *and several Communist Youths.* DYEDOV *and* RAYEVSKY *are on the platform. The rumbling noises of a meeting.*

DYEDOV. Citizens! Citizens! You've heard the report of Comrade Rayevsky, who's come here on special assignment. We have the amounts of wheat and rye each one of you has to sell to the State. I'll read it. Period.

KOTIKHIN. But what about questions? Can't we ask questions?

SHILOV. That's right!

KATERINA. Answer our questions.

GRUNKIN. We demand questions.

OLKHA. It's not clear....

DYEDOV (*speaks quietly with* RAYEVSKY). Questions are permitted. But let's have a little order, citizens. This is a meeting, not a bazaar.

KOTIKHIN (*rising*). May I?

DYEDOV. Ask your question, Kotikhin.

ROMANOV. He has no right to ask questions. He's been deprived of his vote.

ZOTOVA. Don't give him the floor. He has no right.

MISHKA AFANASYEV. Don't give him the floor.

KOTIKHIN. As you like. I just wanted to clear things up for the citizens.

KATERINA. Why shut him up? His vote has been taken away from him— but his tongue hasn't been ripped out. Let him ask.

GRUNKIN. Questions are for the common good, to make things clear for everyone.

SHILOV. Don't restrict the meeting, Chairman.

RUMBLE OF VOICES. Let him ask his question! Let's have the question!

(RAYEVSKY *speaks quietly to* DYEDOV.)

DYEDOV. Let's have your question.

KOTIKHIN (*takes off his hat and reads from notes*). The comrade delegate was talking about sacrifices. Well, I just don't get it? Are we talking about selling our grain or just giving it away, sort of like a contribution to build a church?

(*Laughter.*)

RAYEVSKY. I was talking about selling grain to State and cooperative agencies.

KOTIKHIN. But you did mention sacrifices. So it turns out that selling grain at government prices is just the same as sacrificing it. Turns out we're just giving it away.

SHILOV. And where are we supposed to get it?

GRUNKIN. Eight rubles for wheat.

KATERINA. If only we *had* something to sacrifice. But we're all going to be beggars. We'll be begging off each other.

RAYEVSKY. I was talking about the sacrifices we all have to make to industrialize the country. Come on, now, you know that industrialization is for us, for all of us.

GRUNKIN. And how are we supposed to industrialize? On a full belly or on an empty one?

KATERINA. I'm hungry, folks. I haven't eaten for three days.

KOTIKHIN. So it turns out you need a lot of money for industrialization? And that's why they're demanding more grain from the peasants? Is that about right?

RAYEVSKY. That's right.

KOTIKHIN. But why the peasants, may I ask? Why not reduce the salaries of the workers and the government employees? How come the worker gets new houses, clubs, theaters, and the peasant keeps only his tiny strip of land?

(*Noise.*)

OLKHA. You forgot about the tax. The peasant is taxed. And if you're not on time, you pay with your neck.

KATERINA. They wouldn't think about that. All they want is grain.

RAYEVSKY. Comrades!...

GRUNKIN. Somehow we used to get factory goods, but where are they now? What's the matter? Have the factories closed down, or all the workers died? I'm looking for answers.

(*Laughter.*)

RAYEVSKY. The thing is...

OLKHA (*interrupts*). Why have you used up all the leather for your briefcases? We don't even have boots.

DYEDOV (*shouts*). Citizens, stop this racket! Ask your questions one at a time. You're not giving us a chance to answer.

KATERINA. Enough sweet talk.

DYEDOV. I won't allow any more questions. Period. Whoever wants to can ask his questions from here. (*Points to the platform.*)

GRUNKIN. I'll speak from here. I have a loud voice. Citizens, we've been sending our Red shipment of grain. We've paid our taxes. We're happy to give our last kopeck to the State, but we have nothing. Am I right, citizens?

RUMBLE. Right! We've no more grain! Enough! We've fulfilled our quota!

KATERINA. I'm hungry, friends, I'm hungry....

GRUNKIN. If they won't listen to talk and reason, let them take it by force. Am I right, citizens?

(*Noise, shouts of approval.*)

ROMANOV. What is this? Let me speak! (*He runs up to the platform and easily jumps on top of it. He's all worked up.*) Why aren't we saying anything? Why aren't we partisans saying anything? Kotikhin, why are you pouring wax in our ears and smearing our mouths with honey? Who's supposed to be selling that grain? Those of us who have about three grains of barley, or those of you who have to repair your barns because they're full to bursting and with bags buried underground besides?

KATERINA. What a liar!

ROMANOV. Why is everyone following one guy around, like a flock of sheep? Nothing to say, Ivan Gerasimovich? You're sitting there on your log, but I know your bite....

DYEDOV. Wait, who is that, driving a wagonful of grain in the middle of the day?

(*The whole crowd turns around and looks.*)

Young Communists, find out! Period.

(*Several* KOMSOMOL MEMBERS *run off. The crowd watches intently.*)

SHILOV. They've caught up to him.

OLKHA. They're bringing him here. Why, could that be Mikhailo Kvasov?

(*Agitation. Shouts: "Kvasov!" "Mishka!" "Mikhailo!" A few people run toward the wagon.*)

ROMANOV. Did you see? He was on his way to the market. A regular counterrevolutionary White shipment—four wagons. The rat!

VOICES. A fine time he found. What's he up to? That's a lot of grain. Mishka has lost his mind. Looks like wheat.

(*Several* KOMSOMOL MEMBERS *drag in* MIKHAIL KVASOV. *Those who ran to the wagon follow them.* MIKHAIL *is brought up to the platform. The crowd tightly surrounds the newcomer.*)

DYEDOV. Kvasov, Mikhail! Where are you taking nearly twenty tons when the State needs grain?

MIKHAIL. Not guilty before the State.

ROMANOV. Perhaps he's taking it to the collecting station.

MIKHAIL. I was bringing the grain here.

(*Agitation in the crowd.*)

VOICES: What do you mean, "here"? Why bring grain here? Why here?

ROMANOV. Don't talk to us in riddles. We might figure one of them out.

KOTIKHIN. And just who is this "we"? What's your address?

ROMANOV. I'll send you my address in a letter. You'll read it on the envelope. You bourgeois holdover!

DYEDOV (to MIKHAIL). Where were you taking the grain to? Answer, period!

MIKHAIL. In accordance with the Soviet slogan, "aid to the poor," I brought the grain here to the village commune. (To the crowd.) Citizen villagers, knowing the bitter need of the peasants, through my own hard work, as a tiller of the soil myself, I humbly offer you this grain. Take it, for the love of God.

(Bows low on three sides. There is a second's pause, during which everybody, as if drawn by some invisible force, turns to face the loads of grain.)

KATERINA. Hey guys, free wheat. Free! (Rushes for the grain.)

(The crowd, as if caught up in a whirlwind, rushes to the wagons. A few PARTY MEMBERS and KOMSOMOL MEMBERS remain near the platform with MIKHAIL KVASOV. IVAN GERASIMOVICH KVASOV sits on the log.)

(Curtain.)

SCENE 5

KVASOV's house. RAYEVSKY is alone. He's writing. A knock at the door. PASHA walks across the room and opens the door. RAYEVSKY looks on with anticipation. KVASOV enters.

RAYEVSKY. Oh, it's you?

KVASOV. Yes, good morning.

RAYEVSKY. Thank you.

KVASOV. How did you sleep? Our featherbeds are soft.

RAYEVSKY. Aw, to hell with your featherbeds! I tossed and turned all night long.

KVASOV. Not used to it. As for us, we sleep just fine on them.

RAYEVSKY. They're stuffy.

KVASOV. That's good for you.

RAYEVSKY. Have you seen Olga this morning?

KVASOV. I didn't happen to. (*Pause.*) Where are you planning to go?

RAYEVSKY. People are coming to see me. The Chairman and some others.

KVASOV. I see, I see.... It was a real shame to see our citizens' lack of class consciousness yesterday.

RAYEVSKY. Come on, now, cut it out. You were very pleased about it. I can see right through you.

KVASOV. Me? Where'd you get that from?

RAYEVSKY. And who pulled that trick with the grain? Wasn't it your son?

KVASOV. That's not fair. I swear before God, that's not fair. I've just come from seeing him. I chewed him out the way only a father can. Why'd he go and bring it during the meeting and cause confusion? Well, nothing to be done for it, he won't even listen. You know how children are these days. He's only waiting to get his share, and then... to hell with his father.

RAYEVSKY. I'm going to have him arrested today for disrupting the meeting.

KVASOV. That's not fair, either. He had good intentions. However, as you wish. I'd say the law doesn't apply to that sort of incident. But you know better, you're closer to the law.

(*Pause.*)

Pasha, go to your room.

PASHA. I haven't gotten in your way yet, but look out, I will.

KVASOV. Go, I said. I've asked you nicely.

(PASHA *gets up abruptly.*)

RAYEVSKY. Why do you keep sending her out? You shut her up in the house and order her around. But she's all grown up.

KVASOV. She's my daughter.

RAYEVSKY. And that gives you the right to beat her down? Knock it off!

Forget the old ways. Olga and I are going to take her to the city with us when we leave.

KVASOV. If she wants to go, she'll go.

RAYEVSKY. Will you come, Pasha?

PASHA. Why talk nonsense? (*Leaves.*)

RAYEVSKY (*calls after her*). I'm serious, Pasha. I mean it, really. (*Sits down at the table.*)

(*Pause.*)

KVASOV. What's happening next, my dear comrade?

RAYEVSKY. We're going to get the grain. I'll go from door to door myself. I'll take witnesses with me. I'll dig up every vegetable garden. I'm not in the habit of retreating, damn it!

KVASOV. That's just the sort of attitude I was afraid of. Comrade, believe an old man. I know everybody here. I know what everybody has —not just what's in his barn, but what's in his stocking, in a pitcher, or buried under a floorboard. We haven't got a hundred and twenty-five, honest to God. I talked to the peasants today. We'll give what we can to the authorities—but without making a big fuss about it, without a meeting. We'll collect thirty-five, but there's no way to get any more than that.

RAYEVSKY. What do you mean, thirty-five? I'll turn the whole village inside out.

KVASOV (*to the icons*). Lord, save the soul of your servant, Pavel, and take pity on it!

RAYEVSKY. Stop acting foolish! What's going on?

KVASOV. I can't even get the words out of my mouth.

RAYEVSKY. Listen, stop fooling around. This is no time for jokes.

KVASOV. Comrade delegate, they'll kill you, the damn fools. If you go from door to door, they'll kill you. I know they will.

RAYEVSKY. Well, that doesn't scare me.

KVASOV. But they won't scare you. They'll get you with a sawed-off shotgun from behind some corner. Night or day, makes no difference. See, our village is desperate. Such restless people! You've seen for yourself.

(*There is a sharp rap at the window.*)

RAYEVSKY (*starts*). What's that?

KVASOV (*goes to the window*). He's here. Romanov's here. He's a rotten apple. Biggest troublemaker around. He's missing an arm. A guy like that ought to settle down some, but no, he spits his rage out at everyone, like a dragon breathing fire. Shall I let him in?

RAYEVSKY. Let him in, let him in. He was just starting to say something about you yesterday.

KVASOV. He can say whatever he wants.

(KVASOV *opens the door and comes in with* ROMANOV.)

ROMANOV. Hello, comrade Rayevsky. But I'm not going to talk to you in front of this louse. Order him to get out.

RAYEVSKY. Well, you stop insulting him. We're in his house.

ROMANOV. His house was built with our hands. Let him be crowded for once. Pretty soon we'll crowd him out completely.

KVASOV. I'll leave, comrade Rayevsky, for your convenience. You're so hotheaded, Kolya. Look out, you may find *yourself* in a jam one of these days.

ROMANOV. What are you going to do? Throw me into a well? I haven't forgotten!

KVASOV. There are laws against lying like that.

ROMANOV. And are you going to be the one to twist the Soviet law against me?

KVASOV. Even you will get it some day. Go ahead, talk.... (*Leaves.*)

RAYEVSKY. What well were you talking about?

ROMANOV. When the Whites were here, he betrayed twelve men. He hacked them to pieces himself. Then he threw them into a well. I know this for a fact. But there aren't any witnesses. No one will speak. They're afraid. There was an investigation, but there were no witnesses, so he slithered out of it like a snake. I'll give my other arm this very minute if he's not the one who did it.

RAYEVSKY. That old man?

ROMANOV. That old man! He's the head of the whole monster. May I drop dead this minute if I'm not telling you the truth.

RAYEVSKY. Is that so? And where do you live?

ROMANOV. When you were coming into the village, did you happen to see a royal palace? It's dug into the ground—I guess you wouldn't notice it with the naked eye.

RAYEVSKY. So that mud hut is yours.

ROMANOV. All mine. I have royal blood in my veins. Kolka Romanov. Couldn't you tell?

RAYEVSKY. Well, are you a Party man?

ROMANOV. I'm a one-armed man.

RAYEVSKY. I'm not joking.

ROMANOV. If you're not joking, I'll tell you. I was thrown out.

RAYEVSKY. Why?

ROMANOV. Because.

RAYEVSKY. Come on, why?

ROMANOV. For being wild, for being young. It doesn't matter. I'll get back in.

RAYEVSKY. No, you really should get back in the Party.

ROMANOV. I'll come back with a whole Romanov regiment. I've organized a regiment. We have uniforms, and shoulder-knots too. But we don't have enough boots. So we stand at attention in our bare feet.

RAYEVSKY. How soon will this event take place?

ROMANOV. You'd best get our membership cards ready.

RAYEVSKY. Looks like maybe you've had a bit too much to drink?

ROMANOV. My whole life I've had a bit too much. You just go ahead, crawl into my hole, take a look at the walls. They're weeping, shedding tears. And then you start to get sad and whimper like a dog. But you have a bit to drink—and everything gets a little cheerier. The walls are higher, the earth is warmer.

RAYEVSKY. Why don't they move you somewhere else? You're an invalid, after all.

ROMANOV. Where would they put me? But when we build our communal housing, I'll have my own little apartment, three rooms and a can.

RAYEVSKY. Are you folks organizing a collective farm?

ROMANOV. Of course. You think it will organize itself?

RAYEVSKY. But when?

ROMANOV. We're making preparations. Soon we'll go on the offensive. Ah, comrade! My life has become so cheerful. There's a wind, I'd even say a strong wind. It's a cheerful wind. And my hut even isn't even a hut any-more, but a sailing ship, and I'm the skipper. The sails rustle, the mast bends, the boat tosses me up and down, but I keep it going forwards. The waters are flooding the town, the houses are floating and the peasants are sitting on the roofs. "Kolka," they cry, "reel us in.... Kolka, take us with you." And I keep on reeling them in, keep on going. Pretty soon I'm car-rying the whole village with me—and I'm laughing, and I'm crying....

RAYEVSKY. You're crying! What's wrong with you?

ROMANOV. Not exactly out of happiness, not exactly out of foolishness.... Hey, are you going to collect the grain, or what?

RAYEVSKY. We have to collect it, of course. I'm not sure that we'll get the whole hundred and twenty-five.

ROMANOV. What do you mean, not sure you'll get it. Heck, you could get two hundred and twenty-five, easy, if you needed it. You've got to go from door to door.

RAYEVSKY. I don't know. I don't think...

(*A knock at the door.*)

Just a moment, I'll get that.... (*Opens the door and lets* OLGA *in.*) Olenka, where have you been? I was so worried.

OLGA. You sleep till God knows when! I walked around the village, and farther, into the fields.

RAYEVSKY. Why didn't you wake me up? I would have gone with you.

OLGA. I didn't feel like it, somehow.

RAYEVSKY. Are you upset?

OLGA. It hurt me yesterday to see our defeat.

RAYEVSKY. You mean—my defeat.

OLGA. I said our defeat.

RAYEVSKY. We're a long way from defeated yet. I told you—it's an ele-mental force.

OLGA. But I thought you would conquer it immediately.

RAYEVSKY. It reared up—it roared yesterday. You know, when I was sitting on the platform yesterday, I felt like I was on a ship, on the captain's bridge, during a storm. Waves were rising and then breaking against the planks.

OLGA. What's next, do you think?

(*A knock at the window.* DYEDOV, LOKTEV, *and* ZOTOVA *enter. They all exchange greetings.*)

LOKTEV. We need to talk.

RAYEVSKY. I don't know the situation as well as you do. What do you suggest?

OLGA. Let's sit down.

(*They sit down.*)

DYEDOV (*to* ROMANOV). You can leave. Drop by again later.

LOKTEV. What did he ever do to you? Let him stay.

ROMANOV. I can go. I'm missing an arm....

ZOTOVA. Stay here, Kolka. (*To* DYEDOV.) Don't you dare kick a partisan out. Comrade Rayevsky, you tell him.

RAYEVSKY. Stay here. Now then, I'm waiting, comrades.

DYEDOV. The situation is just the way I reported. The whole population is in revolt. They don't have any grain. We've got to beat a retreat. Period.

LOKTEV. And not collect any grain?

DYEDOV. What makes you say that? We can make a collection. We can go from door to door and collect it one kernel at a time.

LOKTEV. So there are only a few kernels left in the whole village?

DYEDOV. Whatever our comrade delegate decides, whatever he orders, I'll collect it.

ROMANOV. Comrade Chairman, may I ask a question.

DYEDOV. Go ahead.

ROMANOV. How come you're twisting and turning, like the Devil in a frying pan? Give it to us straight now—do the kulaks have grain or not?

DYEDOV. Nikolai Romanov, the time's long gone since you were allowed to be rude to people.

ROMANOV. I'll say this up to my dying breath. I'll even say it afterwards. I'll poke my head out of the grave, and I'll shout out to the whole village. The kulaks have grain. (*Shouts.*)
The kulaks have grain!

RAYEVSKY (*irritably*). What are you shouting for—you think we can't hear you? You're not in your grave yet.

DYEDOV. Shouting like that only gets in the way of Soviet power. Who got up at the meeting yesterday? The kulaks? Period. You need to understand agricultural economics, comrade Romanov. Of course, you never did have your own farm. There's a lot you don't know.

ROMANOV. I lost my right arm because of your kind of farming. Go ahead and cuss me out, Dyedov, cuss me out, Comrade Chairman. All the kulaks call me an idler.

LOKTEV. That's enough out of you! Comrade Rayevsky, we have to make a decision. There is grain, that's for sure. Now what should we do next?

ZOTOVA. Arrest the kulaks—and we'll have the grain in one day.

RAYEVSKY. What do you mean, arrest them—without cause?

ZOTOVA. Until they hand over the grain.

DYEDOV. If we arrest them today, there will be a huge riot by nightfall.

RAYEVSKY. A riot?

DYEDOV. It's very simple. The disturbance could spread to the whole district. And who will be held responsible—the Secretary of the local Komsomol, Zotova? Pardon me, but she'll stay on the sidelines. Or maybe the hothead Kolya Romanov will be held responsible? No, sir. Dyedov will be held responsible, and comrade Rayevsky will be held responsible....

(RAYEVSKY *gets up and walks around the room.*)

RAYEVSKY. True....

LOKTEV. Well, what'll it be, then?

RAYEVSKY. The situation is more serious than you think, comrades. Yesterday we saw before our eyes a unified peasant mass, united and organized.

ZOTOVA. A kulak mass. I told you—the whole village is kulak.

RAYEVSKY. There are two ways we can go. We can actually start making arrests and searching. I was the one who wanted to put on the pressure, but I have become convinced that Dyedov is right. We'll set the whole village against us, and not only will we fail to collect any grain, we may also find ourselves faced with terrible consequences.

LOKTEV. We should have spent some time preparing.

RAYEVSKY. The second method—and, in my opinion, the only correct one from the Bolshevik point of view—is to remember that our alliance with the peasant is far more important than thirty-five or forty-five additional tons of grain. I propose, therefore, that we set ourselves to the task of collecting the largest amount of grain possible, and that we not be embarrassed if we end up collecting only thirty-five or forty-five tons.

DYEDOV. Period.

ROMANOV. Ugh, comrades, comrades! (*He unexpectedly runs up to the table and puts his arm on it.*) Here, Dyedov, chop it off! Chop off my other arm! I have no need for it. You won't let me raise it. I have an ax in my hand. And there are people to strike with that ax. But you won't let me! Chop off my arm, Dyedov, chop it off!

MIKHAILOV (*enters wearing a military coat and a flat, round fur cap*). You folks opening up a butcher shop or something? What are you going to chop off? Hello, Pavel! Comrade Loktev! Hello, Olga! (*To* ROMANOV.) Ah, Your Majesty, so you're the one who's rioting? Dissatisfied with your subjects again?

ROMANOV. I'm in no condition to joke, comrade Mikhailov. I have only two years to live. Has my whole life really been for nothing?

ZOTOVA. Are you here for long, Mikhailov? Will you speak at the Party meeting?

MIKHAILOV. I'm going round the districts, to speed up the grain collection. What have you got so far, Pavel?

RAYEVSKY. Basically, nothing. We had a little delay, because of certain local circumstances.

MIKHAILOV. What do you mean, a delay? There shouldn't be any delay here. There's plenty of grain in this village.

DYEDOV. There *was* plenty of grain.

MIKHAILOV. And who are you?

DYEDOV. Chairman of the local Soviet—Dyedov, Mikhail Pavlov.

MIKHAILOV. Then, Mikhail Pavlov, you ought to know that there *is* plenty of grain here, not that there was.

DYEDOV. Yes, sir.

LOKTEV. For the time being we've failed.

MIKHAILOV. What? What do you mean, failed?

LOKTEV (*hands him a sheet of paper*). Here, read yesterday's report!

MIKHAILOV (*reads, shakes his head, frowns*). How about that.... (*Returns the report to* LOKTEV. *To* DYEDOV.) Is Mishka Kvasov in jail?

DYEDOV. I was waiting for an order.

MIKHAILOV. Waiting? Arrest him! Call a meeting for tonight, send out the officers right now.

DYEDOV. Yes, sir.

RAYEVSKY. In my opinion, a meeting for tonight, without any preparation, is pointless.

MIKHAILOV. You should have organized the preparation long ago, comrade Rayevsky.

LOKTEV. That's what I said, too.

MIKHAILOV. That's what you said, too. You should have acted, not said.

LOKTEV. But, you see, comrade Rayevsky...

MIKHAILOV. Rayevsky! Rayevsky! You are the Secretary—when you disagree with someone, you should be able to convince him. And if you can't, telephone the District Office. Demand, insist. Otherwise you're just some pushover from Tula. And now that the kulaks have beaten us in front of the whole meeting, it's a bit late to be preparing. We must turn the tables immediately.

RAYEVSKY. You won't have only the kulaks to deal with, but a united countryside.

MIKHAILOV. There's no such thing, Pavel. Countryside—that's just a geographic and poetic concept; there is no such sociological concept.

RAYEVSKY. That's a good theory, but when it comes to grain, there's a whole angry river of peasants flowing against us.

MIKHAILOV. That's a false impression, Pavel. Many currents—many waters—many different eddies. You have to know how to steer your boat.

ZOTOVA. And I say that this is a kulak village.

MIKHAILOV. You're not the one saying that. You only think you're the one saying it.

ZOTOVA. Well, how about that, Maria Dmitryevna! Then who is?

MIKHAILOV. The kulaks.

ZOTOVA. I strangle kulaks with my own hands—and yet I talk like one?

MIKHAILOV. That kind of thing happens. Let's get going, comrades! Romanov, you'll have to run a few errands. Dyedov, get the list. Make sure it's the latest list. Loktev, call all the active members together right away. But first of all, let's get out of this house!

(*He,* DYEDOV, LOKTEV, ZOTOVA, *and* ROMANOV *go.*)

RAYEVSKY (*after them, loudly*). There's going to be a riot.

MIKHAILOV (*turns around*). We'll fight fire with fire.

ROMANOV. I won't give my arm up yet, Comrade Chairman! (*Raises his arm.*) I think I'll need it.

(*Curtain.*)

ACT 4

The village square. Toward sundown. In the center of the square is NIKO-LAI ROMANOV, *digging. The peasants—men, women, and children— are assembling in the square. They come singly and in groups. They stop near* ROMANOV *and look on in astonishment.*

FIRST PEASANT WOMAN. What are you doing, Kolya?

(ROMANOV *doesn't answer her question or any of the others that follow. He keeps digging.*)

SECOND PEASANT WOMAN. Kolyushka, what are you making?
FIRST YOUNG PEASANT. Guys, Kolka is digging for treasure.
SECOND YOUNG PEASANT. Treasure!

(*Laughter.*)

Kolya, let me help! We'll split it.
SHILOV. No, seriously now. What are you doing, Kolya?
KATERINA. Why won't he answer, the devil? He's up to no good!
FIRST PEASANT. What did you lose, Kolya?
SECOND PEASANT WOMAN. No one knows. He just digs and keeps his mouth shut.
KOTIKHIN. A clown, a regular clown.
SOTIN. You just wait, Vasily Afanasyevich, maybe it won't be so funny.
THIRD PEASANT. Hey guys, I bet he's digging an early grave for himself.
THE WHOLE GROUP. A grave?

(*Laughter.*)

FIRST PEASANT GIRL. Or perhaps he's digging up a dowry for his Nyushka.

(Laughter.)

KATERINA. Ugh, my dears, this will come to no good....

FIRST PEASANT. Maybe you're digging another hut for yourself? Just tell us, Kolya, and we'll take up a collection of boards for you.

(Laughter.)

A LITTLE BOY. I know. He's digging a radio.

FOURTH PEASANT *(approaching)*. What's he doing?

SECOND YOUNG PEASANT. Building a second church.

(Laughter.)

SECOND PEASANT WOMAN. Come on, tell us, Kolya, don't torture us.

VOICES. Tell us, Kolka! Come on, say something! What are you doing? Doesn't want to say, the devil!

KOTIKHIN. We ought to chase him out. Disorderly conduct and public drunkenness.

SOTIN. He wouldn't have snuck some moonshine at your apiary, Vasily Afanasyevich?

THIRD YOUNG PEASANT. What's going on here, guys?

SECOND YOUNG PEASANT. Here's the news! Someone slaughtered a calf with a cucumber.

(Laughter.)

FIRST PEASANT WOMAN. Kolyushka, the whole village is asking. Tell us how come you're digging?

SECOND PEASANT. Don't be so proud, Kolka!

AN OLD MAN. Kolya, why are you stirring the earth? The earth doesn't like it.

GRUNKIN. Kolya, do you maybe have some grain buried somewhere that you want to sell to the State?

(Uproarious laughter.)

FIRST PEASANT. Oh, this is killing me! (*Laughs loudly.*)

FIRST PEASANT WOMAN. He's got grain here, grain. (*Laughs loudly.*)

KOTIKHIN. Grain! (*Giggles.*)

ROMANOV (*shouts wildly*). Shut up, all of you! (*To* KOTIKHIN.) And especially you, you rat, shut your trap!

(*Silence.*)

I'm building a railroad.

VOICES. What? What did he say? What's that he's saying?

SHILOV. A ra-il-road? With that spade?

(*Restrained laughter in the crowd.*)

SECOND PEASANT WOMAN. He's lost his marbles. Poor little Kolyushka!

OLKHA. A fine time to joke around. What a fool!

ROMANOV. Me a fool? And you're not a fool? And what are all these people around me? They're the fools. (*Points all around him.*) I'm a fool—because I'm building a railroad by myself. But here they are—fifteen hundred fools—Kvasov and his buddies are fleecing them, but they follow him around, and even bow to the ground before him—"Thank you, master...." He can get the best of the whole village, but I can't build a railroad by myself? Can that be?

KOTIKHIN. So that's what you were leading up to?

KVASOV. You're all riled up, Kolya. You shouldn't call all the peasants fools. You're putting yourself above everyone else.

KOTIKHIN. From the inside, citizens, the worm is gnawing away at us from the inside. That's why he's digging up the earth.

SOTIN. There are worms and then there are rats. Kolka's not alone. What do you say, guys?

VOICES. Right! Good job, Kolka! Enough bowing to Kvasov. The murderer!

KATERINA. I said no good would come of it.

GRUNKIN. Now they've started bawling, the idlers. An idler drinks his farm away, go ahead and give him another one. Give him what someone else has earned with good honest work, and he'll drink that one up too. That's what's waiting for you.

KOTIKHIN. Well, Kolya's the one who said it—the whole village is filled with fools.

ROMANOV. There's a word for guys like you, Kotikhin. We have a word for guys like you!

KORYTKO. You had no call to go making a scene, Kolya, no call whatsoever. This is no joking matter.

KVASOV. What matter?

KORYTKO. About you, for instance.

KVASOV. What about me?

SOTIN. It's long past time for everything about you to be out in the open.

KOTIKHIN. And if it's in the open, you'll steal it.

SOTIN. Uncle Kotikhin, I'll pop you just once—and there'll be a well where you're standing.

OLKHA. You quit throwing your fists around! Quit throwing your fists around! You're at a meeting, not a brawl.

KORYTKO. You see what has happened, Kolya, instead of a much-needed discussion? You shouldn't have done that!

ROMANOV. Cuss me out, go on, cuss me out. I'm missing an arm.

KOTIKHIN. What is this, peasants? An idler and a drunkard want to get the best of us! They've made fools of the whole village. Threatening to beat us up. May we never see that in *our* village.

ROMANOV. May we never see *you* again on the face of this earth. (*Jumps at* KOTIKHIN.)

(*A scuffle breaks out.* MIKHAILOV, DYEDOV, RAYEVSKY, OLGA, LOKTEV, ZOTOVA, *several* PARTY MEMBERS, *and* KOMSOMOL MEMBERS *enter.*)

MIKHAILOV. Stop! Stop, I said!

(*The crowd breaks up.* ROMANOV *is dragged away from* KOTIKHIN.)

KOTIKHIN (*plaintively*). He drew blood. Blood.

ROMANOV. I'll get you yet! I'll get you yet! I'll smear you with honey and throw you on an anthill!

MIKHAILOV. Stop rioting! I'll have you removed from the meeting!

ROMANOV. Hmpf, too bad I don't have the other one. I'd...

MIKHAILOV. What's going on here?

OLKHA. A little quarrel. A peasant always makes his point with his fist.

KORYTKO. Kolya here put on a show, but all he did was stir things up.

MIKHAILOV (*to* ROMANOV). You're always getting hot under the collar. What's the rush?

ROMANOV. I don't have long to live.

KVASOV. You're right about that!

MIKHAILOV (*turning around abruptly*). Ah, Kvasov!

(KVASOV *bows.*)

Dyedov, let's get the meeting started. Hello, Ignat Vasilyevich. (*Greets* KORYTKO.) Why didn't you speak up at the meeting yesterday? Do you see what's happened now?

KORYTKO. Hello, Dmitri Petrovich. No one called on me, or I would have spoken up.

MIKHAILOV. That's bad. You have to take matters into your own hands. If you see a mess, you have to speak up.

KORYTKO. I thought it would pass. It all happened so quickly.

MIKHAILOV. I see. (*Goes toward the platform.*)

KVASOV (*to* GRUNKIN). Did you bring it?

GRUNKIN. I have it with me.

KVASOV. Where?

GRUNKIN. Here. (*Pats his pocket.*)

KVASOV. Don't be late. Go up as soon as he's done. Don't give him time to gather his wits.

GRUNKIN. On the button. He won't know what hit him.

DYEDOV (*climbs up on the platform*). Citizens! We will continue yesterday's meeting which was interrupted by a kulak conspirator who is now locked up. (*Agitation in the crowd.*) The Secretary of the Regional Committee, comrade Mikhailov, has the floor.

MIKHAILOV. Last time I was here was the spring of last year. Remember, that's when we were trying Proshkin for speculating in grain. He had bought up all the grain at a ruble twenty kopecks in the autumn, and later sold it back to you at four and a half rubles. He'd sold six, maybe seven hundred bushels. What would that work out to? Could someone take a stab at it?

SECOND PEASANT. Mishka Afanasyev. Figures jump around in his head like flies.

MISHKA. If it's six hundred (*mumbles*) one thousand nine hundred and eighty—and if seven hundred (*mumbles again*) two thousand three hundred and ten.

MIKHAILOV. Thank you. You're good with numbers. I ask you, then. If you're going to make two thousand rubles, could you do what Mikhail Kvasov did yesterday, and give away one hundred and twenty bushels in order to shut everyone up?

(*Silence.*)

I ask you. Why do the poor and middling peasant, when they know that the State needs grain in order to strengthen agriculture, sell it at the official price, when the market has the same price, while the kulak not only hoards his own, but, benefactor that he is, overbids the State and buys up all the grain in the village?

OLKHA. Tell us.

MIKHAILOV. Because the peasant has to buy boots for the winter. He needs clothes. He has to pay his taxes. He has to make repairs. So the kulak waits. The kulak waits for the kulak spring. When the market price goes sky high, the kulak brings his grain to the market.

ROMANOV. White wagonloads filled with white flour.

MIKHAILOV. What do you think—is that fair? The peasant sells for a ruble fifteen kopecks, and the kulak for five, six rubles. No—you can sell to the State at the same price as everybody else.

VOICES. Yeah! Right! They can sell like everybody else.

(*The crowd moves closer to the platform.*)

GRUNKIN. We have no kulaks here!

(*Pause.*)

MIKHAILOV. If there aren't any kulaks, then let's divide the grain assessment equally among everyone in the village. I have a list of names here that I wanted to propose. Here's how it works: We need a hundred and twenty-five tons of grain. We could exempt eighty percent of you and still get all the grain from the twenty percent left over. And out of those twenty percent we could get seventy tons from the biggest kulaks—but if there aren't any kulaks here, we'll collect it from the whole village instead.

SHILOV. What do you mean, the whole village?

FIRST WOMAN PEASANT. No, no. That's not right!

VOICES. Get it from the twenty percent! Let the rich squirm a little! Let the eighty percent off!

SECOND PEASANT. Get it from the kulaks! That's fair, citizens!

VOICES. That's the way to do it! That's fair! Get it from the kulaks!

THIRD PEASANT. Let them sell like everybody else.

OLKHA. Kvasov has a thousand—I have only fifty. Should we both be giving ten? He fixes up his calfskin boots, and I have to sew some rags together for a winter coat.

KVASOV. You have a short memory. Who helped you last year?

OLKHA. You helped a little, but then you took me for all I was worth—and locked it up in your barn.

(*Laughter.*)

KORYTKO. Excuse me, citizens.

DYEDOV. Korytko, Ignat! Climb up here and say your piece!

(KORYTKO *comes forward.*)

KVASOV (*to* GRUNKIN). It's time.

GRUNKIN. I'm going. (*Loudly.*) Comrade Mikhailov, allow me to ask a question.

MIKHAILOV. Go ahead.

GRUNKIN. I need to get closer to you.

MIKHAILOV. Come on.

(*The crowd separates for him.* GRUNKIN *slowly walks up to the platform. He has everyone's attention. Right next to the platform, he shoves his hands into his pockets and brings out two fistfuls of grain.*)

Well?

GRUNKIN. My son and I split up the farm. I do things the old way—my son set things up the new way. Take a look—here's the wheat—which is better?

(MIKHAILOV *stretches out both hands.* GRUNKIN *fills them with wheat.* MIKHAILOV *observes attentively. The crowd watches him in silence.*)

MIKHAILOV. You want to catch me, eh? This one is spring wheat, this one is winter wheat. (*Laughter.*) You're a practical joker, I see. Well, I've got a joke for you, too. (*Puts his hand in his pocket and takes out a handful of grain.*) Here, take a look at this grain.

GRUNKIN (*looking*). Oh, Mother of God! Where did you find grain like that?

SHILOV. Give it here! Show it to us!

(*The peasants crowd in, feel the grain, and pour it from hand to hand.*)

FIRST PEASANT. Come on, give it here!

THIRD PEASANT. You're crowding us out—let us take a look.

SECOND PEASANT. Now, that's what I call grain!

OLKHA. What grain! What is it, a sample from America?

MIKHAILOV. I picked this up at the Lenin Collective Farm. Dropped by on my way here. Not a bad harvest. Eighty in some places, ninety in others.

GRUNKIN. Ninety! They're lying!

MIKHAILOV. Go and see for yourself.

OLKHA. And even if they only got eighty—it's nothing like what we get. Ours is awful.

ROMANOV. No big deal; we'll have a harvest like that soon.

KOTIKHIN. Kolya will shepherd us to the kolkhoz.

SOTIN. Don't worry, he won't take *you* there.

AFANASYEV. They'll send you packing.

OLKHA. Will you take me?

ROMANOV. You'll go yourself.... You won't just go—you'll run.

OLKHA. Me?

KORYTKO. Why not? You, too. Citizens, I have an idea. This is the idea. I get up in the morning, spend two hours looking for my boots, and they're right in front of the stove. The State needs grain. You there, Vasily Pavlovich—when you were building your house, for two years you denied yourself everything. You borrowed from anybody you could find. Well, then, what do you expect the State to do when they have to build a whole five-year plan.

OLKHA. Fair enough.

KORYTKO. That's just the way it is. Except that we give the State very little and still barely have anything left over for ourselves. In other words, everything's falling apart.

VOICES. Right, that's true....

KATERINA. What can we do about it?

KORYTKO. I thought we could economize, citizens. Now follow me here. We have a thousand lots, houses with additions. We stretch out for six miles, but just think if we could plow that land! If, say, we demolished our huts and built one or two big buildings instead.

KATERINA. No... no...

THIRD PEASANT. Shsh!

KORYTKO. We have about two thousand dogs. Figure it out: If you convert it to grain, each one eats a pound a day. In a year—twenty wagonfuls.

SHILOV. For dogs?

KATERINA. Pshaw! The devil! I ought to throw a rock at 'em....

KORYTKO. And God forbid a horse should ever die. That's a killer right there. But if we have five hundred of them, owned in common.... With small-scale agriculture, the land's broken up, and you've got to do everything yourself. But with large-scale agriculture, you can distribute everything fairly. Look at nature: Even the ant doesn't drag straws by itself. And he's also one of God's creatures. That's what I'm thinking, citizens.

KOTIKHIN. You're getting carried away, Minister. Tell us about the grain!

KORYTKO. We need to sell the grain to the State, citizens. Especially those of us who have a little extra. And how much grain there is—that we know.

KVASOV. Now he's going to try to prove it.

KORYTKO. What everyone knows, Ivan Gerasimovich, needs no proof. Just try to prove that the sun rises, stays in the sky all day long, and as soon as the day ends—it goes down to the Japanese. What does proof have to do with anything?

KOTIKHIN. You trying to say you don't have any at all?

KORYTKO. You're right, I have some. And as long as you've brought it up, let's see you match me. I'll give half of my supply and you give half of yours.

OLKHA. That's fair. Give nine tons.

KOTIKHIN. Where would I get eighteen tons? You won't find even nine.

SECOND PEASANT. He fed nine to the bees.

(*Laughter.*)

SOTIN. Let's finish up. Read the list of names.

MIKHAILOV. I don't think we need to burden the whole meeting with the list, citizens. We'll turn it over to the local Soviet and its committees. Let them decide. What do you think?

SHILOV. Yes, I guess that's right.

OLKHA. Can we be there when they decide?

MIKHAILOV. The door's open for everyone but kulaks.

KOTIKHIN. They're trying to separate us like sheep, folks. Peasants should just be divided into idlers and hard-workers only. They thought up kulaks in the city....

MIKHAILOV. Kotikhin!

KOTIKHIN. Yes?

MIKHAILOV. What's that you're saying about the city?

KOTIKHIN. Oh, nothing. I'm just worried about a couple of things. Can I ask you to explain some things?

MIKHAILOV. I know what kind of explanations you want. Go ahead.

KOTIKHIN. Why does the countryside get all the hardships? Why is it never the city? Why are the workers the favorite sons of the State, while the peasants—who feed the whole nation—are the stepchildren?

MIKHAILOV. So, the workers live better?

VOICES. God grant *us* a life like that! Better than us! If only we lived like that! Not the way we do!

OLKHA. If only we lived like that—getting wages.

MIKHAILOV. You want wages! Fine. Dyedov, take a piece of paper and write. We're building a brick factory in our district. We need two thousand workers. Anyone who wants to leave his farm, sign up, and we'll transfer you to the city to work in the factory for wages. Whoever wants to, raise your hands.

(*Pause. Silence. The peasants, looking uncomfortable, look away.*)

Well? (*Looks around; everyone is turning aside.*) There are no volunteers. It's all hot air. Alright, then, are you done?

OLKHA. Yes, I guess we're done. You just hurry up with those lists.

MIKHAILOV. Actually, I'm leaving. Comrade Rayevsky will stay here. He'll take care of it.

DYEDOV. Period.

(*The peasants disperse, talking with one another.*)

MIKHAILOV (*leaves the platform and goes toward* OLGA *and* RAYEVSKY). Well, there you go. No revolt. Olga, could I have a word with you.

(RAYEVSKY *moves away.*)

OLGA. Well?

MIKHAILOV. Olka, would you like me to stay here for a day?

OLGA. You know what's best, Mikhailov.

MIKHAILOV. I can leave, or I can stay for a day. We'd stay together at Korytko's.

OLGA. We won't stay together, Mikhailov....

MIKHAILOV (*after a pause*). I get it.... So there it is.... In that case, well... I suppose I'd better leave.

OLGA. As you like...

MIKHAILOV. But Olka.... How badly it all turned out.... No, it's clear the sooner I leave, the better.... Dyedov!

DYEDOV. Here.

MIKHAILOV. Are the horses ready?

DYEDOV. As you ordered.

MIKHAILOV. Goodbye, comrades.

(MIKHAILOV *leaves hurriedly.* DYEDOV, LOKTEV, ZOTOVA, *and the* KOMSOMOL MEMBERS *leave with him.*)

RAYEVSKY (*walks up to* OLGA). What did he want?

OLGA. Doesn't matter. Just the same, Pavel, he did win.

RAYEVSKY. Did you tell him that?

OLGA. Yes.

RAYEVSKY. He saw for himself that we didn't get the job done.

OLGA. Not we—you.

RAYEVSKY. Just a few hours ago you said—we.

OLGA. But then there was a conference where you got spooked that there might be a revolt. You and Dyedov talked about responsibility, but he wasn't afraid to call a meeting right after our setback—and he won.

RAYEVSKY. Well—nobody likes a loser.

OLGA. I still just don't get it. All of a sudden you lose your head, as though someone else had taken your place. You say things you shouldn't, and you start acting the opposite of your real self. That's not you, Rayevsky; you're completely different. How did this happen? What are you doing?

RAYEVSKY. Nothing. My collar is a little tight. It's choking me. Well, go on.

OLGA. You probably tied it too tight.... Necktie.... Maybe yours really is the same color as all the others, exactly the same?

A BOY (*running up to* RAYEVSKY). Here's a note for you, uncle. (*Gives him a note and quickly runs away.*)

RAYEVSKY. What could this be about? (*Reads it, furrows his brows.*) Hold on! Where's that boy? (*Looks around.*) Dyedov! Sound the bell. Call back the peasants!

OLGA. What is it?

RAYEVSKY. Just wait.... Hey, guys, Young Communists! Hurry up! Get everybody back here!

(*The* COMMUNIST YOUTHS *run. The village bell starts ringing, and the peasants, surprised and afraid, start to gather.* RAYEVSKY *gets up on the platform by himself and stands there, glowering and stiff.*)

OLKHA. What's wrong?

SHILOV. Why are you calling us?

RAYEVSKY (*clearly and distinctly*). I just got a note. Here's what it says. (*Reads.*) "Mr. Delegate: We scared you away from one meeting. But you're still here. We advise you to start gathering boards for your coffin. You don't have long to live. Your bullet has been cast. The time has come for you to enter the next world and steal grain there. Just you wait!" That's an expensive note. It's going to cost you thirty-five tons of grain. If by morning you don't bring me the author of this note, I will add thirty-five tons to the hundred and twenty-five. And if I get any more notes—seventy.

(*Pause.*)

OLKHA. How do you figure: who knows who wrote the note, but we all have to pay for it?

RAYEVSKY. Silence! I'll show you who a bullet has been cast for.

(*Gets down from the platform and, without turning, marches away right through the crowd, which makes way for him.*)

(*Curtain.*)

SCENE 7

KVASOV*'s house.* OLGA *is cleaning a revolver.* RAYEVSKY *is at the table, writing.* ZOTOVA *is standing near him.*

RAYEVSKY (*finishes writing and gives the paper to* ZOTOVA). Here, give this to Dyedov and get everybody together immediately. And get the weapons ready. I'll be there right away.

OLGA. We're coming with you.

RAYEVSKY. You'd better not risk it, Olga.

OLGA. You think I'm just going to hide? The Browning is ready.

RAYEVSKY. Let's go. (*To* ZOTOVA.) Your guys know how to fight?

ZOTOVA. They'll hold their own! Loktev has been running from house to house ever since he found out about the disturbance. He's trying to calm the peasants down.

RAYEVSKY. That coward! Go, Zotova.

ZOTOVA. On the double! (*Runs out.*)

RAYEVSKY. Well then, a state of war! Aren't you scared, Olga?

OLGA. Not at all.

RAYEVSKY. Do you feel the storm rising? I wish they'd hurry up with my horse!

OLGA. You'll go on horseback?

RAYEVSKY. In 1919 I galloped by myself into a mutinied battalion. They were waiting for a detachment to return and getting ready for a battle. I galloped up to them, all alone, and right in front of everybody I shot their commander. This battalion ended up joining our division.

OLGA. You're starting to look taller.

(MIKHAILOV *enters, removing his things on the way. He goes up to the door to* KVASOV*'s room, opens it, and looks in.*)

RAYEVSKY. There's no one besides the nun.

MIKHAILOV (*shuts the door*). What's this mess you've made? What's wrong with you, do you want to be tried? Loktev phoned me at Ryzhovo, and I raced back.

RAYEVSKY. There was nothing to worry about.

MIKHAILOV. I suppose you know that all hell has broken loose in the village and that there could be a riot tonight.

RAYEVSKY. I have taken measures to suppress the revolt.

MIKHAILOV. Have you reversed your order?

RAYEVSKY. I gave orders to arm the Young Communists.

MIKHAILOV. Have you reversed your order?

RAYEVSKY. I'm no coward. You know that perfectly well!

MIKHAILOV. I suggest you reverse that absurd order immediately and make sure the whole village hears about it.

RAYEVSKY. That won't happen.

MIKHAILOV. I could do it myself, but I don't want to make a fool out of you. You're the one who has to stay here and collect the grain.

RAYEVSKY (*flaring up*). I won't reverse the order, and I won't allow you to do it. To retreat, to reverse the order just because we are being threatened with a revolt would be cowardly and a discredit to the Party. Everyone has a limit, after all....

MIKHAILOV. Calm down, Pavel! Crazy orders and unwillingness to correct mistakes are a discredit to the Party.

RAYEVSKY. First you have to prove that a mistake was made. You yourself used to impose fines on a city when our soldiers were killed there.

MIKHAILOV. I imposed fines on our enemies. You mean to tell me you're among enemies here?

RAYEVSKY. Let them give up the kulaks.

MIKHAILOV. You've driven them to unite with the kulaks. You've set the whole village against you. How dare you use the grain collection as a punishment? What are you—an English lord visiting one of his colonies? Did you learn this stunt abroad?

RAYEVSKY. So you think we ought to let them shoot us?

MIKHAILOV. Who shoots? The kulak, who is always shouting that we're taking grain by force—that we're stealing. You have done everything you could to help him. We need to fix that. You must show that your order is not in line with Party policy.

RAYEVSKY. How am I supposed to work after that?

MIKHAILOV. So you consider it more important to maintain your personal integrity than to follow the correct line?

RAYEVSKY. I won't reverse the order.

MIKHAILOV. You will reverse it.

RAYEVSKY. No!

MIKHAILOV. Reverse the order, Pavel, we don't have time for this. If you don't, I'll do it myself and put you under arrest.

(RAYEVSKY *grabs his cap and rushes toward the door.*)

Throw on a coat, it's cold.

(RAYEVSKY *puts on a sheepskin jacket and leaves.*)

OLGA. Mikhailov, can I have a word with you?

MIKHAILOV. Yes.

OLGA. Were you happy when you heard about what happened here? Did your heart pound with joy? Did it?

MIKHAILOV. I got very upset and rushed back here. I was afraid of unrest.

OLGA. It's a simple question. Were you happy?

MIKHAILOV. More riddles. Happy at what?

OLGA. At another chance to gloat—at the chance to humiliate Pavel—at the chance to take a mean, petty revenge—because he's smarter, because he's more vital, because he's a thousand times better than you....

MIKHAILOV. You know, Olga, this really is insulting. What vile things you've thought of me lately!

OLGA. You're taking revenge on him because of me. Do you hear? I'm not addressing you, the man in a shell, but Mikhailov, the inner man, the real Mikhailov. You're taking revenge on him because of me. That's why you came here.

MIKHAILOV. How vile, Olga! If you can't understand what's happened here and can only drag it all down to a squabble between rivals—we have nothing to say to each other.

OLGA. Once again the Secretary of the Regional Committee giving a speech—Mikhailov is hiding.

MIKHAILOV. There aren't two Mikhailovs, Olga. Drop that nonsense. There's just one man.

OLGA. And that man is the Secretary of the Regional Committee?

MIKHAILOV. Yes, that's the one.

OLGA. But you've failed, Mikhailov. You wanted to turn me against him, you wanted to force me to return to you, but you've done the opposite. You will forever—do you hear? forever—be a stranger to me. I will go to the man humiliated and hunted by you, but a real man, the man I love. (*Quickly puts on her coat.*)

MIKHAILOV. I guess I really didn't know you very well. This is so hypocritical.... But hang on, I'm going to the Club.... I ordered Loktev to get together some peasants.

OLGA. I'm not going with you. (*Leaves.*)

MIKHAILOV. Suit yourself....

(*Pause.* MIKHAILOV *slowly puts on his things, talking to himself.*)

So, comrade Mikhailov.... A couple of questions. Well? Olga is a stranger to you? Well, I guess so.... How did you see things before?... Well... it didn't occur somehow.... Fair enough... And how do you feel about this *stranger* now?... You no longer love her?... Yes, yes, you.... (*In a different tone of voice.*) Well, I've got to go.... They must all be there by now.... No, but answer the question.... (*In the same tone of voice.*) Well, enough, enough... I've got to go. (*Exits.*)

MOKRINA (*enters, looks around*). They're gone.

KVASOV (*enters*). Ugh! (*Sits down.*) My heart is pounding! Death is knocking at the door.

MOKRINA. Pray.

KVASOV. Our prayers do not please God—they don't reach Him.

MOKRINA. Have hope.

KVASOV. I want to. Here's what I want you to do, Mother—go to the shed and knock. Tell them all to come here. Tell them I'm waiting.

(MOKRINA *exits.* KVASOV *kneels and prays, making low obeisance.* MOKRINA *returns to the house, followed by* KOTIKHIN, GRUNKIN, PROSHKIN, ZUBOV, SHILOV, *their boys, and two other peasants. They cross themselves in front of the icons and sit down.*)

KOTIKHIN. Ivan Gerasimovich.... Well, what is it?

(KVASOV *doesn't answer. He continues to pray.*)

Ivan Gerasimovich!

(KVASOV *prays.*)

Ivan Gerasimovich, the Kingdom of God is eternal, but we have less than an hour. We're all here.

KVASOV (*rises*). Hello, everybody. Mikhailov is here again.

ZUBOV. Is that right?

GRUNKIN. Again?

KOTIKHIN. Cunning, very cunning, this Regional Chief. And not very good-natured either, not a bit open-minded. He got the better of us at the meeting. And now he's here again.

PROSHKIN. Mikhailov hasn't forgotten Proshkin, but I haven't forgotten him either.

KOTIKHIN. And how did the two of them get along?

KVASOV. There's a rift between them. Fire and ice.

KOTIKHIN. Couldn't we stick a knife in them? Have you given that any thought?

KVASOV. We don't have time to sharpen the knives. We need an ax. You keep sneaking around like a fox, Vasily Afanasyevich, when we need to be bears.

KOTIKHIN. The bear's broad chest is too good a target for a gun.

KVASOV. Hide behind the logs. Knock oak trees on the hunter. Arouse the beasts. Even squirrels should throw cones. The forest is huge and there aren't many hunters.

KOTIKHIN. If only the beasts in this forest got along, Ivan Gerasimovich. But the hare will never go with the wolf.

KVASOV. Force the hare, scare him into it. (*Addressing everybody.*) We have gathered here, my guests, in secret, in our very own village, as if we were the outsiders. But who are we? We are the ground and foundation. Our grain feeds all of Russia. We're the ones who clothe Moscow, provide her shoes, and feed her. But who orders us around? Bums, beggars, drunkards. People in Moscow have little to worry about. For them, Russia is just a field for their experiments. They want to raise a special kind of cereal from Europe. On that field, as far as they're concerned, we are the weeds—the broom-rape, the wild grass. They've started pulling us out. They're tearing us out by the roots. They're mowing us down with a scythe. The hour has come when we either have to lie down under the scythe or shout to all Russia: "You're wrong, you Moscow agronomists! We're not weeds—we're oaks!" (*Pounds the table with his fist. Pause.*

More quietly.) You'll break your scythes on us. You know the saying—if the straw around the village is dry, strike a match and it will go up in flames. With God's help, we will start the fire.

ZUBOV. Right.

SHILOV. Isn't it a bit early for that?

GRUNKIN. This is the best time. Rayevsky was right when he said the note was costly. But who it will cost....

PROSHKIN. Mikhailov will never leave our village. He likes the climate.

KVASOV (*to* KOTIKHIN). And you?

KOTIKHIN. I won't back out. But let's not be stupid, fellas, let's not be stupid. First things first, we can't forget the bottle. A little bottle can do an awful lot. It can make a rich man poor and a poor man rich. We need to throw a little party.

GRUNKIN. We should... we really should....

KOTIKHIN. And we'll have to bless folks. A peasant's always happier at work when he knows God's on his side. That's a tricky one, too. Tomorrow there'll be a lot of peasants at church for the holiday. We'll tell the father to announce a confession hour. And while each peasant confesses sins he didn't commit and hides the ones he did, just whisper in his ear, "Here's what you gotta do.".... With God then, and tomorrow we'll begin.

KVASOV. Tomorrow won't work. We have to begin today, fellas. We'll start right now.

ZUBOV. How now?

GRUNKIN. What do you mean now?

SHILOV. It's awful!

KOTIKHIN. What's the hurry, Ivan Gerasimovich? Tomorrow's a better bet.

KVASOV. Mikhailov's here to reverse our hero's order. They won't have time to let people know today, but tomorrow the whole village will find out—tomorrow you won't be able to stir up anybody.... We move today.

PROSHKIN. You let me have Mikhailov.

KVASOV. And now let us beg forgiveness for Mikhailov's soul.

(*Crosses himself. Pause.*)

ZUBOV. And for Rayevsky's.

KVASOV. Don't touch that one. With Mikhailov out of the way, our hero
will screw things up so badly tomorrow that not only our village, but
the whole district will revolt.

ZUBOV. Is Mikhailov at Korytko's?

KVASOV. That's right. Now let us send the boys out to get things ready and
dig up the rifles and sawed-off shotguns. We'll meet in Kotikhin's apiary.

KOTIKHIN. We should get together the ones we can count on right away.

KVASOV. Send the young guys. God be with you, my guests, God be with
you.

SHILOV. Hold on....

GRUNKIN. What's wrong, Vasya?

SHILOV. Hold on, hold on.... Ivan Gerasimovich, what's going on?... I
can't... I can't... I don't quite understand....

KVASOV. What is it, Vasily?

SHILOV. Well, so we're fighting about the note, because it's not fair to add
another thirty-five tons.... But now... it seems like Mikhailov's changing
it back.... He must understand it's not fair.... And now we're going to....
(*Makes a gesture.*) But why? Ivan Gerasimovich.... If he's on our side...

GRUNKIN. You come have a drink with me, Vasya, then you'll understand.

SHILOV. No, hold on, hold on.

KVASOV. The time has come to act, Vasily.... The time for talk has passed.
Get going; leave one at a time. Never together. To think we can't show
our faces in our own village! Oh, for shame!

(*The peasants leave one at a time.*)

MOKRINA. It's that Kolka who keeps making trouble, the devil. If he
weren't his mother's child, I'd strangle him with my own hands.

KVASOV. Kolka is only the nail in the horseshoe. We've got to whip the
horse.

SHILOV. Whose horse, Ivan Gerasimovich?

KVASOV. Get going, Vasily, get going.

(GRUNKIN *leads* SHILOV *out.* KVASOV *shuts the door behind them, picks up an ax, kneels, and during* MOKRINA*'s story pries up one of the boards and takes out a rifle and a revolver.*)

Oh, for shame. Tell me something, Mother.

MOKRINA. What can I tell you, Ivan Gerasimovich? I'll tell you what I saw last night. I felt depressed yesterday evening; I could not get to sleep for a long time. The dogs were howling out behind the gardens, and behind the stove a cricket was chirping—crick-et, crick-et. And then—I don't know how I lost track—but suddenly there was no cricket, but little angels touched their light fingers on strings finer than anything ever seen by the eye of man—strings made of starlight. Then a beautiful garden in full bloom was revealed to me, with babbling springs, bright, clear lakes, and little crystal boats. And the flowers in this garden grew not out of the ground, but floated along the heavens and perfumed the air. And then a shimmering table was revealed to me—spread with a cloth of clouds, and around this table sat a radiant host of people, and in the center, on a throne shining like the sun, sat our Lord God, and I dared not raise my eyes to face my Lord, and I fell to the ground. And the Lord God said to me: "Maiden, raise your eyes and see." And I did so. Just across from the Lord, dressed in white raiment embroidered with diamonds, with a purple halo around his head, was our Tsar. "Great Tsar," I asked, "will the Kingdom of the Antichrist last much longer? Will you come back to your flock soon?" And the Tsar arose and stretched out his arm, and I...

(PASHA *appears in the doorway. She leans against it and stares at* KVASOV. MOKRINA *looks at her silently.*)

KVASOV (*does not turn around*). And what did you do? (*Pause.*) What did you do? (*Turns around, the rifle still in his hand, and sees* PASHA. *Pause.*) A-ah... my daughter. What kind of club have you been out to, anyway?

PASHA. I was watching the performance here.

KVASOV. Mother, didn't you lock the door?

PASHA. The door was locked; I came in with the peasants in the dark.

KVASOV. And what were you looking for?

PASHA (*nodding her head at the rifle*). Not what you found.

KVASOV. Spying on your father?

PASHA. I'm interested in everything.

KVASOV (*threateningly*). Pashka!

PASHA. You christened me yourself.

KVASOV. My memory fails when I'm angry; I might even forget you're my daughter.

PASHA. If you did, I'd thank you.

KVASOV. Bitch!

PASHA. And you, standing under the icons.

KVASOV. I'll kill you, Pashka!

PASHA. Isn't Mikhailov enough for you?

KVASOV. Aha! So you must have heard?

PASHA. I'm not deaf.

KVASOV. Well, then, Pashenka?

PASHA. It won't happen! I'll block your bloody plans. I'm going to tell them everything.

KVASOV. And let your father face a bullet—send your father to his death?

PASHA. Give it up!

KVASOV. You're in my way.

PASHA. You're in *my* way. You've kept me locked up in the house like a wooden coffin.

KVASOV. This is no time to get even.

PASHA. Are you in a hurry? You'll still have time to murder him. I'm going. (*Starts to go.*)

KVASOV. Where?... Pasha! Hold on! Pasha!

PASHA. You said yourself, I'm in the way.

KVASOV. Listen to me, Pashenka. Why are you destroying your father's life? Is it not for you, Pashenka, that I scrape the soil with my bare hands? That I tear the bark off trees with my teeth? Think!

PASHA. I never asked you to do that. (*Goes to the door.*)

KVASOV. Pasha! One last word—just one last word—then you can go.

PASHA. Well?

KVASOV. Who are you going to see? Do they even see us as human beings? We're just animals to them. We're the clay on their shoes. Why do you think they made fun of you?

PASHA. Made fun? Who made fun of me?

KVASOV. That hero of yours, the one with the medal. And his pasty-skinned wench.

PASHA. What do you mean, they made fun of me? Tell me!

KVASOV. He was mocking you in front of his wench. "What a country bumpkin she is," he says, "fat and pug-nosed... and clings to me like a cat..." he says, "...and I go and invite her to the city with us."

PASHA (*listens with her hands pressed to her chest and her eyes wide open*). You're lying!

KVASOV. And his wench laughs. "Bring her along," she says. "Bring her along—we need a cook in the city!"

PASHA (*with tears in her eyes*). A cook...

KVASOV. And he says: "You'll see, if I want her to, she'll even cook for us..." he says.

PASHA (*with tears, desperately*). You're lying! That can't be! He couldn't!

KVASOV. I swear by our Holy Lord—by our most holy Mother of God....

PASHA. You shut up, shut up! Let me collect my thoughts. Mocking me in front of her...

KVASOV. In front of her, my daughter, in front of her...

PASHA. You shut up. Don't you say another word. So that's what kind of a man you are, Pavlik! Clinging, am I? You're the dummy, with your painted block head and your whitened teeth! (*Cries.*)

MOKRINA. Go ahead and cry, Pashenka, cry! You'll feel better.

PASHA. Shush, you! I'm not crying. Start burning it all up, Father.... Let them feel the flames.... Don't let them come here again—let the fire race across the dry grass all the way to the city, let the fire blaze all over. And we'll laugh while the glass shatters in their houses. Their buildings are all high, but we'll start wrecking them. We're oaks, right, Father? Oaks!

KVASOV. Together, daughter, we'll start together.

(PASHA *feverishly throws on a kerchief over her head and puts on her coat.*)

But where are you going?

PASHA. I'm leaving. Don't worry. I'll be at the apiary. (*Leaves.*)

(MOKRINA *goes to shut the door after her.* KVASOV *kneels slowly.*)

KVASOV. Mother of God, Holy Intercessor, forgive the terrible false oath
I swore to my daughter!

(*Curtain.*)

ACT 5

A peasant hut made into a reading room. The benches are pushed off to the side. ZOTOVA, ROMANOV, MISHKA AFANASYEV, *and* KOMSOMOL MEMBERS *are in the room. They are smoking.*

ROMANOV. Zotova!

ZOTOVA. Yes?

ROMANOV. Isn't it time to change the guard?

ZOTOVA. We just sent one out.

ROMANOV. Ugh! What is there to do around here?

AFANASYEV. Well, now—here's a nail coming out of the wall—drive it back in with your head.

(*Laughter. Two peasants enter, one of them carrying a rifle, the other a stick with an iron point.*)

FIRST PEASANT. Hi guys! Are we going to go wreck stuff?

SECOND PEASANT. The bastard's lost his mind!

ROMANOV. Order, order! Have a seat.

FIRST KOMSOMOL MEMBER. Why hasn't Rayevsky come?

ZOTOVA. He'll come when it's time. Maintain discipline.

FIRST KOMSOMOL MEMBER. I am.

ROMANOV. Just make sure you don't lose it.

(*Laughter.* SOTIN *enters, carrying a club. There is a little boy with him.*)

SOTIN. Comrade Zotova. (*Bows.*) You just let me at Proshkin. I was one of his farmhands, so I brought this little stick with me.

SECOND KOMSOMOL MEMBER. Watch the backswing on that, Uncle Pyotr, or you'll knock us all to hell.

(*Laughter.*)

SOTIN. Don't worry—she only swings one way.

(*Swings the club the other direction. The kids scream in alarm. Laughter.*)

ROMANOV. Isn't the boss coming?

(MIKHAILOV, KORYTKO, *and* OLKHA *enter.*)

MIKHAILOV. As you were! What's going on here?

ZOTOVA. Mikhailov? Well how about that, Maria Dmitryevna! I thought you left?

MIKHAILOV. Leave *you* guys *here?* And you, what are you doing here with that shaft?

SOTIN. I'm going to fight with it.

MIKHAILOV. Who are you going to fight?

SOTIN. Whoever is against us.

MIKHAILOV. And you, too?

VOICES (*together*). Us too!

MIKHAILOV. Go home! In an hour the village will be calm. Comrade Rayevsky has reversed his unfortunate order.

ROMANOV. Reversed it?

ZOTOVA. He didn't tell me.

AFANASYEV. Good for him!

MIKHAILOV (*looking around*). Any peasants here? (*To* ROMANOV.) Are these all members of your unit?

ROMANOV. That's right....

MIKHAILOV. And these are Komsomol members?

ZOTOVA. Yes.

MIKHAILOV. And there's no one else? I gave orders to get the peasants together. What's wrong?

ZOTOVA. Loktev raced house to house....

MIKHAILOV. But there's no one here. What could have happened? (*To* OLKHA.) What do you think?

OLKHA. Something's up....

MIKHAILOV (*to a* KOMSOMOL MEMBER). Go get Dyedov. (*He runs out.*) Not good, not good.... What's going on, Ignat Vasilyevich?

KORYTKO. They're all riled up, Dmitri Petrovich. You know how the peasant is. If everything's fair, he might raise a fuss at first, but in the end he'll do what you ask him to. But if you're not fair, then he'll fly off the handle.

OLKHA. Take me, for example—if I hadn't known you, I wouldn't have come, I'm telling you. In the days of the Tsar—then maybe I would have put up with it, but now—no.

ZOTOVA. This is counterrevolutionary!

OLKHA. That I can't say—you could be right—you studied that stuff in school. But this is my government. I took their side. Why should I suffer from them? It's like getting hit in the face by your own left hand.

MIKHAILOV. You yourself know that nothing big has ever been accomplished without some slipups.

OLKHA. Well, that's true.... We understand that... but there are so many slipups. So the peasant holds a grudge.

MIKHAILOV. Against whom?

OLKHA. That's just it—he doesn't know. If he knew, he'd take it out on someone.

(DYEDOV *and the* KOMSOMOL MEMBERS *enter.*)

MIKHAILOV. Have you informed everybody?

DYEDOV. About what?

MIKHAILOV. That the order has been reversed.

DYEDOV. Not at all—I've received no such instructions.

MIKHAILOV. What do you mean? Hasn't Rayevsky been to see you?

DYEDOV. Not at all.

MIKHAILOV. That can't be true!

DYEDOV. It is.

MIKHAILOV. So that's how you do things here, my friends!

DYEDOV. Guilty as charged.

MIKHAILOV. I'm not blaming you. So that's why the peasants aren't here. Attention, folks! Go to the village immediately! Knock at every door and announce: "The comrade delegate has reversed his order. Mikhailov is here. Tomorrow all the lists will be decided on at the Soviet!" Hurry, guys, we can't be late....

LOKTEV (*runs in, breathing hard; his speech is disjointed*). The kulaks have freed Mishka Kvasov. There is a whole mob of them. They're all drunk. They've gone up to the hill. They have rifles and knives.

ZOTOVA. But wasn't there a policeman there?

LOKTEV. They killed him.

MIKHAILOV. We're too late. Dyedov!

DYEDOV (*frightened*). A revolt! A revolt! I said there would be. What's going to happen now? Lord!

MIKHAILOV. Shut up! (*To* SOTIN.) Can you shoot?

SOTIN. I served in all the wars.

MIKHAILOV. Take the Mauser. Stand by the door. (*Gives it to him. Speaks to* KORYTKO *and* OLKHA.) You see, my friends, how this nonsense has turned out. I'm going to assign a few boys to you. You're going to have to walk all around the village. We can't let the kulaks drag the peasants in after them.

KORYTKO. You pick out the boys and we'll go.

OLKHA. The things people are capable of....

MIKHAILOV. Zotova, pick out five men.

ROMANOV. Pick out three for me, too. I'm going to check the guard.

MIKHAILOV. Pick out the boys, Zotova.

ZOTOVA (*picking the boys*). You go, Petya, and you, and you.

KOMSOMOL MEMBER. I don't want to race out. I want to stay here with you.

ZOTOVA. I'll give you... Ninka, you go.

NINKA. I'm with Romanov.

ZOTOVA. Go with Romanov, you go.

KORYTKO. So long, Dmitri Petrovich.

MIKHAILOV. All right.

(*The groups leave.*)

ZOTOVA. If we could only ring the bell....

MIKHAILOV. I'll ring your bell! Loktev, the weapons!

LOKTEV. The guns are in that room, in the Party cell.

MIKHAILOV. How many? (*To the* KOMSOMOL MEMBERS.) Stand back. Attention! Single file!

LOKTEV. Three Berdans, six shotguns, and one Monte Cristo.

MIKHAILOV. Afanasyev, you go with Loktev. Bring the guns this way! Girls, step out of the line!

FIRST KOMSOMOL GIRL. We're not moving. We're staying with the boys.

SECOND KOMSOMOL GIRL. We want guns, too.

FIRST KOMSOMOL GIRL. We...

MIKHAILOV. Silence! Zotova! Is this your idea of discipline?

ZOTOVA. Why are you discriminating against us? Are we worse than the boys or something? We're going anyway.

FIRST COMMUNIST YOUTH. Better let them come. They'll whine.

MIKHAILOV. We'll sort this out later. For now, divide up the cartridges.

(*The Komsomol girls go into the Party cell room and drag out cases, powder, and cartridges.* LOKTEV *and* MISHKA AFANASYEV *bring out the guns and put them on the table.*)

DYEDOV. It'd be... uh... it'd be good if we could phone the city.

MIKHAILOV. Go ahead and phone.

DYEDOV. What do you mean, go? The telephone is in the council building. They'll kill me.

MIKHAILOV. Sit down and shut up. Do you have a pistol?

DYEDOV. Yes.

MIKHAILOV. Give it here.

DYEDOV. But what'll I do without a pistol?

MIKHAILOV. We'll hide you under the bed. Alright then! (*Takes his pistol.*) Guys! Get your guns.

(*The whole file makes a break for the table.*)

Stop! Where are you going? Back! Zotova, pick out the best fighters.

ZOTOVA. Vanka—take a Berdan. (*He leaves the line and takes a rifle.*) Mishka—a Berdan.

MISHKA. I'd rather have a shotgun.

ZOTOVA. You take what I tell you to. A Berdan hits at a thousand paces.

LOKTEV. A thousand paces?

ZOTOVA. Get lost! Stepka—a shotgun. Andrey—a Berdan. Vanyechka—a shotgun.

LOKTEV (*distributing the cartridges*). Pack 'em tight, don't skimp on the paper.

MIKHAILOV (*to* LOKTEV). Does the liquor merchant live right here, next to the store?

LOKTEV. Yes, here....

MIKHAILOV (*to* AFANASYEV). Go, bring him here. (MISHKA *exits. To* LOKTEV, *quietly.*) Is it a big mob?

LOKTEV. It's hard to say exactly.

MIKHAILOV. What do the peasants say? You went from house to house?

LOKTEV. They say nothing.

MIKHAILOV. Nothing.... That's bad.

(MISHKA *enters with the liquor merchant. The latter is sleepy and has thrown a jacket over his night shirt. He is frightened.*)

Are you the liquor merchant?

AGENT. Four years now, without a single citation.

MIKHAILOV. How was business yesterday and today?

AGENT. I think you'll be pleased. I don't want to blow my own horn, but I can tell you that I sold more yesterday and today than I did for the last year.

MIKHAILOV. Who was buying?

AGENT. A lot of people. Vasily Afanasyevich Kotikhin took three pailfuls himself. In order to keep up the output I practically didn't go to bed last night. And this morning I got up at the crack of dawn. I do my best....

MIKHAILOV. To hell with your best! Do you have any vodka left?

AGENT. Hardly any. How much do you need?

MIKHAILOV. You're a blue-ribbon jackass. Zotova! Go over there and pour it all out into the ground. Make sure not a single drop is left.

AGENT. What do you mean—pour it out? If you please! (*To* ZOTOVA.) Where are you going?...

ZOTOVA. Get lost! (*Leaves.*)

(KOLKA *runs in, and with him are several peasants armed with scythes, pitchforks, and shotguns.*)

ROMANOV. I've done some reconnaissance. They are apparently waiting for reinforcements. The whole mob is in Kotikhin's apiary. They're bringing the peasants right with them.

ONE OF THE NEW ARRIVALS. The drones are swarming.

THIRD COMMUNIST YOUTH. Comrade Mikhailov, give those of us who don't have guns permission to tear down the fence and use the boards.

MIKHAILOV. What will you do with the boards?

FOURTH YOUNG COMMUNIST. For now we'll just keep 'em handy. Whoever gets shot, we'll take his gun.

ZOTOVA. Don't you interfere, Mikhailov. Let them all go!

ROMANOV. Damn it all! And what a beautiful day! (*To* SOTIN.) Uncle Pyotr, let's smack 'em one!

SOTIN. We'll crack 'em one!

ROMANOV. Oh, you sweetheart you!

(*They kiss.*)

MIKHAILOV. Easy now, warrior. Attention! Listen! I'm going to do some reconnaissance!

ZOTOVA. As if we'd let you go out alone!

LOKTEV. Comrade Mikhailov, I'll go.

MIKHAILOV. Silence! This is no laughing matter. Loktev! Take command of the red detachment of the village of Thundering Well. If I'm not back in ten minutes, send out another reconnaissance squad and advance toward the enemy lines. Go in chain formation, maintain complete silence, don't shoot unless necessary—and if you have to shoot, shoot only at the kulaks. Is that clear?

(*He steps away, goes toward the door.* LOKTEV *follows him.*)

LOKTEV. Comrade Mikhailov, it's more dangerous for you to go than anyone else. Let me go. They'll string you up if they catch you.

MIKHAILOV. I have to go. Have you thought of Rayevsky and Olga?

LOKTEV. Hey, right, where are they?

MIKHAILOV. That's just it. They're in Kvasov's house. Do you realize what may happen?

LOKTEV. Still unreasonable for you to go. How do you think you're going to make it to Kvasov's?

MIKHAILOV. Unreasonable? You know, there are circumstances when reasonable behavior borders on the criminal. (*Smiles.*) A friend once told me that. Goodbye!

(*Shakes* LOKTEV*'s hand and exits.*)

(*Curtain.*)

SCENE 9

First Episode

In front of KORYTKO*'s house. There are logs in the yard. To the right a fence and part of the street are visible. It is a moonlit night. A group of peasants slowly approaches. The group consists of those who were at* KVASOV*'s (scene 7), plus several other old and young men. They're carrying sawed-off shotguns and Berdan rifles.* KVASOV *carries a rifle,* MIKHAIL *a pistol. Several of them have double-barreled guns. Except for* KVASOV *and* KOTIKHIN, *everyone is drunk. One of the young men holds an accordion. They talk in half-whispers.*

KVASOV. Shhh.... Quiet.

KOTIKHIN (*to* MISHKA). Check the street.

MISHKA (*goes toward the street and looks*). No one.

PROSHKIN. Let me, I have the right....

KVASOV. Shhh.... I'll look through the window. (*Walks to the window and looks inside.*)

GRUNKIN. Is he there?

KVASOV. He's here.

PROSHKIN. Let me.

KVASOV. Pavel Ivanovich, stand by the gate.

KOTIKHIN (*tinkers with the door*). The door's latched. I need a knife.

PROSHKIN. I'll do it with this. (*Pulls out a long, fine blade.*)
KVASOV. Open it quietly.

(PROSHKIN *sticks his knife into the crack, raises the latch, and opens the door a little.*)

PROSHKIN. That's how we do things around here.
KVASOV. Well, God bless. You go, Sofron Kuzmich! And you, Mikhail! And you, Petka!
ZUBOV. Petka's still young—don't send him.
KVASOV. Shhh.... Quiet. Am I sending my son, Pavel Ivanovich? Then don't hide yours!
PETKA. I'll go.
KVASOV. Go. Remember what I told you. Don't shoot. Just as a last resort. Just knock Korytko out. But if he recognizes you—finish him.
GRUNKIN. Why Korytko?
KOTIKHIN. For his sweet-talking. Don't forget, Sofron Kuzmich.
PROSHKIN. I remember.
SHILOV. I'm scared.
KVASOV. As soon as you open the second door, we'll strike up the music so no one can hear in case there's screaming or gunshots.
MIKHAIL. Play something happy! We're on our way. (*Goes to the door.*)
KVASOV. Christ save us!

(*They all cross themselves.* PROSHKIN, MIKHAIL, *and* PETKA *enter the house, leaving the door open behind them. Pause.*)

SHILOV. I'm scared.
GRUNKIN (*drunk*). Well, I'm happy!

(*It is quiet. Then the creaking of the second door can be heard as it opens.*)

KVASOV. Andreyka!

(*The* YOUNG PEASANT *begins to play the accordion. At first dissonant and quiet, the song grows stronger and more desperate. Two of the peasants*

ANDREYKA.

> I don't want beer, I don't want wine,
> Cheer up, my boy, and cock your gun.
> Just let me drink my own moonshine,
> And then we'll have a little fun.

CHORUS.

> Oh, life is a prison,
> A dark dungeon cell,
> A valley, an aspen
> A funeral bell.

ANDREYKA.

> So drink, men, drink, full steam ahead,
> Cheer up, my boy, and cock your gun.
> No matter what, you'll end up dead,
> For now, we'll have a little fun!

(OLGA *and* RAYEVSKY *run up to the fence. They begin to speak during the refrain.*)

CHORUS.

> Oh, life is a prison,
> A dark dungeon cell,
> A valley, an aspen
> A funeral bell.

RAYEVSKY. They're killing him. He's there!

OLGA. He can't be there.

RAYEVSKY. Look! The door's open. He's there, they're killing him!

OLGA. No.... Maybe not....

ANDREYKA.

> At dawn the cackling crow calls 'round.
> Cheer up, my boy, and cock your gun.
> By night, you're six feet underground,
> For now, we'll have a little fun!

RAYEVSKY. Let me go, Olga! I'll attack them!

OLGA. Pavel, don't you dare. They'll kill you, too. What are you going to do by yourself?

RAYEVSKY. I have to, you see... they're strangling him! He has a lame leg.

CHORUS.

Oh, life is a prison,

A dark dungeon cell,

A valley, an aspen

A funeral bell.

OLGA (*holds* RAYEVSKY *tenaciously, not releasing him*). I won't let you go! Look, this is crazy, they're all armed. The whole village is revolting. Let's make a run for it. At the outskirts of the village we'll get a wagon and return with a military detachment.

RAYEVSKY. I will die with him. (*Rips loose from her.*)

ANDREYKA.

So laugh and sing and roar and drink,

Cheer up, my boy, and cock your gun.

Face death straight on; don't whine or blink,

You die just once and then it's done.

OLGA. Come back! No, no! It's a pointless death.... I won't let you go, Pavel. Remember, he said, pointless heroism and cowardice are just two sides of the same coin. *He* would escape. Show some courage, let's escape!

RAYEVSKY. He would—but I can't. (*Pushes* OLGA *away and jumps over the fence, holding his revolver.*) What are you doing, you bastard?

KOTIKHIN. There's no bastards here, just peasants.

(*The kulaks surround* RAYEVSKY.)

RAYEVSKY. Where's Mikhailov?

KVASOV. We're not Mikhailov's keepers. But what are you worrying about?

(*Hits* RAYEVSKY*'s hand with the butt of his rifle, knocking the revolver loose. The younger peasants hit* RAYEVSKY *on the head with clubs from behind and grab him.* OLGA *screams and falls down.*)

Hands behind your back.

(*They tie* RAYEVSKY.)

KOTIKHIN. Here, shove this rag in his mouth.
KVASOV. Put him over there, by the fence. Get going, guys, get going.

(RAYEVSKY, *tied up, is carried to the fence and placed against it.*)

CHORUS.
Oh, life is a prison,
A dark dungeon cell,
A valley, an aspen
A funeral bell.

(*The stage revolves slowly, until the interior of the house faces the audience. The singing dies down as the second episode begins.*)

Second Episode

It is totally dark. Singing and accordion music offstage. One can hear the jingle of the latch and the squeak of the opening door. Footsteps.

MIKHAIL (*in a whisper*). Shut the door, so he can't escape.
PROSHKIN. He won't escape.
PETKA. Where could he go?
MIKHAIL. Shut up!...
PROSHKIN. I'm going to the bed. We ought to strike a match.
PETKA. Better not.
MIKHAILOV. Would you like some light, guys? (*Pause.*) I'm asking you, do you want some light?
PROSHKIN. No light. We'll find you like this.
MIKHAILOV. Oh-ho! So it's you, Proshkin? What took you so long?
PROSHKIN. You recognize me?

MIKHAILOV. Of course! Well, what's new?

PROSHKIN. We brought you thirty-five tons. Take it!

MIKHAILOV. That's good. And here I thought you were bringing me a second note.

MIKHAIL. We haven't settled up on the first one yet.

PROSHKIN. We will. Where are you? (*Walks, stumbles into a bench, which falls.*) God damn you!

MIKHAILOV. Be careful! There's no hurry, you've got plenty of time to cut my throat. Why do you want to kill me? (*Pause.*) Why, I'm asking you?

PROSHKIN. I have my reasons.

MIKHAILOV. Come on, why?

PROSHKIN. I want to hear you clear your conscience.

MIKHAILOV. Maybe you could let me go—I'm still young!...

PROSHKIN. That's enough, Mikhailov! Come here, Mishka! You better not shoot, Mikhailov. If you go quietly, we'll end it easy for you. If you fight, then it'll be a hard death. I mean it.

MIKHAILOV. No, of course not, why would I shoot? Here, let me get you a light. (*Scratches a match and lights a candle.*)

(*The house is lit, and along the walls, in the corners, and next to* MIKHAILOV *at the table stand* PEASANTS *and* KOMSOMOL MEMBERS *with their guns pointed at the entering kulaks. In the silence the music and singing offstage become more audible.*)

MIKHAIL. Why you! (*Lowers his gun.*)
MIKHAILOV. Take them!

(*The kulaks are surrounded.* SOTIN *walks up to* PROSHKIN *and grabs him around the chest with both arms.*)

SOTIN. I waited a long time for you, Sofron Kuzmich. (*Shakes him, at first gently, then harder and harder, adamantly and mercilessly.*)

(*The house revolves slowly, and the third episode begins.*)

Third Episode

In front of the house. The singing ends. The kulaks crowd around the door.

SHILOV. Good Lord, what's going on there?

KVASOV. They're taking their time.

ZUBOV. And not a sound.

A YOUNG PEASANT (*looking through a crack in the shutter*). They've lit a candle.

GRUNKIN. What's going on there?

(*The group crowds around the window.*)

A YOUNG PEASANT. O, mother! Ivan Gerasimovich, the whole Komsomol branch is in there! Our guys are done for!

SHILOV. Run for it, brothers!

(*The crowd dashes from the house.*)

KVASOV. Stop! Where are you going? Who's there to run away from? Stop!

KOTIKHIN. We've got to do something. He's tricky, that Regional Chief!

KVASOV. No trickier than us. Get ready. No one's coming out of this house. Get some logs, pile them up against the door, prop them against the windows.

(*They quickly pick up the logs. The people inside begin to pound on the door and windows.*)

PASHA. Go ahead, pound all you want! You wanted to burn them, well, what are you waiting for, burn them!

KVASOV. I will burn them. You won't outsmart me, Mikhailov! Pour the kerosene!

(*One of the young peasants jumps up and splashes kerosene on the logs.*

The village bell begins to ring. The crash of broken glass is heard. Kulaks hold the logs in place.)

MOKRINA. Burn them, Christians, set them on fire! Let them writhe in pain, the devils!

KVASOV. Faster, faster! Don't you hear? They've started ringing the alarm.

KOTIKHIN. Ivan Gerasimovich, your son is in there.

KVASOV (*suddenly remembering*). In there....

PASHA. Well, Father, you wanted to burn them? Scared now?...

(*The people inside the house are trying to knock out the shutters with the butts of the rifles. The kulaks lean against the logs.*)

ZUBOV (*leans out the gate*). What's going on? The people are running to the bell.

KVASOV. Holy Mother of God! Set the fire! I don't care, just set the fire!

SHILOV. Stop, Ivan Gerasimovich, you mean burn them alive?

GRUNKIN. Citizens, citizens! What are we doing?

FIRST PEASANT. Hold on!

SECOND PEASANT. What are we doing?

MOKRINA. Burn them!

GRUNKIN. Hold on, citizens, I'm sobering up.

KVASOV (*to* GRUNKIN). Shush! I'll kill you like a dog!

THIRD PEASANT. What's going on?

ZUBOV (*leaning out the gate*). They're running here. Kolka's leading them.

KVASOV. Start the fire!

SECOND PEASANT. Don't you dare!

GRUNKIN. Ivan Gerasimovich, I bow to you. (*Bows.*) Thanks for the vodka. But I won't let you set the fire!

KVASOV (*wildly*). Won't let me?

(*A group of peasants falls on* KVASOV. *The kulaks and young peasants group around him in defense.*)

SECOND PEASANT. Hold him, he'll kill someone!

(ZUBOV *shoots out the gate.* KVASOV *hits* GRUNKIN *in the face and knocks him down. The peasants fall on the kulak group. There is a fight. The shutters get broken.* MIKHAILOV *appears in a window holding a Mauser.* SOTIN *is at another window with a club.* KOLKA *jumps over the fence holding a pistol. His "unit" and other peasants pour in after him. The fence falls over. The* KOMSOMOL MEMBERS *spring out the door and join the fray. The kulak group is pressed together.*)

MIKHAILOV. Tie all of them.

(*The kulaks are tied up.* SOTIN *turns* KVASOV *and tightens the knots.*)

SOTIN. Is this too tight? You just tell me, Ivan Gerasimovich, and I'll loosen it up.

KVASOV (*through clenched teeth*). It's fine. Thank you.

OLGA. Where is Rayevsky?

MIKHAILOV. I haven't found him.

(*Pause. Commotion in the crowd.*)

GRUNKIN. Oh, he's—here he is.

(ROMANOV *and a* KOMSOMOL MEMBER *free* RAYEVSKY.)

ROMANOV. Sweetheart, what were you lying there for, little dove!

MIKHAILOV (*loudly*). Why didn't you reverse your order?

RAYEVSKY. We'll talk about that later.

MIKHAILOV. Yes, there will be a talk. You're dismissed. Leave for the Regional Office immediately.

OLGA. He faced certain death just to save you. He attacked the whole mob by himself, all for you... and that's all you have to say to him?

MIKHAILOV. Thank you, Pavel! But you're still going on trial. (*Harshly.*) I'm sorry, Olga, I don't have time to talk to you right now.

OLKHA (*walking up to* KVASOV). Well, citizens, this is what we've been shouting for.... We've been shouting our heads off, and Ivan Gerasimovich Kvasov went and singed the Soviet state here (*pointing to* MIKHAILOV).

SHILOV. You're right, Vasily Pavlovich, you're right....

OLKHA. So now what are we gonna do, stand on the sidelines? That's not right—it's just not right.... We need to have our say. I'm going to tax myself thirty bushels. I'll put it on the wagon right now, and I call on all of you to do the same.

SHILOV. That's right, Vasya! I was telling him all along, citizens.... "What are you doing, Ivan Gerasimovich?..." I'm bringing fifty bushels!

GRUNKIN. Villagers... citizens... I have grain. Ivan Gerasimovich Kvasov stored it at my place. "You tell them it's yours," he says. Well, if it's mine, then I'm giving it to the Government.... I'm bringing one-hundred bushels....

SHILOV. Let's leave now; we'll be in the city by morning.

ROMANOV. To the city, damn it! To the city! Ah, what a life!... What a glorious calling! Mikhailov, what should we do with the kulaks?

MIKHAILOV. Take them away!

KVASOV. It's a little early to celebrate. One way or another—it's us or you. We can't both go on living.

MIKHAILOV. Then I'm worried for your sake. You've got it figured wrong, Ivan Gerasimovich. You wanted to kill Mikhailov, but you got it figured wrong. You thought there was only one Mikhailov—but look how many Mikhailovs there are! Look at all the Mikhailovs! (*Points all around him.*) Look at all the Mikhailovs! (*Points to the audience.*) You can't burn us!

(*Curtain.*)

The Guests

A Drama in Three Acts

Leonid Zorin 1953

Aleksey Petrovich Kirpichov [Alyosha]
nearing seventy
Vera Nikolayevna
his wife, age sixty-five
Pyotr Alekseyevich Kirpichov [Petya]
their son, age forty-five
Varvara Alekseyevna
their daughter, age thirty-two
Nina Konstantinovna
Pyotr's wife, age thirty-nine
Sergey [Seryozha]
twenty-five years old
} Pyotr's children from his first marriage
Tyoma [Artemya]
nineteen years old
Pavel Pavlovich Trubin [Pashenka]
forty years old
Mikhail Aleksandrovich Pokrovsky
age fifty-five
Nika
nineteen years old

The action takes place in a small town at the beginning of the fifties.

ACT 1

The owners' industrious hands have converted the yard behind the house into a little garden. At the back of the stage is a terrace, and on it, a table and a few wicker armchairs. By the terrace fence there is a small table with a telephone from the house. The doors to the room are opened wide; in the room, by the exit onto the terrace, we see a piano. There is a little table in the garden. A linden tree shades the table. Around the table are the same wicker armchairs. Near the terrace, behind some elder bushes, is a bench. On the left, a gate, barely visible behind the dense bushes. In the garden, in the armchair, is VARVARA. *Voices can be heard from the room.*

ALEKSEY PETROVICH'S VOICE. You gave me this shirt, now find the cuff-links.

VERA NIKOLAYEVNA'S VOICE. The cuff links are in the box.

(VERA NIKOLAYEVNA *walks out.*)

VERA NIKOLAYEVNA. Did you find them?

ALEKSEY PETROVICH'S VOICE (*annoyed*). There are boxes all over the place.

VERA NIKOLAYEVNA. In the long red one. (*She listens to find out whether her husband will ask her anything else—but no, it is quiet.*) He found them.... He's calmed down. Varvara, what are you doing, lying around like that?

VARVARA. I'm enjoying the relaxation you lured me with in all your letters.

VERA NIKOLAYEVNA. You found time....

VARVARA. Don't worry, Mother. Everything's washed and cleaned. All swabbed down, as the sailors say.

ALEKSEY PETROVICH'S VOICE. Mother!

VERA NIKOLAYEVNA. Well, what do you want?

ALEKSEY PETROVICH'S VOICE (*somewhat aggressively*). I suppose I should put on a tie, too?

VERA NIKOLAYEVNA. I'd put one on.

ALEKSEY PETROVICH (*in the window*). For crying out loud, it's practically a diplomatic reception.... (*Disappears.*)

VERA NIKOLAYEVNA (*seeing him off with an attentive glance*). Don't you get in my way.... (*Takes her head in her hands.*) Hmm, there's something here I just don't understand.

VARVARA. Trouble at the Kirpichovs'.

VERA NIKOLAYEVNA. Varvara, don't make me angry. Spectators shouldn't throw stones.

VARVARA. Me, a spectator? What are you talking about? I just sat down. I'm an active participant in the ongoing events.

VERA NIKOLAYEVNA. My head's going in circles. It's all so unexpected. How many years has Pyotr been gone, and, suddenly, look out, "The four of us are coming." Him and his wife, and Tyoma. Who's the fourth? Nothing but riddles. He's completely forgotten how to write letters. Now just think, where am I going to put all of you?

VARVARA. Think, Mom, think. Your son, a man of great responsibilities, is coming to visit you. That puts a great responsibility on you, too.

VERA NIKOLAYEVNA. Everyone frets in his own way. One gets in a bad mood, another makes jokes.

VARVARA. It's a misfortune to have a teacher for a mother. A professional student of human nature.

VERA NIKOLAYEVNA (*smiling*). A hard profession.

VARVARA. You're a student of human nature twice over. The teachers understand the children, and you understand the teachers. Where can we hide?

VERA NIKOLAYEVNA (*motioning toward the window*). There's the one who's nervous.

VARVARA. Father? Oh, yes. And he hides it even worse than I do.

VERA NIKOLAYEVNA. He got up in the middle of the night. I understand, he can't lie still. It's hard to know what to think. And then... Seryozha.... He read the telegram, and it's as if he became a different person. (*Short pause.*) What will it be like when they see each other?

VARVARA. Don't worry, don't worry. It'll all work out.

VERA NIKOLAYEVNA. No, it's a mess. No train number, no car.... He should have thought of us, too.

ALEKSEY PETROVICH's VOICE. Mother, Mother...

VERA NIKOLAYEVNA. I'm coming. I'm coming. (*She goes into the house.*)

VARVARA (*alone, declaiming*). Trouble at the Kirpichovs'. Alarm at the Kirpichovs'. (*As if interested.*) And what's befallen the Kirpichovs? (*Answering.*) The Kirpichovs are expecting guests.

(*During the last words enter* TRUBIN. *He is nearing forty.*)

TRUBIN. Excellent verses, precise, clear. Realistic. "The Kirpichovs are expecting guests...." (*Satisfied.*) A good welcome.

VARVARA. You're not a guest, are you?

TRUBIN. I am. Why, don't I look like one?

VARVARA. I don't know. I haven't sized you up. Who invited you?

TRUBIN. A wonderful young man, Seryozhinka Kirpichov, invited me. I arrived yesterday, called him from the hotel, and he invited me then and there. Unfortunately, I ended up having a lot to do and had to postpone my visit.

VARVARA. Now I see.

TRUBIN. And are you a guest too, or... the host?

VARVARA. The host... that's not quite right.

TRUBIN. Then the young host?

VARVARA. That's closer

TRUBIN (*with a smile*). In other words, you're related to Seryozha Kirpichov....

VARVARA. His aunt.

TRUBIN. Excuse me... who?

VARVARA. His aunt. And a strict aunt at that. Are you surprised?

TRUBIN. No, not at all. However...

(*Enter* SERGEY.)

SERGEY. Pasha!

TRUBIN. Who do you think you are, calling me Pasha? Little twerp....

SERGEY. Pal Palych.

TRUBIN. Pal Palych.

SERGEY. Trubin.

TRUBIN. Trubin.

SERGEY. Well, I'll be—

TRUBIN (*finishing*). Damned. He remembers everything about Trubin. Come here, Seryozhinka.

(*They embrace.*)

Well?

SERGEY. Everything's perfect. I was expecting you yesterday.

TRUBIN. I was busy.

SERGEY. And this morning I was searching for you.

TRUBIN. This morning I wasn't around.

SERGEY. Will you stay with us for long?

TRUBIN. Not very.

SERGEY (*looking at* VARVARA). You've met?

TRUBIN. Your aunt? Almost.

SERGEY. Varya, this is Pal Palych Trubin.

VARVARA. I heard.

TRUBIN. That's not everything.

SERGEY. No, that's not everything. This is the war correspondent who wrote about me.

TRUBIN. There, now I've been described fully.

VARVARA. There you are. Listen, you'll get no peace until you tell us with your own mouth, without any pretty newspaper talk, how Seryozha looked.

TRUBIN. I personally was interested in his age. There was nobody younger than him in the detachment. You weren't even seventeen then, right?

SERYOZHA. Just about.

TRUBIN. That's what he said then, too.

VARVARA. He's a fugitive, mind you. Ran away from home. Like a first-grader. Did you know about that?

TRUBIN. I found out later.

(*Pause.*)

VARVARA. Silence. That psychological moment when a third person gets in the way. The rude frontline soldiers want to reminisce like men about bygone days and so forth.

TRUBIN. How do you know that?

VARVARA. From books. I'll be back. (*Exits.*)

TRUBIN. Your aunt is good-looking.

SERGEY. We're friends. Well, Pashenka, sit down.

TRUBIN. I'll sit down. You've really changed, Sergey. You know, you've got that slightly arrogant independence of a man with a diploma.

SERGEY. I do have a diploma.

TRUBIN. What are you?

SERGEY (*edifyingly*). You have to follow the fate of your heroes.

TRUBIN. Well, true, true... I write so much, I don't have enough energy left for letters. Answer me, Sergey. I have to keep asking and asking you.

SERGEY. I'm a literature teacher, Pashenka.

TRUBIN. So you're teaching literature? I seem to recall you wanted to write it.

SERGEY. I did. But I don't have it in me.

TRUBIN. Aha! It turns out you're capable of tough decisions?

SERGEY. As you see.

TRUBIN. Well, I'll be damned. (*Surprised.*) Seryozha. Seryozhka Kirpichik, tenderfoot, hey-y, where a-r-r-r-e you? A grown man is sitting across from me; he thinks like an adult. Listen, explain to me, why are you here? In the letter I got in forty-six, you wrote about it cryptically: I'm living with my grandfather. But you're a Muscovite.

SERGEY. I was. It's a long story, Pasha.

TRUBIN (*shrugs his shoulders*). I'm not in a hurry.

SERGEY. Another time. But to make a long story short, my mother died not long after the war. Soon afterwards, my father married... a... but he'd been married to her for a long time. Unofficially, so to speak. But in forty-five, he made it official. Basically, I didn't want to return. He didn't really insist, either. I live with my grandfather.

TRUBIN. And your brother? You had a brother, right?

SERGEY. My brother's with my father.

TRUBIN. Do you write to each other?

SERGEY. On holidays. Actually, no.

TRUBIN. I see.

(*Pause.*)

SERGEY. That's the way it goes, my dear old friend, as they say in "the high style." (*Laughs forcedly.*)

TRUBIN. Listen, what about your grandfather? Alive and well?

SERGEY. He's seriously ill. Though he doesn't want to admit it. At five in the morning he's already on his feet. People write to him constantly....

TRUBIN (*pensively*). The same old Kirpichov.

SERGEY. Same old, Pashenka, same old.

TRUBIN. I can't believe it. Has he been living here for long?

SERGEY. They settled here back before the war. When he got sick. He's come within a hair's breadth so many times. The government gave him this house.

TRUBIN. Same old Kirpichov. Seryozhka, you're used to it, for one thing, and for another, regardless of your diploma, you're just a smug kid. But we old folks can't sit still when we hear your grandfather's name. It's Kirpichov, after all! Knight of the revolution. A squeaky-clean name. Our enemies' worst nightmare. Hero of five-year plans. Seryozhka, you're just a young fool.

SERGEY. Why are you telling me off?

TRUBIN. Damn right I'm telling you off. You have a man like that for a grandfather. You see him day by day. Write. Take notes. Observe.

SERGEY. How do you know? Maybe I am writing.

TRUBIN. You're fibbing. You're ashamed, so you fibbed. Give me a light. (*Starts smoking.*)

SERGEY. Tell me about yourself. How's the family?

TRUBIN. I don't have a family, Seryozhenka. I'm alone.

SERGEY. And where's your wife?

TRUBIN. My wife.... My wife is now someone else's wife. My wife left me. She was stolen.

SERGEY. Forgive me. I didn't know.

TRUBIN. I forgive you, but not her. On the other hand, God bless her; I'm no prize either. Traveling husband.

SERGEY. How did you end up here?

TRUBIN. An assignment. Have you heard that they're opening up a school here—not a school, but a temple for youths.

SERGEY. I've heard about it so much that I'm going to work in it.

TRUBIN. So my fine magazine decided to celebrate this event

(*Long whistle.*)

SERGEY. Twelve.

TRUBIN. Are you in a hurry to get somewhere?

SERGEY. No. People are in a hurry to get here.

TRUBIN. If you don't mind my asking, who?

SERGEY (*grinning*). My father has decided to grace us with his presence. And apparently he's not coming alone.

TRUBIN. Aha..... That's what the poem was about.

SERGEY. What poem?

TRUBIN. "What has befallen the Kirpichovs? The Kirpichovs are expecting guests." Your aunt recited it to herself.

SERGEY. Yes. The Kirpichovs are expecting the Kirpichovs. The province awaits the capital. Before us stands a hard but honorable duty: to contend with Crimea and greater Moscow.

TRUBIN (*observing him*). You're in a difficult mood.

SERGEY. Difficult situation is more like it.

TRUBIN. Pull yourself together. A father's a father. He wants to see you, his parents, his sister. That's natural.... And... you don't need to bristle. (*Pause.*) I didn't know you were having such a convention. Oh gosh!... I set up a meeting with someone.

SERGEY. Where's the meeting?

TRUBIN. Well, here, at your place. Since you asked me over for the whole day. A citizen visited me yesterday evening. To get some advice from a representative of the Moscow press. We weren't able to finish our conversation, and I told him to come here.

SERGEY. Well, that's no big problem. If you set it up, you set it up.

TRUBIN. By the way, Seryozha, you wouldn't be able to find me three hundred rubles, would you? I'm being transferred on Monday.

SERGEY. I'll find it. I have that kind of money.

TRUBIN. Without batting an eyelash. You can tell right away: a grandson of means.

SERGEY. My grandfather has nothing to do with it. I live on my own means. I was just planning to close a purchase.

TRUBIN. Well, wait for three days. I really need it.

SERGEY. I see.

(*Enter* VERA NIKOLAYEVNA.)

VERA NIKOLAYEVNA. Seryozha, don't go far. I need to talk with you.

SERGEY. Yes, Grandmother. Pashenka, this is Vera Nikolayevna Kirpichova, my grandmother and boss.

TRUBIN. Your boss, too?

SERGEY. Only recently. In the public school system. I'm one of her subordinates. Besides that, she's my guide and mentor in the secret labyrinths of pedagogy.

VERA NIKOLAYEVNA. Arkady, my friend, don't talk so pretty.

SERGEY. It's a fact, Grandma, and Turgenev has nothing to do with it.... (*Ceremoniously.*) And this is Pal Palych Trubin.

VERA NIKOLAYEVNA. Varya already told me.

SERGEY. But she didn't tell you the main thing: Trubin's going to write about the new school.

VERA NIKOLAYEVNA. In that case you'll have to have a conversation with me.... (*Concerned.*) Hey Seryozha, I was just thinking—maybe we should drop over to the station after all?

SERGEY. I'm not going.

VERA NIKOLAYEVNA (*reproachfully*). Sergey!

SERGEY. I'm speaking from the best intentions. It's plain to see they want to surprise us. Make a dramatic entrance. It would be downright rude to spoil a plan like that.

VERA NIKOLAYEVNA (*nodding her head with concern*). Yes. You really are speaking from the best intentions.

SERGEY. Grandmother, don't get angry. (*Kisses her.*) Pasha, let's go. I seem to recall I owe you—

TRUBIN (*softly*). What do you owe me?

SERGEY (*whispering*). Did you ask me for money or not?

TRUBIN (*figuring it out*). Money.... Aa-ha.... Very discreet. (*Grabs him by the shoulders.*) Well, show me the road.

(SERGEY *and* TRUBIN *exit into the house.*)

VERA NIKOLAYEVNA (*pensively looks at her grandson, then, walking up to the window, softly*). Alyosha!
VOICE OF ALEKSEY PETROVICH. Com-iing!

(*Enter* ALEKSEY PETROVIC—*tall, very thin, white-haired, which suits him. His forehead and cheeks have straight, sharp wrinkles. He's leaning on a cane. In a black suit and a tie.*)

VERA NIKOLAYEVNA. With a tie and everything....
ALEKSEY PETROVICH (*querulously*). I should have put on the full regalia, too. A parade's a parade, after all.
VERA NIKOLAYEVNA. You've started to grumble, Aleksey Petrovich. Are you getting old or something?
ALEKSEY PETROVICH (*quiet, grinning*). How much older could I get? (*Sits down next to his wife; she puts her hand on his shoulder.*) I was just answering some letters....
VERA NIKOLAYEVNA. With all your correspondence, you ought to have secretaries.
ALEKSEY PETROVICH. Wait, that's not what I mean.... They write... asking for advice... I could take some advice myself these days.
VERA NIKOLAYEVNA. What do you mean by that? (*Forces a laugh.*) Something new....
ALEKSEY PETROVICH. Oh, I was just... idle talk.... (*Softly.*) I've been uneasy since morning....
VERA NIKOLAYEVNA. Well you calm down. You're supposed to greet guests cheerfully.
ALEKSEY PETROVICH. With hospitality and songs? (*Claps his hands.*) "Take my home and take my bed, the host has nowhere to lay his head." (*A little irritated.*) Calm down... my first-born hasn't calmed me down very much.

VERA NIKOLAYEVNA (*takes his hand in hers*). Just hold on. We haven't seen him for many years. Pyotr's already on his way. Soon he'll be here.

ALEKSEY PETROVICH (*suddenly smiles*). And do you feel like seeing him? Is your heart pounding? Well, Mother?

VERA NIKOLAYEVNA (*deliberately calm*). Just the same as you, Alyosha.

(ALEKSEY PETROVICH *laughs.*)

And you're right that "the host has nowhere to lay his head." (*Animated.*) Everyone's coming at once. First Varvara, now Pyotr. And with three others.

ALEKSEY PETROVICH. That's alright. We'll find room.

VERA NIKOLAYEVNA (*after a pause*). Now Seryozha... worries me. He's nervous....

ALEKSEY PETROVICH. Father and son are meeting.

(*His wife looks at him attentively. He's noticed.*)

You don't have to worry. Sergey's a grown man. He's no pup; he has clear head. Where is he?

VERA NIKOLAYEVNA. He has a guest from Moscow. A journalist who was with him in the detachment.

ALEKSEY PETROVICH. Another young man?

VERA NIKOLAYEVNA. He's pushing forty.

ALEKSEY PETROVICH Very young.

VERA NIKOLAYEVNA. Seems to me Sergey's infatuated with him. He looks at him with wide eyes....

ALEKSEY PETROVICH. That's fine. We'll invite the journalist for lunch. So Sergey remembers he's in public.

(*Enter* SERGEY *and* TRUBIN.)

SERGEY. Grandfather, this is Trubin. Before coming to you he buttoned his jacket all the way up, cleared his throat, and looked in the mirror.

ALEKSEY PETROVICH. You're babbling, Sergey. I don't like it. (*Extends his hand to* TRUBIN.) Glad to see you. How do you like it here at our place?

TRUBIN. At the moment—I feel very awkward. Seryozha told me that you're expecting....

ALEKSEY PETROVICH. Well, so what....

TRUBIN. I'm just thinking I should have come another time, but now....

ALEKSEY PETROVICH. But now, if you don't have any urgent business, we won't let you leave. It's true, my son is coming with his family. You're a Muscovite. You must know him.

TRUBIN. Personally—I haven't had occasion. A friend of mine, a newspaper man, was telling me how he bumped into him once not long ago. Basically—I've heard of him.

ALEKSEY PETROVICH. He's a well-known man.

(*Honking is heard. Enter* VARVARA.)

VARVARA. Observation post reporting: A car has stopped.

ALEKSEY PETROVICH. Is that somebody for you, Mother?

VERA NIKOLAYEVNA (*displeased*). What are you talking about? I'm off today.

VARVARA (*interrupting*). No, my simple-hearted parents, no. They're not coming for you, they're coming to you. Pyotr Aleksandrovich Kirpichov with his family.

VERA NIKOLAYEVNA. They've arrived!

(*Animated voices can be heard. Enter* PYOTR ALEKSEYEVICH KIRPICHOV. *Tall, stout, round-faced, he is the very picture of masculine good health.*)

PYOTR. Hello, folks! Someone show Nikolai where to park the car.

(*Exit* VARVARA.)

How're you getting along? (*Animated.*) Father, you're looking great, looking great. And Mom's even better. (*Kisses his mother and father.*) Where did Varvara go? (*Squeezes both of them tightly.*) Oh, my goodness....

VERA NIKOLAYEVNA (*laughing with joy*). Petya... gently... you'll crush us.

ALEKSEY PETROVICH (*agitated, softly*). Well now... our son's arrived.

PYOTR (*cheerfully*). I have. (*Walks to his son.*) Seryozha... wel-l-l, look how you've... hello.

SERGEY. Hello, Father.

(*Handshake.*)

PYOTR (*not releasing his hand*). This kind of occasion calls for a kiss. (*Kisses him.*) You've really shot up. Ye-es... a Kirpichov. Say what you like: a Kirpichov.

VARVARA (*returning*). Hello, brother. (*Kisses him.*)

PYOTR. Varvara. Great. You're visiting here, too? (*Embraces her, pats her, and rocks her from side to side.*) You're looking great. Where'd you go?

VARVARA (*cheerfully*). You're instructions have been carried out.

PYOTR. What instructions?

VARVARA. I showed him where to park the car and unloaded your things.

PYOTR. My deepest gratitude.

(*Presses her to his chest. Enter* NINA KONSTANTINOVNA, TYOMA, *and* NIKA. *Both women are wearing sunglasses.* TYOMA *has a cap pulled over his forehead.*)

Here's my offspring and my household. Introduce yourselves to whomever you don't know.

(*The women take off their glasses.* TYOMA *unfastens his cap.*)

VARVARA. I pretty much know them. More or less.

PYOTR. We'll make it more. My Nina Konstantinovna. Faithful sidekick. I ask you to love and welcome her. This is Tyoma. Sergey will recognize him, but Grandma and Grandpa won't at all. You knew him as an infant, but look at the guy I've brought you now. This is Nika. We're all attached to her, but especially Tyoma is. Which is natural. We decided, since they're such friends, not to separate them for the summer. Especially since it was in our power.

ALEKSEY PETROVICH. And allow us to introduce comrade Trubin. Seryozha's friend.

PYOTR (*extends his hand*). Kirpichov.

(*During the greetings small groups take shape.*)

NINA KONSTANTINOVNA (*walks up to* SERGEY). So, good day and good luck. I didn't know how you would take my coming along, and I wasn't sure about coming, but I figured sooner or later we'd have to meet.

SERGEY. That's probably true.

NINA KONSTANTINOVNA. You don't look like Pyotr. No... you don't.

SERGEY. Yes. Friends and family say that I look like my mother.

NINA KONSTANTINOVNA (*glances at him, falls silent*). Well, now you've seen the woman on account of whom you didn't return to your own home....

SERGEY. That's not exactly right.

NINA KONSTANTINOVNA. All the same, I want to give you the opportunity to see for yourself that I'm not some kind of cobra. (*Walks off to* VERA NIKOLAYEVNA.)

TRUBIN (*to* SERGEY). Boy, do I feel like a fifth wheel at this party. Listen, Seryozha, I'm leaving. I'll meet my man at your gate.

SERGEY (*softly*). Pasha, I'd like you to stay.

TRUBIN. Okay, but you have only yourself to blame.

TYOMA (*walks up to them*). Well, brother, hello again.

SERGEY. Hello. You've gotten big, Tyomka.

TYOMA. I think so, too. (*Goes up to* NIKA.) I keep telling her that Tyoma's childhood has ended.

TRUBIN. She doesn't believe it?

TYOMA. Not really.

SERGEY. She doesn't really not believe it, or she believes it—but not really?

NIKA. Both versions suit me. Do you live here year-round?

SERGEY. Year-round.

NIKA. It's—pleasant here. (*Looks attentively at him.*) I never thought that Tyoma would have a brother like you....

SERGEY. Well, there you have it. Now think it over—at your leisure.

NIKA (*slowing slightly*). With your permission.

NINA KONSTANTINOVNA. We've given you a real task, Vera Nikolayevna. And how *are* you going to find room for all of us?

VERA NIKOLAYEVNA. It's nothing, dear, we'll manage.

ALEKSEY PETROVICH. It's all very simple. We're in our room, you and Pyotr in the room next-door. We'll send Nika to Varya, and Tyoma to Sergey. There's the whole stationing plan for you.

PYOTR (*hugging his father*). A real strategist. (*Looks around.*) I'm tired after the trip—it's nice here. A garden, flowers, and no farther than the terrace (*nods at the telephone*), civilization.

VERA NIKOLAYEVNA. What, are you sick of it?

PYOTR (*with a sigh*). Sorry to say.

VERA NIKOLAYEVNA (*smiling*). That's the spare phone. In the summer we're out here all the time—so we don't have to run into the room for every call.

PYOTR. By the way, I apologize ahead of time. I'm going to be getting some calls from Moscow. (*Spreads his hands.*) There's no escaping civilization.

VERA NIKOLAYEVNA. All—business?

PYOTR. It's insatiable. My body's here; my head's there. Split personality. (*Takes his mother by the shoulders.*) Maybe you'll kick me out before it's too late? Your guest is disruptive.

ALEKSEY PETROVICH. No problem; we'll pull through.

PYOTR. In that case we might as well transport our things. (*Slyly.*) There's a little something there for you....

ALEKSEY PETROVICH. Well, we'll have a look. Seryozha, Tyoma, follow me—we're unpacking.

PYOTR. I take it there's a direct path from the street to your house?

ALEKSEY PETROVICH. Yes, and we're using it. (*Walks, singing.*) "What can we house painters do—we work for a day and walk for two."

(*Exit everyone except* PYOTR *and* NINA KONSTANTINOVNA.)

PYOTR. We ought to tell Nikolai to take a look at the car. Just as a precaution.

NINA KONSTANTINOVNA. You can tell him later.

PYOTR. He's a bungler and a real slacker. He won't lift a finger if you don't tell him to.

NINA KONSTANTINOVNA. Well, that's going a bit too far.

PYOTR. Don't argue, I know better than you. (*Yawns, stretches.*) So we've arrived. I'm glad. I was really starting to miss my folks.

NINA KONSTANTINOVNA (*displeased*). Better late than... for the last seven-odd years you could have introduced your wife to your parents.

PYOTR. You've already said that. I'm not at the age where you need to go get your parents' blessing. And my folks, as you can see, are a different type. They're not too hung up on formalities. My father met my mother in a transit prison. And they got married in Siberia. As far as my father goes, he grew up an orphan; my mother's parents threw a fit. The daughter of poor but noble parents, and suddenly she ups and marries a typesetter!... (*Laughs.*)

NINA KONSTANTINOVNA. That's a romantic story, of course, but I still don't understand why the eldest son, the pride of the family, delayed his visit for so long.

PYOTR. That's not the point.,,, I'm telling you about our family, about its traditions, but you go on talking about something completely different.... (*Pensively.*) Moscow. Moscow, damn it. It sucks you in. You can't break loose. I'm standing here now.... I can't even believe it.... Silence.... Blue sky. No calls, no meetings. Even the annoyances have evaporated....

NINA KONSTANTINOVNA. There you have it... and you kept thinking: should we go or not....

PYOTR. I was right to think that. However much trouble Moscow is, it's still calmer there. We don't have the sort of good people in the ministry, and it's not, as they say, the sort of historical moment, to be in the countryside enjoying the fresh air. You've turned me toward idle thoughts.

NINA KONSTANTINOVNA. That's my main purpose in your life, you know. That's what I came into it for. (*Embraces him.*) But still, you're exaggerating....

PYOTR. Hardly. You don't know our people. Nikita's going to call me from time to time—well, that's no big deal. But when I get a call from...

NINA KONSTANTINOVNA. Don't disturb yourself. You mustn't. Tell me, what did you think of your son?

PYOTR. Well, what... he's a grown man. War, independence—that builds character, you know. I also left my family early.

NIKA KONSTANTINOVNA. He's not happy about our coming here, not at all....

PYOTR. You're exaggerating... how could he not be happy? I'm his father, he's my son. We haven't seen each other for a long time. Of course, he's embarrassed, out of sorts, even though he's grown up, he's still young.... You need to give him time.... Let him get used to us, loosen up—then we'll have a heart-to-heart talk.

NINA KONSTANTINOVNA (*grinning*). You've... thought all this out pretty well.

PYOTR. That's my job. You have to think a lot of things through. (*Laughs.*)

NINA KONSTANTINOVNA. You're a wise man, I know....

PYOTR (*somewhat edifyingly*). If you want people to believe you, let them get used to you. That's the rule.

NINA KONSTANTINOVNA. Still, there are a lot of us. I feel sort of awkward—we're crowding them.

PYOTR. Nonsense. Apart from my work, it's a great idea for us to be here. I should have made the trip a long time ago. (*Pensively.*) All this separation. But my mother, my father, my son are here.... You know, I want peace and friendship. Forgive and forget. In other words, strengthen the bonds.

NINA KONSTANTINOVNA. Admit it, though: Nika didn't have to be here.

PYOTR. She didn't. But tell me, why shouldn't we make it fun for Tyomka? You can see for yourself, the guy's head over heals in love. This summer could be a fantastic memory for him.

NINA KONSTANTINOVNA. You really love your youngest son.

PYOTR. I sure do.

NINA KONSTANTINOVNA. You were a lot more forceful about inviting Nika than he was.

PYOTR (*shoots a quick glance at her*). It's not his place to invite. That's my job.

(*Enter* VERA NIKOLAYEVNA.)

And here's Mom. Are you doing chores? We just got here, and you've already left us.

VERA NIKOLAYEVNA. Don't worry, Pyotr, I won't leave you. Follow me, my dear guests, I'll show you your chambers.

(*Enter* TYOMA *and* NIKA.)

PYOTR. Show me, show me, I've always dreamed of living in a chamber. (*To* TYOMA *and* NIKA.) Hey kids, don't keep following us. Take a walk by yourselves, no one's going to bother you.

VERA NIKOLAYEVNA. Nika, you must be tired. Varvara Alekseyevna's coming now.

NIKA. Don't worry, Vera Nikolayevna. I'm fine.

PYOTR. They're fine. Well, show me, Mom. And tell me. What's new with you at school? (*Laughs at the unexpected rhyme.*)

(*Together with his wife, exits after* VERA NIKOLAYEVNA.)

TYOMA. Are you really fine?

NIKA. Yes, I'm tired from the ride.

TYOMA. Your good moods always have surprisingly boring causes.

NIKA. Possibly. I'm often bored.

TYOMA. With me?

NIKA. You're repeating yourself.

TYOMA. Are you sorry you came?

NIKA. No, why should I be? I'm very grateful... to you and Pyotr Alekseyevich....

TYOMA (*takes out a pack*). Have a smoke.

NIKA. Thanks. (*Lights up.*)

TYOMA. I'm sick of them. I'll have to get a pipe.

NIKA. You'd better not. You're too young for a pipe.

TYOMA. You're always going out of your way to emphasize my age.

NIKA (*laughing lazily*). A boy's reaction.

TYOMA. I'm a sophomore.

NIKA. You're going to be a sophomore. Speak precisely.

TYOMA. Are we going to keep squabbling for much longer?

NIKA. Forever.

TYOMA (*with an air of suffering*). A happy life awaits me.

NIKA. Are you sure it "awaits"?

TYOMA. What, you're not sure?

NIKA (*slowly*). You know, you're not a bit like your brother.

TYOMA. I don't suffer by comparison, I hope?

NIKA (*not right away*). Give me a light, silly. Mine's gone out.

TYOMA. Listen, that doesn't do your little golden throat any good.

NIKA. Once a year does no harm.... (*Lights up.*) Say... does Pyotr Aleksandrovich really love your stepmother?

TYOMA. With his heart and soul. Why do you ask?

NIKA (*shrugging her shoulders*). No reason.... (*Grinning.*) By the way, Nina Konstantinovna insists that I call her by her first name. I just can't force myself to do it.

TYOMA. How come? That's what I call her.

NIKA. You're different.

(*Enter* VARVARA.)

VARVARA. So, Nika, you and I'll be living together. Our room isn't too huge, but we'll get by. The main thing is, it's good company.

NIKA. You're right.

VARVARA. Muscovites are demanding, but I think we'll get along. I'm reasonable—I won't drag you down. Are you a patient person, too, I hope?

TYOMA (*smile*). How can I put this?...

NIKA. She's asking me.

VARVARA. You don't have to answer that kind of question either. (*Glancing at the cigarette in her hand.*) Smoke often?

NIKA. Not really....

VARVARA. If it's because of stress, I'll keep quiet, but if it's just to be cool, I'll object. I like fresh air. However, I assume it can't be too stressful yet. (*Businesslike.*) Well, let's go. First I'll take you to clean your feathers and then—we'll relax.

NIKA. Thanks. I'm okay. You know, it's a wonderful time of year. There's nothing better than relaxing in July.

(*They go.*)

VARVARA (*on the way*). August is worse?

NIKA (*with a barely noticeable smile*). August just isn't the same.

VARVARA (*shrugging her shoulders*). I don't know.... On the other hand, you know best. (*Turns around.*) Nephew, the other nephew will come and take you in his charge.

TYOMA. Thank you. I'm an independent, original man.

(NIKA *and* VARVARA *disappear into the house.* TYOMA *sits down in the wicker armchair, lights up, and then softly whistles some indistinct melody. Enter* SERGEY *and* TRUBIN.)

You coming for me, paleface?

SERGEY. You're the paleface. We'll put you right.

TYOMA. Do you want to teach me, young pedagogue?

SERGEY. You object?

TYOMA. No, why should I? We're all peaceful folk in my little village.

SERGEY. There's that Moscow chic. Can you sense it, Pavel?

TRUBIN (*imperturbably*). That just how we Muscovites are.

TYOMA. I came to visit my brother, but he's a teacher. Tough luck. But never mind. We'll take the blow without flinching. Sow, Sergey. Be a sower of the wise, the good, and, of course, the eternal.

TRUBIN. And you—don't plan to sow?

TYOMA (*ironically*). Where? I'm a lowly student. A mere nursling of the Institute of International Relations.

SERGEY. So how about it, diplomat, you want to go wash up?

TYOMA. Hang on, I'll finish my smoke.

(TRUBIN *glances at his watch, walks up to the wicker gate, opens it, looks.*)

SERGEY (*querulously*). Your button is on its last legs. (*Softly.*) Our stepmother doesn't do a good job looking after you.

TYOMA. Nina? Not at all, she's a cool chick. (*Touches his button.*) I'll tell Nika—she'll sew it back on.

(TRUBIN *returns. To* TRUBIN.)

So, you're a Muscovite?

TRUBIN. For the last forty years.

TYOMA. Where's your place?

TRUBIN. In Molchánovka.

TYOMA (*thinking*). Not bad. We live on Mozhaiskii Street. Do you know the new buildings?

TRUBIN. I've seen them.

TYOMA. It's nice and quiet there, calm. Of course, it's not quite the suburbs, but still....

TRUBIN. The suburbs—that's paradise.

TYOMA. We celebrated the new year at our dacha. On Mount Nikola. Well, it's awesome. Quiet all around, white snow—it's really something. It's especially nice there during the winter—it gets tiresome in the city, you know....

SERGEY. And I can see you're tired out....

TYOMA (*not listening*). It's more boring in the summer. Everyone goes in the summer. Change of scenery, as they say. Well, I've finished my smoke. Let's go, teacher. To tell the truth, I'm tired. The others took a rest when we stopped, but, just between us, Nikolai and I got smashed but good. How he drove the car after that, I can't imagine.

SERGEY. Brother, you're a real democrat. Getting drunk with the chauffeur.

TYOMA. With Kolya? He's not a bad guy. Just lazy. (*Yawns.*) To hell with him. I drive okay myself, you know, only I don't have a license.

SERGEY. You do. You have a license to the world. Let's go. Wash up and take a rest.

(TYOMA *leaves.*)

Pavel, I'll be right...

TRUBIN. Good.

(SERGEY *and* TYOMA *exit. Taking a cigarette holder out of his pocket,* TRUBIN *starts singing.*)

Celery is a wonderful vegetable
But carrots are better for you....

(*The cigarette holder falls on the ground.*)

I'll be damned!

(*Bends down, looks for his cigarette holder. The wicker gate opens, and a graying, stooped man enters. He's wearing an extremely threadbare suit, in his hands a light-colored, dirtyish hat.*)

THE MAN WHO HAS ENTERED. Please forgive me for disturbing you. Is this thirty-two Lermontov Street?

TRUBIN (*gets up from the ground, with the cigarette holder in his hand*). That's right, that's right, thirty-two Lermontov Street. Come in, comrade Pokrovsky.

POKROVSKY. Comrade Trubin... forgive me, I didn't recognize you at first....

TRUBIN. It would have been hard to. Have a seat.

POKROVSKY. Thank you very much. Don't trouble yourself.

TRUBIN. No trouble at all. Have a seat. I apologize for breaking off our conversation so quickly yesterday. Extraordinary circumstances.... But you could see that for yourself.

POKROVSKY. I'm the one who should apologize—I'm always tearing you away from your work.

TRUBIN. Well, fine. Let's stop apologizing and start talking. And let's start from the beginning. To get the big picture.

(*In the window is* VARVARA. *They don't see her. She sits and listens to the conversation. Enter* SERGEY *from the house.*)

Seryozha, this is Pokrovsky... Mikhail Aleksandrovich, right?

POKROVSKY. Yes, yes. Quite correct.

SERGEY. Pleasure to meet you.

TRUBIN. You can tell the whole story with Sergey here. He's a close friend of mine.

POKROVSKY. Of course. It's not a secret, after all.

TRUBIN. By the way, Mikhail Aleksandrovich, when you came in you were asking whether this was the right street. So you're not from around here?

POKROVSKY. No, not at all. I live in Voronezh. My wife's cousin and her husband live here. My wife went to visit them a month ago. A few days ago she got sick, and so... they sent for me. I'm thinking of taking her back when she gets better.

TRUBIN. I see.

POKROVSKY. I just happened to hear about you from my relatives. An acquaintance of theirs works on the editorial staff of the local newspaper. My wife convinced me to turn to you.

TRUBIN. So tell me about it.

POKROVSKY. As I already said, I'm a lawyer. I've been living in Voronezh for thirty years, and for all thirty I've been a public defender. Basically, everybody there knows me. (*With a smile.*) I even enjoy a certain popularity, if I may say so.

TRUBIN. Of course, you may. You're just telling it like it is.

POKROVSKY. At the beginning of January, I was invited to participate in a case—a big case—one of the lawyers suddenly fell ill and was forced to turn the case down. I set about my duties and just barely started finding my way to the heart of the matter, which, by the way, I found quite bewildering, when I was suddenly dismissed from the defense, together with the other two lawyers.

TRUBIN. On what basis?

POKROVSKY. I am in search of that basis myself, but they accused my colleagues and me of advising our defendants to elect a course of action that would mislead the court and place the investigation in doubt and so forth. They alleged that a note was found to that effect.

TRUBIN. A note—to the defendants?

POKROVSKY. Exactly. I tried to demonstrate that, with regard to me, no such charge could be brought. In thirty years not a single smudge has stuck to me—everyone can confirm that—and I have a completely solid reputation. Later, when I saw that they were more inclined to believe my accusers than me, I tried to demonstrate—this was humiliating, but I had no choice—that I was just plain physically incapable of participating in this whole affair, because I became involved in the Shevtsova case only in January.

TRUBIN. Excuse me, you said—the Shevtsova case?

POKROVSKY. Quite correct—the Shevtsova case. Ekaterina Shevtsova. Did you want to say something else?

TRUBIN. No. No, nothing. Keep going.

POKROVSKY. Basically, defending myself turned out to be much more difficult than defending others. Where did my logic and persuasiveness go? My argument had no effect, and I was dismissed from the public defender's office.

TRUBIN. So what did you do next?

POKROVSKY. I decided to assert my rights. I was fortunate. Soon after all this, comrade Krasnoshchekov—from our Republic's ministry—visited Voronezh, and I was able to get a reception. But comrade Krasnoshchekov told me that he didn't see any basis for changing the decision of the local court.

TRUBIN. He didn't?

POKROVSKY. Quite correct—he said he didn't. I didn't let things lie, no. I went to Moscow, to the Union Ministry, to comrade Kirpichov. I left only when I was sure that my letter found its way into his own hands. I was simply not able to wait there for the decision... (*with a smile*) because of difficult financial circumstances.

(*At the name of Kirpichov,* SERGEY *starts forward, but with a gesture unnoticed by* POKROVSKY, TRUBIN *tells him to keep quiet.*)

TRUBIN. And what was the answer?

POKROVSKY. The answer came after several repeated inquiries. I was informed that comrade Kirpichov advised me to turn... to comrade Krasnoshchekov.

(*Everyone is silent for a while.*)

TRUBIN. So, to this day you...

POKROVSKY. Quite correct. To this day—the status quo, the same situation. For the first time in many years, I am idle. It's not life but a continuous vacation, so to speak. I'm not used to it, you know, and on the whole... it's an unpleasant sensation. Honestly, I don't know what else to do. (*Slowing slightly.*) And besides all that—forgive me for digressing—it's highly unsettling. Although I haven't even been able to delve deeply into this case, which is so fateful for me, it nonetheless seems to me that it was conducted not at all by the books. My impression is that a good deal of it was botched right from the start.... However, I've spoken about this many times. (*Spreads his hands.*) This is not the time to talk about that, but it's difficult not to think about it....

(*Pause.*)

TRUBIN. Seryozha, I forgot my cigarette holder back there. Do me a favor and bring it, please.
SERGEY. In the living room?
TRUBIN. That's right.

(SERGEY *exits.*)

Listen, Mikhail Aleksandrovich, while we're alone.... Just don't be offended—I'm no diplomat—you probably need some money?

(POKROVSKY *is embarrassed, doesn't know what to answer.*)

Let me lend you this small amount—unfortunately, I don't have more. Pay it back when you're able to.
POKROVSKY. What do you mean, what do you mean—I'm telling you, this is impossible.
TRUBIN. Why impossible? What does that mean, impossible? Everything is possible on this planet.
POKROVSKY (*decisively*). No. I thank you for your concern, but—no.... Let's not argue about this. (*Shakes his hand.*)
TRUBIN. Well, okay then, we won't. (*Querulously.*) All the same, there's no good reason.

(*Enter* SERGEY.)

SERGEY. I couldn't find any cigarette holder.

TRUBIN. I found it. I sent you off for no good reason. (*To* POKROVSKY.) Here's the thing, Mikhail Aleksandrovich, will you be here for long?

POKROVSKY. No, not very long. My wife isn't feeling well... her cousin is also... ill.... (*With a guilty smile.*) We all have a case of nerves, you know.... We're thinking, at the end of the week....

TRUBIN. Leave me your number. I'll call. I might even be able to help somehow.

POKROVSKY (*writing on a page from a small notebook*). There you are. You should ask for Vera Semyonovna or Evgeny Arkadievich, and they'll call for me. If you're curious to look at all the papers, I have them, of course.

TRUBIN. Fine. That's good to know.

POKROVSKY. Thank you very much and forgive me for taking up so much of your time....

TRUBIN. That doesn't matter... let's just hope it all works out.

POKROVSKY. Yes, without hope, life is hard. All the best.

SERGEY. Take care.

POKROVSKY Once again, please forgive me. (*Leaves.*)

(*Пауза.*)

TRUBIN. What do you think of him?

SERGEY. He seems like a decent person. He just apologizes a lot... and in general... he's really very submissive.

TRUBIN. Submissive.... Well yes... submissive. (*Angrily.*) He doesn't have any money, that's why he's submissive. When your pockets are full of air, but you have to prove something, convince someone, even your walk changes. That's a well-known fact. (*Falls silent.*) He sent his wife to her cousin—apparently things became unbearable. And he got the cold shoulder here, that's obvious. Parasites... hmm, yes... a nasty situation.

SERGEY. And all the same he's sort of resigned himself... he's sagged... I can see it myself.

TRUBIN. Probably. You have something there. He's an intellectual of the old school, so to speak. But that doesn't mean that you can just do whatever you like with him.... (*Pauses.*) The interesting thing is, I've already heard about this Shevtsova case. And in a light very unflattering to the prosecutors.

SERGEY (*not immediately*). Pavel.... Are you talking about all of this because you don't want to talk about my father?

TRUBIN. No, I'm not that subtle. Let's talk about your father. I don't mean to tell him what to do, but in any case, dammit, he needs to finish this thing honorably. (*Smiles.*) To tell the truth, I invited Pokrovsky here to draw Aleksey Petrovich into his case. But since Kirpichov the Second is here.... (*Suddenly, with irritation.*) Well that's just my luck... I always have to get involved in some fiasco.

SERGEY. Pasha... ugh, I don't feel right.... And I don't want to go into the house.

TRUBIN. You get a hold of yourself. You're a man, after all.... We're going to act calmly, soberly, and, above all, with the utmost dignity.

THE VOICE OF VERA NIKOLAYEVNA. Seryozha! Pavel Pavlovich! Lunch!

TRUBIN. Com-ming! (*Softly.*) You go ahead. I'll finish my smoke and come, too.

(SERGEY *wants to say something, thinks better of it, leaves.* TRUBIN *sits, smokes, hums from time to time under his breath:* "I'll be damned, I'll be damned...." VARVARA *comes down. Sits down nearby in an armchair.*)

VARVARA. Why aren't you at the table?
TRUBIN. Just another minute....

(*Pause.*)

VARVARA (*looks attentively at him*). Have you hit forty yet?
TRUBIN. Alas.
VARVARA (*looking at his head*). You've managed to get a little gray.... I suppose you've had to live through a thing or two.
TRUBIN (*looks her over*). Well, no more than others. Why do you ask?
VARVARA. Because I like you. (*A short pause. Stands.*) I heard your conversation.

(TRUBIN *looks intently at her, falls silent. Happy sounds and laughter are heard from the room. Animated voices interrupting each other.*)

I'm going to go see what's "befallen." (*Leaves.*)

TRUBIN (*alone, slowly*).
And what's befallen the Kirpichovs?
The Kirpichovs are expecting guests....

(Curtain.)

ACT 2

Twilight. They had tea in the house not long ago. The clearing of dishes from the rooms can be heard. In the garden on the terrace are TYOMA, SERGEY, ALEKSEY PETROVICH *and* VERA NIKOLAYEVNA, PYOTR KIRPICHOV, NINA KONSTANTINOVNA, TRUBIN, VARVARA, *and* NIKA.

NINA KONSTANTINOVNA. Yesterday it was a little stuffy here, but today the weather is wonderful. Warm, but still cool enough. Tyoma, come here.

TYOMA (*on the terrace, near the radio*). Predictable. Zero-zero. No one knows how to score.

TRUBIN. Somebody must know how.

TYOMA. The coaches have gone AWOL. Their game plans are pretty much always primitive.

ALEKSEY PETROVICH. It's twenty years since I've been to a soccer match.

PYOTR. Nina and I, we go often. On the other hand, back there everybody goes. You don't need to visit anyone—you'll meet them at the stadium. Whenever there's a soccer match, the offices empty right out. Everybody goes to cheer for "Dynamo."

TYOMA. I still say it's boring away from Moscow. The northern bleachers are emptying out now. The crowd's dispersing. You can see *everybody* there. The cream of the capital. The streetlamps are on, Gorky Street is humming.... Nika and I usually go to "The Loft" around this time—to discuss ice cream sundaes and so forth.

VARVARA (*muttering*). Around this time you and I, around this time...

TYOMA. Red muscatel goes really well with a sundae.

PYOTR. He's the regular among us. Whenever we happen to eat supper together, he orders. A real master. (*With irony.*) I think all the maitre d's know him.

VARVARA (*stands*). I think we were hoping to hear Nika.

PYOTR. We were hoping to, and we will. Everything is within our power. Sing, star of the conservatory.

TYOMA. Shine, shine.

NIKA. I warn you, it won't be much fun to listen to.

VERA NIKOLAYEVNA. That's for us to judge. Sing, dear.

NIKA. You have only yourselves to blame. Tyoma, play with me.

(TYOMA *has taken a chair from the terrace, moved it over to the piano which is in the room. He accompanies* NIKA, *who sings a serenade of Drigo's.*)

PYOTR (*he has been listening with rapture*). Bravo, bravo. First rate.

TYOMA. We'll take it.

NINA KONSTANTINOVNA. Darling, just darling.

VARVARA. Simply wonderful.

SERGEY. I liked it, too.

NIKA (*glances at him; softly*). You? That's—unexpected.

(SERGEY *shrugs his shoulders.* VARVARA, *observing this scene, smiles.*)

TYOMA. Ugh, Nika, now you're going to get a big head. You're even a hit in the backwoods.

NIKA. What are you jabbering about? Put the chair back.

TYOMA. Pavel Pavlovich, you'll have to write about Nika, too, just like you wrote about Seryozha. If not now, then in the future.

TRUBIN. Who knows? Maybe the occasion will arise.

NINA KONSTANTINOVNA (*laughing*). There now, they've provided you with press, too.

PYOTR (*edifyingly*). The press is a powerful force. It can raise you up or trample you in the mud. You have to think about it from a civic point of view.

TRUBIN. There's no occasion to object to that.

PYOTR. There are sound cadres in our press, without a doubt. Many comrades worthy of the highest esteem. But there are also people who are completely irresponsible. You know... sensationalists.

TRUBIN. And you've met those types.

PYOTR. I've had occasion. I can't say that I often socialize with our writing brethren, but I've had occasion to. Quite recently, fate brought me together with a certain comrade Ptitsyn.

TRUBIN. I know him.

PYOTR. My condolences. We bumped into each other in a case where the efforts of others like him stirred up an unhealthy noise you wouldn't believe.

TRUBIN. You don't mean the Shevtsova case, do you?

PYOTR (*looks at him with interest*). You—know about it? (*Short pause.*) Where from, if it's not a secret?

TRUBIN. Volodya Ptitsyn, the sensationalist, is a close friend of mine.

PYOTR. Aha....

TRUBIN. I've known Ptitsyn for many years. Of all the people I know, he's one of the most upright.

PYOTR. I see—if he's a friend...

TRUBIN. And the Shevtsova case, out of all the ones I know of, is one of the filthiest.

PYOTR. Is that so? You like strong expressions?

TRUBIN. Sometimes. But I prefer accurate ones.

ALEKSEY PETROVICH. And what, exactly, is the heart of the matter?

TRUBIN. The heart of it? How can I put it... briefly? Of course, I'm not an expert, but from what I know, it's clear to me that we have before us a case of arbitrariness. First at the local level, and then higher up.

PYOTR. If all your expressions are that accurate, I don't envy your readers.

TRUBIN. Instead of punishing the local Prishibeevs,[1] a few people in the capital are trying to influence the Supreme Court.

PYOTR. Come now, you yourself said that you're not an expert—how can you arrive at such conclusions?

TRUBIN. I just have a little bit of life experience—that's all. And so it seems to me that some of your colleagues think more about keeping their reputations clean than about a person's fate.

PYOTR. You're blowing hot air. (*With ironic pathos.*) "A person's fate." (*Smiles.*) There are different sorts of people, you know. And as far as clean reputations, that's no matter for irony. That respect must be preserved.

TRUBIN. I agree. How to preserve it, that's the question.

PYOTR. Well, we know—how....

(*A pause.* ALEKSEY PETROVICH *paces.*)

VARVARA (*observing* TRUBIN). Tranquillity doesn't come easily to you.

TRUBIN (*cracks his knuckles, a little annoyed*). I don't make a good guinea pig.

VARVARA. I'll be the judge of that.

ALEKSEY PETROVICH (*stops*). Pyotr, you say that it's well known how to preserve respect. It's not well known to everybody.

PYOTR. What's your point?

ALEKSEY PETROVICH. My point is, you know, there are different views on the matter. I'm not familiar with this case that Pavel Pavlovich has been telling us about. But it reminded me of another case....

PYOTR (*joking*). It was lo-o-ong ago....

ALEKSEY PETROVICH. Back in 'eighteen, it's true. But it'll do you no harm to hear it.

PYOTR (*hurriedly*). Tell us, tell us.

ALEKSEY PETROVICH. So... one fine morning I ascertained that a man under investigation, an inventor, a former general, was a completely decent and honest man. A certain Grinin was conducting the case, conducting it slowly and badly. To make a long story short, I ordered the general to be freed with an apology.

PYOTR. I see.

ALEKSEY. Some time passes, and I find out that this man is still in the same situation. I remember, it was a wonderful spring day, and there was some sort of gloomy news in the papers. I sent for Grinin. There were many people in my office for various purposes. Grinin comes in, all neat and spiffy, with an easy smile. People got up to leave us alone. But I didn't excuse them. I ask him, "Why didn't you carry out my order?" With the same smile, he said, "Well, we find it inexpedient. To find this brass innocent would undermine our prestige." (*Falls silent.*) The rest seems like a dream. I whipped out my Browning from the holster....

NINA KONSTANTINOVNA. Oh my!

ALEKSEY PETROVICH. At the last second... someone pulled my hand aside.

VERA NIKOLAYEVNA. What's wrong, darling?

NINA KONSTANTINOVNA. It's getting scary.

VERA NIKOLAYEVNA. Lord, what do you have to be afraid of?

PYOTR. Well, Father, your story isn't relevant. First of all, it's not nineteen-eighteen now, and second, if we act in that manner....

SERGEY. I liked the story....

PYOTR (*angrily*). Your head's screwed on wrong. Don't take it personally.

ALEKSEY PETROVICH (*stands up*). I'm going, Mother. I'm tired. (*Goes. Suddenly stops.*) To this day I'm sorry I didn't shoot him. (*Leaves.*)

VERA NIKOLAYEVNA (*after a pause*). Father's upset.... (*Goes after her husband.*)

TYOMA. Nika...

NIKA. Wait....

NINA KONSTANTINOVNA. Comrades! Citizens! You're all too serious. You don't know how to relax. You keep talking business, nervous, chilly business. You need to unwind. That's all there is to it. Who's coming with me—for volleyball?

TYOMA. Me!... I'll show you my latest moves.

VARVARA. We'll see, little nephew. Nika, you coming with us?

NIKA. Of course.

SERGEY. Aha! I thought you could only sing.

NIKA (*looks at him and sits down again*). That's right. I was kidding. (*Looks aside.*) I'm staying here.

NINA KONSTANTINOVNA (*throws her a quick glance*). And you, Pyotr?

PYOTR (*not right away*). I guess I'll stay here.

(NINA KONSTANTINOVNA *and* TYOMA *leave.*)

VARVARA (*to* NIKA). Too bad you changed your mind.

TRUBIN (*to* VARVARA). Take Seryozha and me.

VARVARA. Let's go. But if you miss I'll kick you off the team.

TRUBIN. Got it. Let's move, Sergey.

SERGEY. Let's go. (*To his father.*) Just don't leave. I need to talk to you.

PYOTR. I'm very glad. Finally.

(SERGEY, TRUBIN, *and* VARVARA *leave.*)

How do you like this theatrical production?

NIKA. Not much.

PYOTR. Exactly. This journalist is apparently a rogue... and the old man is acting strange. (*Indulgently.*) On the other hand, what will we be like at that age?

NIKA. You have a long way to go before you get there.

PYOTR. Thank God for that. Come here.

NIKA (*approaches*). You want to tell me some special secret?

PYOTR (*laughs*). Something like that. Ugh, Nika, sweetie, I'm bored. That's all the secret there is.

NIKA. You already said that.

PYOTR. I'll say it another thousand times. I've made it through forty-five years. Fathered two sons. And what's the point? One's a little wolf, the other's just a lamb. (*Laughs.*) What, you don't like this? (*Embraces her.*) Well, marry him just the same.

NIKA (*frees herself from his arms*). You think that will bring me such great pleasure?

PYOTR. Well, here's the thing... not all pleasures in life are the same. And then, he's not stupid, no, he's sharp... and mature.... Yea-ah.... He just keeps missing the mark. I suppose you've spotted it yourself.... (*Laughs.*) I've gotten informal with you—well, that's no big deal, after all, I am a little older.... (*Preoccupied.*) He has no backbone, see—no backbone.

NIKA. Are you hiring me as a spine for your son?

PYOTR. What? (*Laughs.*) That's it—bull's-eye! Well, so what? You just look, and he'll straighten up. The main thing is to have a smart man around. That means a lot, brother. Now his mom... she was the same... life with her was good at first.

NIKA. At first? And afterwards?

PYOTR. And afterwards—it's a long, complicated story. You wouldn't understand. You're smart, but you wouldn't understand. Your age won't allow you to. Your brain is mostly in your tongue.... But it should be right here.... (*Strokes her head.*) It'll work out with age.

NIKA. I like my own age just fine.

PYOTR. Your age suits you. Everything's blossoming.... (*Strokes her.*) Why are you looking at me like that?

NIKA. No reason... after lunch you always have... peculiar eyes. (*Interrupts herself.*)

PYOTR. Eyes?... For you—I have tender eyes. Well-intentioned, as they say.... Now at work—their expression changes. That's true.

NIKA. Are people afraid of you, Pyotr Alekseyevich?

PYOTR. Yeah, a little. That's no obstacle to getting things done. Just the opposite.

(*Enter* NINA KONSTANTINOVNA.)

NINA KONSTANTINOVNA (*not right away*). I'm coming for help. We're losing.... You ought to play, Pyotr, run around—it'll do you some good.

PYOTR. It won't do your team any good.

NINA KONSTANTINOVNA (*significantly*). That doesn't matter. The main thing is, it's better for *you* out *there* than *here*.

PYOTR (*falls silent, then forces a smile, gets up*). Well, if that's how it is, I'll go cover myself with shame. (*Leaves, humming the last lines from the serenade that* NIKA *sang.*)

NINA KONSTANTINOVNA (*as if preoccupied*). Pyotr Alekseyevich has gotten clumsy, I've noticed.

NIKA (*turns away*). What have you noticed?

NINA KONSTANTINOVNA. I haven't noticed anything else. He has young eyes and a young head. And for a woman of my years, it's sometimes more important *not to notice*. If I had been noticing, I hardly would have become Pyotr Alekseyevich's wife. But at one time I really wanted to. You're nineteen, Nika?

NIKA (*suspiciously, coldly*). Yes, Nina Konstantinovna.

NINA KONSTANTINOVNA. Just call me Nina, I told you you could. Nineteen... is a good age. And it's good to be so beautiful.... And it's good when there are so many hopes... and so much ambition.... I only hope it doesn't ruin you. But to preserve the remains of the past—that's bad. A suntan won't help, neither will exercises in the morning, nor friendship with young people. Nothing at all will help.

(*Pause.*)

NIKA. Shall I leave?

NINA KONSTANTINOVNA. That's up to you. By the way, send Pyotr Alekseyevich to me.

(NIKA *leaves.* NINA KONSTANTINOVNA *sits, smokes. Enter* PYOTR.)

PYOTR. Why'd you take it into your head to embarrass the girl?

NINA KONSTANTINOVNA. The thought never entered my mind. I see you're looking for some diversion? Don't think that I'll be getting in your way.

PYOTR. Woman talk.

NINA KONSTANTINOVNA. Not at all. It's just that your attention isn't so important to me anymore.

PYOTR. Aaah, you're angry.

NINA KONSTANTINOVNA (*shrugging her shoulders*). Angry? As they say, what was once will never be again.

PYOTR (*pats her on the sides*). What was once is far gone, more like.

NINA KONSTANTINOVNA. You're really a jerk.

PYOTR (*laughs*). Nothing you can do—it's my working-class background.

NINA KONSTANTINOVNA. Ugh, Pyotr, don't play the peasant with me. Save it for work. I know your true colors.

PYOTR. Well, alright, alright...

NINA KONSTANTINOVNA. What were you talking about with Sergey?

PYOTR. We weren't able to get very far. Someone came and got in the way. Basically, he's decided to do some charity work here, Sergey has. He insists that I grant some lawyer an interview.

NINA KONSTANTINOVNA. A victim?

PYOTR (*ironically*). No, a victor. By the way, I recall the incident. I'm going to have to set Krasnoshchekov straight. And if I'm going to set him straight, I'll do it good and proper.

NINA KONSTANTINOVNA. Krasnoshchekov? From the Council of the Republic?

PYOTR. Exactly. Remember, at the Zernov's dacha, Nikita Vasilievich was telling us about him.

NINA KONSTANTINOVNA. He said he was a man with a future.

PYOTR. I've met him a few times. He's a damn snake. Watch out you don't put your fingers anywhere near his mouth.

NINA KONSTANTINOVNA. I'd also like for things between you and your son to smooth over.

PYOTR. You'd like.... Maybe I'd like that, too. He's already grown up, found his place, a crafty guy, if you ask me—everything could work out fine. (*Grumbles.*) Quarrels... dissension... I can't stand them. He's my son, understand... my very own.

NINA KONSTANTINOVNA. You're right, right. Frankly—this whole business is really poisoning my life.

PYOTR. Sure is.... You and I are good people, thank God. (*Hugs her.*) We take everything to heart. (*Touched.*) Here's how it is: I'd say I'm fairly tough, and my work doesn't encourage tenderness, but a soul never changes.

NINA KONSTANTINOVNA (*puts his head on her chest*). That's just why I fell in love with you, for your soul.... For everyone else you're Pyotr Kirpichov—tough, powerful, but for me you're....

PYOTR (*squeezes her tighter*). I know, Ninok, I know.... You're my safety-valve.... All these worries, all these worries—all around.... Did you hear that weirdo, Seryozha's friend, talking about the Shevtsova case.... Ugh, I left at a bad time!... (*Nervously silent for a while.*) You think it started from outside. But all around... your own colleagues... are stirring up trouble. (*Mournfully.*) For some people, a vacation is rest; for others, it's insomnia. I've put out the fires for now, but what it'll be like later—who can say? I tried to call Nikita—couldn't get him.... (*Pensively.*) And it's all on account of that Krasnoshchekov. He pointed it out himself, he himself came for support, and now go ahead, just poke him—he'll remember it all like this: "It was you," he'll say, "who were working with Shevtsova; it's none of my concern." Go ahead, pick a fight with him now.... Because of Sergey....

NINA KONSTANTINOVNA. You just think it over... think hard.... You're smart, you know life, people, you won't do anything stupid.

PYOTR. It's a tough thing—a position of responsibility. It has its own morals, its own code. You want to be kind, soft—but it won't let you, no. The state machinery—it's an orchestra, you know: You want to play, follow the baton. Fall into rhythm.

NINA KONSTANTINOVNA. That's very deep. Very. Here comes Sergey. I'll disappear, okay?

PYOTR. Go. Wait... give me your hand. (*Kisses her hand.*)

(NINA KONSTANTINOVNA *exits. Enter* SERGEY.)

SERGEY. You're here?

PYOTR (*in the same softened state*). I've been waiting for you, son. Every-one keeps getting in our way. (*Hugs him, presses him to his chest.*) Ahh, my eldest... my sorrow... sit down.

SERGEY (*hiding his agitation*). I'm sitting. Well, what do you say, Father?

PYOTR. The years are passing. Passing relentlessly. And look what an ea-gle you are now. Some people move up in the world, some just go down-hill.... Hmm...

SERGEY. You're in a poetic mood.

PYOTR. Melancholy, more like.

SERGEY. Don't sell yourself short.... You're the one who's moving up in the world.

PYOTR. Well, don't flatter me. We all walk under God.

SERGEY. You pin your hopes on God, but you don't slip up, either.

PYOTR. No one gets to slip up. They hold that against you, brother. (*Pauses.*) We haven't seen each other in a long time. That's your fault.

SERGEY. Perhaps it is.

PYOTR. Everything about you is different from other people. You weren't seventeen—and you ran out to the front. (*Edifyingly.*) You walk to the front, you don't run. I respect your impulse, I've carried a rifle myself, but all the same.... Now you're grown up. You know what I mean.

SERGEY. That's all in the past. And it's a little late for us to sort out who fought and who "carried a rifle."...

PYOTR. Seryozha! Even you can't say just anything.

SERGEY (*continuing*). You carried a rifle, but you preferred womanizing.

PYOTR. Seryozha! You're speaking with your father!

SERGEY. You said yourself—I'm grown up now. You can't always sidestep everything.

PYOTR. Well, yes, well, true—when it comes to your mother, I am guilty. Guilty... but just don't think that it was all so simple—maybe she her-self pushed me... to the decisive step.... Her nature.... Anyhow, what does it mean to judge, to remember... life... we don't just control it... it con-trols us too.... Nina Konstantinovna also... suffered through all that... she's a good, decent person... yes-s....

SERGEY. You know best.

PYOTR. Know best. Exactly. You just live with your grandfather. What can you say, he's Kirpichov. A great name. Well, just living with him around—you can grow callused. He's eccentric, unapproachable. To-day—did you hear? Why was he going on—about that... Grinin? Well, a fool is a fool. It's all plain to see.

SERGEY. I already said—I liked his story.

PYOTR. He's withdrawn from real, meaningful affairs, your grandfather. True enough, his name carries weight, a lot of weight—it's respected everywhere. But... how can I put this to you.... (*Searches for words, at last—confidingly.*) Your town is quiet, gardens, greenery.... The streets aren't all paved. You see, he—your grandfather—is a man of another time. Life goes on—new content, new forms, new relations.

SERGEY. Our goals are the same as in nineteen-seventeen, I would think?

PYOTR. Goals?... Who's talking about goals?... It's just that the country's not the same.... We ourselves are different....

SERGEY (*slowly, pensively*). Not only different, but also somehow the same....

PYOTR. "Somehow!"... Exactly, junior, "somehow!" There's a difference! I'll tell you, son...

SERGEY. You tell me this: Are you going to talk to Pokrovsky?

PYOTR. That Pokrovsky's become an obsession with you! You're fussing over him, but is he worth it? I know this case—it seems he's a swindler.

SERGEY (*thinks, then decisively*). No.

PYOTR (*weightily*). A swindler. They're all swindlers, those lawyers. I know a little bit better than you do. Unprincipled people.

SERGEY. Think what you're saying....

PYOTR. It's their profession, brother. For twenty years you defend all sorts of rabble....

SERGEY (*interrupts*). It's great how you lump them all together.

PYOTR. Well, if they're still young... our generation... that's different. But these are eagles of the old school....

SERGEY. Are you going to talk to Pokrovsky?

PYOTR. You're pushing it.

SERGEY. I want you to put an end to this ugly business, that's all. Let him in, hear him out, see for yourself. You're expecting a call from Moscow; so you can give the necessary instructions over the phone.

PYOTR. Thought out down to the last detail. You know what that's called, brother? Protectionism.

SERGEY. Don't try to scare me with words. I know a few of them myself. Answer me.

PYOTR. Looks like you've started shouting at me, eh, pal? Isn't it a little early for that?

SERGEY. I can be quiet. And leave.

PYOTR. Well, well, don't get all sore.... (*Hugs him, presses him to his chest.*) My formidable son.... Alright. I'll have a talk with this... character of yours. I'll take a look at him... but no guarantees. Understand?

SERGEY. He's here, Pokrovsky.

PYOTR. Here? For a long time?

SERGEY. No. He just barely arrived.... I'll call him. (*Goes.*)

PYOTR. Call him. (*Grins, slowly.*) You've set it all up so cleverly. (*Starts to smoke.*)

(SERGEY *returns with* POKROVSKY.)

SERGEY. Here is Mikhail Aleksandrovich Pokrovsky. Allow me to leave you two alone.

(PYOTR *shakes* POKROVSKY's *hand, sits down comfortably, nods.* SERGEY *leaves.*)

PYOTR. So, you're Pokrovsky?

POKROVSKY. Quite correct. Please forgive me, comrade Kirpichov, for disturbing you on vacation.... I did not expect to find you here. Everything has happened so unexpectedly.

PYOTR. Happened.... Hmm... yes-s.... You needn't tell me about your case, I've been reminded about it here.... And I have a rough idea of what's going on. Who have you seen?

POKROVSKY. I've seen comrade Krasnoshchekov.

PYOTR. You... uh... sit down. Take a load off your feet. Well, and what did Fyodor Ivanovich tell you?

POKROVSKY. He said that he didn't see any basis for changing the decision of the local authorities.

PYOTR. So-o... you evidently do perceive a basis?

POKROVSKY. I... that decision strikes me as... unjust.

PYOTR. Don't get upset. Speak calmly, clearly.

POKROVSKY. I'll try. You must know about the case of Ekaterina Shevtsova....

PYOTR. Shevtsova? I know about it. You tell me about yourself. Stick to the point.

POKROVSKY. Very well. So then... as I already wrote you, I had filled in for a sick colleague. I couldn't deal with my client at that time. The comrades have all the documentation—I can give it to you. And besides that, my principles... would never allow me.... (*Extends a folder to* PYOTR.)

PYOTR (*doesn't take the folder, gracefully*). You just calm down. Everything is in order. When a person has principles—that's just wonderful. (*Slowing down.*) Of course, the situation is complicated. You see, we've known Fyodor Ivanovich for quite some time and are somewhat inclined to trust him.

POKROVSKY. What do you mean.... It didn't even cross my mind to defame comrade Krasnoshchekov... I assume... he was misled....

PYOTR (*in the same lofty style*). Perhaps. Everything has to be sorted out. Sensibly, deliberately. So you're going to have to be nervous for a little while longer—nothing to be done for it. But we'll resolve your case fairly. If there were mistakes on our side—we'll correct the mistakes. Without fail.

POKROVSKY (*starts talking disjointedly*). Pyotr Alekseyevich, believe me, everything's happened so... I myself don't even understand. I'll be grateful to you.

PYOTR. Yes, yes, of course. I'll talk with Moscow—I'll tell them to prepare the materials for me.... Naturally, we'll write back. Leave your address with Sergey Petrovich. You know him, right?...

POKROVSKY. Yes, comrade Trubin introduced us.

PYOTR. Trubin? The journalist?

POKROVSKY. Quite correct.

PYOTR. I see. (*Pauses.*) Well then... it's settled. (*Stands up.*)

POKROVSKY. Is there any hope for me?

PYOTR. There is, there is. We'll straighten it out.

POKROVSKY. I won't take up any more of your time. All the best to you. The very best.

PYOTR. I thank you. Goodbye.

(POKROVSKY *leaves.*)

Trubin's in on this too. Entire organization.... (*Wipes his forehead with a handkerchief, slowly leaves.*)

(*Enter* SERGEY, *looks around, gestures to someone with his hand. Enter* VARVARA, TRUBIN, *and with them,* POKROVSKY.)

POKROVSKY. I'm terribly, terribly grateful to you....

TRUBIN (*impatiently*). That—can wait.... What did he tell you, though?

POKROVSKY. He spoke very courteously with me.

VARVARA. Did he refuse you or not?

POKROVSKY. What do you mean! He instructed me to leave my address with Sergey Petrovich—he said they'll write me....

TRUBIN (*grumbling*). "They'll write back"... "he instructed."... He didn't instruct anything else?

SERGEY. Pasha, wait a minute.... Did you talk about Krasnoshchekov?

POKROVSKY. We did... naturally.

SERGEY. And what did he say?

POKROVSKY. Wel-ll... Pyotr Alekseyevich said that he has known comrade Krasnoshchekov for quite some time and that he's inclined to trust him.

VARVARA. Inclined.... And inclining his head slightly, he let him know he was free to leave.

TRUBIN. Who are you talking to?

VARVARA. I'm making a poem. From the life of kings.

POKROVSKY. But, as I understand it, Pyotr Alekseyevich admits the possibility that Krasnoshchekov has been misled. (*Gestures with his hand.*) I rambled horribly... not at all the way I should have talked.... If I acted that way in court, I would really have to be thrown out of the bar on my ear. But basically, he told me that there is definitely hope for me. (*Laughs joyfully.*) With your permission—I'll leave. I'm going to go cheer up my wife. She must be worried. I've been on the run since morning, you know.... What's more, they go to bed early there.... I don't want to disturb people. (*Goes, then returns, shakes everyone's hand.*) Thank you. (*Quickly leaves.*)

TRUBIN (*after a pause*). The way I see it, there's no basis for joy.

SERGEY. Why?! He promised, after all.

TRUBIN. He didn't promise a damn thing. It's all a put-on. A gesture. "We'll straighten it out." "We'll write you."... What are we going to straighten out? It's all plain to see.

SERGEY. Pavel, he's an official. He can't answer any other way.

TRUBIN. It's not the form that matters.

SERGEY. No, it's not. It's your prejudice. I'm not blind, after all—I've noticed.

VARVARA. Seryozha! You're talking nonsense!

TRUBIN. No. He's right. I am biased. I have reasons.

SERGEY. But I don't. And I don't understand why I should let you think for me!

VARVARA. Sergey, be quiet!

SERGEY. You hear, I don't un-der-stand!

TRUBIN. Don't shout. There's a lot you don't understand.

SERGEY. Possibly. But you're no oracle either, just a member of the journalists' union, as far as I know. (*In a fit of temper.*) Ugh, you all have that way of judging everything on the fly.

TRUBIN. "You all"? Who?

SERGEY. You—newspaper men. I know that somewhere in your souls you're all a little cynical. You are too... I can tell... yes, yes!

TRUBIN. That I'm a cynical will have to be proved. That you're a fool is beyond doubt. Go take a shower.

SERGEY. You give me a cold shower every five minutes. I'm sick of it. (*Runs out.*)

TRUBIN. The little crank! He's angry that I can't tell him anything good about his father.

SERGEY (*returns*). Listen. I'll bring my father here, and we'll have it out. Bring everything into the open.

TRUBIN (*takes him by the shoulder*). For now, don't go anywhere. Sit down. Teacher.... Not an ounce of self-restraint. Well, what do you have to say now? You'll shout a bunch of slogans—that's it. Sit down, I said. Let's think.

SERGEY. About what?

TRUBIN. There's plenty to think about. About the fact that your daddy doesn't want to quarrel with Krasnoshchekov. About why this Krasnoshchekov is so "irresistible." Who this lawyer is who got sick at such a bad—or good—time. Why were they so anxious to settle with an experienced defense attorney who was supposedly grasping at straws? As you see, there's a broad field for your analysis.

SERGEY. A whole curriculum...

TRUBIN (*pensively*). You certainly won't answer all the questions sitting here.

SERGEY (*slowly*). Maybe you're right. And maybe not. I don't feel like agreeing with you. (*Slowing.*) Anyway, I'm going. Not to my father, don't worry. I just feel like being alone....

TRUBIN. Nothing wrong with that. I'm about to get going myself. Look how dark it's gotten. Another half-hour and I won't find the road back.

SERGEY. You'll find it. Somehow. (*Leaves.*)

VARVARA (*after a silence*). Still, you're right....

TRUBIN. Unfortunately.

VARVARA. Pokrovsky was just glowing.... He bolted to his wife... to cheer her up.

TRUBIN. He was very tired. And most of all from the bad news. It's hard to take that in big doses.

VARVARA. Ye-ess.... Tomorrow he'll have a much more sober impression of the conversation.... (*Pensively.*) And Seryozha also... has illusions.

(*Someone in the house can be heard banging on the keyboard.*)

Tyoma's banging away.... (*Falls silent.*) Are you going to stay around this area much longer?

TRUBIN. No. The Temple of Science is ready to open. I've already spoken with the architect. All that's left is the ribbon-cutting. The teachers will wait around for September, but I'm going to go hand in some stuff.

VARVARA (*suddenly*). I'm also leaving. In the near future.

TRUBIN (*surprised*). I thought you just got here a few days ago....

VARVARA. That's God's honest truth.

TRUBIN. What's up?

VARVARA. What's up is that in this house, which I love more than anything in the world, in which my father lives—I love him more than anything else in the world, too—it's become hard for me to breathe in this house. That's what's up. (*Pauses.*) Do you hear me, Trubin?

TRUBIN. I hear you.

VARVARA (*grumbling*). Sat down in the shadow... can't see him, and he doesn't say a word. If you hear me, why aren't you saying anything?

TRUBIN. I'm thinking

VARVARA. Thinking? What a big-shot. So what is it you're thinking about?

TRUBIN. How unfamiliar you, such a jovial person, seem when you're so angry....

VARVARA. Unfamiliar.... And when did you get the chance to become familiar with me? In two days? I'm not all that cheerful.... (*Pauses.*) And what, you don't understand why I'm angry?

TRUBIN. I understand.

VARVARA. Thank God. So you won't interrogate me.

(*A short pause.*)

TRUBIN. I won't interrogate you, but let me ask you something.

VARVARA. Well, what now?

TRUBIN. I wanted to ask Sergey about this, but just now I changed my mind. Better to go straight to the source.... Are you married?

VARVARA. I'm a widow. Is that it?

TRUBIN. That's it.

VARVARA. Well, there you have it, short and easy to understand.

TRUBIN. Short, but hard to understand.

VARVARA (*querulously*). What's hard to understand?

TRUBIN. It's hard to understand why they've left you a widow.

VARVARA. I see you also think that it's only men who choose. A common misconception.

TRUBIN. I just don't see where else they'd look.

VARVARA. They're looking... don't trouble yourself on their account. Back there in my county seat, two men follow me around and whimper and yelp. They're waiting for me to drive them away.

TRUBIN. That's a gloomy way of looking at it.

VARVARA. I had a husband, a wonderful husband. We got married when we were sophomores, though everyone advised us to wait. He was the greatest guy, the greatest athlete, the greatest person. He was killed in Berlin. And now more than five years have passed, the pain has passed, and if I live alone, it's precisely because I know how good it can be to live as a couple.

TRUBIN. You really aren't all that jolly.

VARVARA (*grins*). No, dearest Pal Palych, I love humanity, I love my work, but my life, like the majority of people's, isn't a smooth road; it's not a ball; it's not a resort. (*Falls silent.*) I work in a big factory, but not a well-known one. Our manager is a procrastinator, which, by the way, is a source of conflict between us. Fires, thunder, lightening, and other natural disasters set in at the end of each month. Everyone yells at each other, and he yells at everyone. Furthermore, since he sometimes forgets that the person he's talking to isn't the only one who can hear him over the intercom, he usually tells him, to everyone's delight, where he can go, how to get there, and what he can do along the way....

TRUBIN (*as if evaluating; satisfied*). Not bad.

VARVARA. And when I come home, completely exhausted, *I* straighten up the room, *I* run to the store, *I* cook dinner, and some despondent citizen appears for dessert and complains about being lonely—oh, how I'd like to tell *him* where he can go, how to get there, and what he can do along the way.

TRUBIN. Well, I'll be damned... it's a legitimate wish.

VARVARA (*more to herself than to her interlocutor*). I have a friend. She's a little, energetic woman with a tender soul. She has three children; her husband also died. We see each other rarely; she's always busy. Well, she never whines. You know, Pal Palych, I've never heard my friends—and I have quite a few of them—complain about having to work a lot.

TRUBIN (*thinking about his own friends*). Never.

VARVARA. And so it's always seemed to me that in the kind of life where the main thing isn't your work but your position, not your accomplishment but your consumption; in the uninspired, dull, self-satisfied life so different from the one that I and millions like me live—there's something foreign and insulting. (*Pauses.*) That's why I feel like running away from my childhood home.

TRUBIN. But how will your running away be interpreted?

VARVARA. My father will understand.... It's not envy, oh no. This will sound ridiculous, but, if you like, it's something like the anger of the Sans-Culottes. Go ahead and laugh! I'm glad that I've amused you! (*Abruptly.*) And where did this high society come from?

(*The sound of a cheerful melody wafts from the house.*)

TRUBIN. Where from? (*Shrugs his shoulders.*) From vulgarity, greed, aggression. From their bankruptcy and our patient patience. When you give a lot to someone you can't expect much from, these kinds of metamorphoses occur.

(*Pause.*)

VARVARA (*softly*). Pavel Pavlovich, when did you join the party?

TRUBIN. On Lake Khasan.

VARVARA (*slowly*). Fifteen years gone by.... We were young then....

TRUBIN (*with a smile*). You especially.... (*Rises.*) Goodbye.

VARVARA. You're going? Already?

TRUBIN. It's time.

VARVARA. Well, all right....

(*For an instant they stand silently facing each other.* TRUBIN *looks at her attentively, then decisively takes her head in his hands and kisses her. Pause. He wants to say something, but she puts her finger to her lips.*)

Go....

(TRUBIN *kisses her hand, leaves. Enter* PYOTR, *humming the melody that he has just heard.*)

PYOTR. Who's here? Is that you, sister? (*Follows* TRUBIN *with his eyes.*)

And is that the journalist who just left? You were having a conversation, were you?

VARVARA. We were.

PYOTR. And I scared him off.... (*Laughs.*) Nothing to be done for it—older brother. I'm on guard duty.

VARVARA. You're our guardian... of order and justice.

PYOTR. That's true. True—from every angle. (*Lazily.*) You be careful with that paperboy. I don't like him.

VARVARA. Why so uncharitable?

PYOTR. He's a puppeteer, as far as I'm concerned. He hides behind a screen, starts up with the strings, and the puppets jump. (*Gloomily.*) Take Seryozha... he's dancing for him. (*Short pause.*) Listen, Varya...

VARVARA. What?

PYOTR (*preoccupied*). Here's the thing.... He, this Trubin, sends me... all sorts of petitioners. Well, they never let me rest—I'm used to that, but I'm afraid he might start sending them to our father. You keep an eye out. (*Catches her suspicious glance.*) The old man is sick. We have to protect him. Both from journalists and from these twits.

VARVARA. These people, don't you mean?

PYOTR (*displeased*). The devil can sort out that riffraff. He's a scoundrel, that much is clear. (*Wants to smoke.*)

VARVARA. Go away!

PYOTR. What—have you gone out of your mind?

VARVARA. You don't want to? Then I'll go. I'm leaving. Just so I don't have to see you.

PYOTR (*stunned, can't find words*). Wel-ll.... Wel-ll.... You're the one who.... It's you who.... (*Raises his voice.*) Who do you think you're talking to, eh? (*Walks onto the terrace, stops, shouts.*) Don't you dare show your face around me! (*Leaves.*)

VARVARA (*tries to smile*). Brother, my brother.... Ahh, if I only had something heavy in my hand.

(*Enter* ALEKSEY PETROVICH *quickly.*)

ALEKSEY PETROVICH. Varvara, what happened here?

VARVARA. A little family fireside chat.

ALEKSEY PETROVICH (*strictly*). Varya!

VARVARA. You know, it's like Dickens: "It was the best of times, it was the worst of times."

ALEKSEY PETROVICH. Varya, what was going on here?

VARVARA. There's one thing that was and is going on. You have a worthless son, and I have the same for a brother. He's about as much like you and everyone you love as a monkey is like a person. Today a wronged man came to him for defense and justice and, to put it plainly, he sent him away with nothing.

ALEKSEY PETROVICH. Hold on... one thing at a time....

VARVARA (*after a pause*). I see that it's painful for you to hear this. I'll keep quiet.

ALEKSEY PETROVICH. Keep quiet? You've already said it all. And why keep quiet? I'd heard it before, too.... Heard a lot.... (*Softly.*) It's hard to believe. (*Pauses. Pensively.*) August is coming up. My month. One year older.... (*Wants to go.*)

VARVARA (*in fits and starts*). Stay a minute.... I told him I would leave here, so I wouldn't have to see him. I'm not going to do that. I'll stay; I want to be with you.... I'm staying.

ALEKSEY PETROVICH. You think I'd let you go? And if I had to choose, don't you think I'd be able to? Silly daughter.... (*Turns, leaves.*)

VARVARA. Papa... I know. (*Quietly.*) My amazing father.

(VERA NIKOLAYEVNA *appears.*)

VERA NIKOLAYEVNA. Something's not right with your father. He passed me looking darker than night.

(*Enter* ALEKSEY PETROVICH *once again.*)

ALEKSEY PETROVICH. Varya. I want to see that man who came to see Pyotr.

VARVARA. You stay calm. Everything will work out.

ALEKSEY PETROVICH (*firmly*). Varya, you bring him to me. (*Leaves.*)

VERA NIKOLAYEVNA. He worries me. Sleeps poorly, eats poorly. He had a seizure today. Things aren't right at home.

VARVARA. Aren't right... that's true. But it won't be that way for long—I'll see to that.

VERA NIKOLAYEVNA. I was worried about Seryozha, but I should have been worried about you....

VARVARA. Mommy, the main thing is: Believe me. Always and in everything.

VERA NIKOLAYEVNA (*hugs her, cuddles*). Oh Varya, Varya...

VARVARA. You're so wise....

(*Long pause.*)

VOICE OF PYOTR. Momma!

VARVARA. You're being called... by your guests.

VERA NIKOLAYEVNA. I need to go....

VOICE OF PYOTR. Momma!

VARVARA. Go. Back there they aren't used to waiting.

VERA NIKOLAYEVNA (*stops; severely*). Varvara, you promise me to get ahold of yourself. (*Leaves.*)

VARVARA. "Get ahold of yourself."... (*Grumbles.*) Get ahold of yourself, or we'll get ahold of you. Oh, I'll be damned, as a certain journalist says....

(*Enter* NIKA, *behind her* TYOMA. VARVARA *opens the wicker gate, goes outside.*)

TYOMA. Nik, hang on.... Where you going?

NIKA. My head hurts.

TYOMA. Just wait.... That's a crock. I spend less time alone with you here than in Moscow. And it's as boring as a museum. What's up with you?

NIKA. Just—a bad mood.

TYOMA. Just—a bad personality.

NIKA. Maybe.

TYOMA. My old man has his quirks, alright. He suddenly gets a bright idea—let's go visit your grandfather! The best trip in the world. Well, what's so fun? I learned about the era of War Communism back in school.

NIKA. Be quiet. It's not funny at all, what you're saying.

TYOMA (*angered*). Too rude for little musical ears?

NIKA. And now you're trying to be cute. That's not funny either.

TYOMA. No, you're getting impossible. Of course, you've come into your own here, but you showed signs even before. The night before we left a bunch of us got together in a cocktail lounge. We had a stag party, and when Zhenya Myasnikov, you know, the son of that....

NIKA. I know.

TYOMA. When he found out that we were going together, he raised a wall-banger—an excellent liquid, by the way—and said: "Milords, let's drink to poor Artemya, who's rushing into the jaws of the tigress." And everyone drank with tears in his eyes. As you can see, no one's fooled by you.

NIKA. So you triumphantly announced that I was going with you?

TYOMA. For Chrissake, it was among friends. By the way—smile, Madonna—Valya Kuroyedov was insanely jealous of me. The poor guy was planning to give himself over to car racing, too, but his parents thought the little pup needed to take a breather.

NIKA. Why were you in such a hurry to blab to everyone that I was going with you? Answer!...

TYOMA. Listen, this is stupid. (*Grins.*) The poor girl was proud....

NIKA (*stunned*). What?

TYOMA. When it comes down to it, what's the big deal? Is it supposed to be a secret? And are we going to get married in secret, too? Like they do in novels?

NIKA. Not in secret, not in the open. Never.... (*Quickly exits into the depths of the garden.*)

TYOMA (*perplexed*). Nika.... You're crazy!... How come?... (*Shrugs his shoulders, gestures with his hand.*) She hasn't been herself all day long.

(*Enter* PYOTR KIRPICHOV *and* NINA KONSTANTINOVNA.)

PYOTR. What's on your mind, young man? (*Slaps him on the shoulder.*) He's really gotten some color these last few days, though, hasn't he, Ninok?

NINA KONSTANTINOVNA. He looks great. No wonder the girls love him.

TYOMA. They're head over heels. What's going on here with Nika is beyond me.

PYOTR. Show a little self-control. A man has to have composure. That's a woman's business—getting mad. (*Laughs, pats his wife.*)

NINA KONSTANTINOVNA. Well, don't be in such a hurry to enlighten him....

PYOTR. Enlighten *him*? Teach the teacher. (*With one arm hugs his son, with the other, his wife.*) It's good to be with your own family. My dearest, my own people. (*Slowly.*) But we probably won't stay around here too long, eh, folks? We'll visit a little longer, and then saddle up.

TYOMA. Now you're talking, old man! Even Nika's starting to go mad here. No, you've got the right idea.

PYOTR. Well, thanks for admitting it. Oh you... Kirpichov Junior.... To tell the truth, you're not a Kirpichov yet, but a little Chirper.

NINA KONSTANTINOVNA. There was a song once, "Little Chirper."

PYOTR. There are a lot of songs in the world. You'll never sing all of them, though you'd like to. You need a big voice for that. Save your voice, son.

NINA KONSTANTINOVNA. Well, that's—obscure....

PYOTR. Never mind, he'll understand. He's a Little Chirper....

(*The gate opens silently, enter* VARVARA; *they do not notice her.*)

TYOMA (*laughing*). Flattery will get you nowhere. Am I going to get some wheels?

PYOTR. Oh you.... (*Also laughing.*) He wants to get married, and he's begging for toys.

TYOMA. So what, am I supposed to spend my whole life hanging on Nikolai's every word? Waiting for him to get in a good mood?

PYOTR. Knock it off, don't snivel. You'll have those wheels; you'll have a horn, too. You need to be reined in, Tyomka. You come by everything too easily.

TYOMA (*impatiently*). The rearing process begins....

PYOTR (*a little angry*). You listen when you're spoken to. You know how to *spend*.....

NINA KONSTANTINOVNA. We're pouring so much down the drain. It's crazy.... This trip's already cost us...

(PYOTR *pensively nods his head in agreement.*)

NINA KONSTANTINOVNA. And, as they say, everything still lies before us.

PYOTR (*spreading his hands*). What can you do? We came to my parents' place. I just wouldn't feel right coming empty-handed....

NINA KONSTANTINOVNA (*irritated*). You're just a big spender by nature... And the expenses we have coming up....

PYOTR. Go ahead and scold, it does me good. (*Puts his hand on her shoulder, decisively.*) We'll cut back, we'll cut down—I promise. (*Hugs his wife and son.*) Let's go home, folks.

(*All three exit.*)

VARVARA (*glancing after them*). Lord, how I hate the bourgeois....

(*Curtain.*)

ACT 3

Night. There is light in only one of the windows. Music, barely audible, carries from somewhere in the distance. NINA KONSTANTINOVNA, *in a nightgown, stands, leaning on the terrace fence, with her hand behind her head.* PYOTR *enters in pajamas, with slippers on his bare feet.*

PYOTR. How come you're up? I opened my eyes, and the bed was empty....

NINA KONSTANTINOVNA. For some reason I just can't sleep.... I don't know why....

PYOTR. You're talking just like a little girl.

NINA KONSTANTINOVNA. Lay off.... You're speaking in that style again.... Why do you need it... with me? (*Nestles up to him.*) It's quiet.... I don't feel quite right somehow.... What happened with you and your sister?

PYOTR. No big deal. She's all grown up, but she's still such a... flake. I put her in her place, though.

(*Pause.*)

NINA KONSTANTINOVNA. Petya, let's leave.

PYOTR. They'll be offended.

NINA KONSTANTINOVNA. Another day gone by, and we're still just as awkward and uncomfortable. The people here aren't friendly. You know, I wanted this reunion myself, but why fool ourselves—it hasn't come off....

PYOTR (*sullenly*). There's a light in my father's window.

NINA KONSTANTINOVNA. Nika's... acting strange somehow... agitated about something.... Tyoma's nervous....

PYOTR. Hang on. I'm expecting a call from Moscow. Zernov should be calling. Then I'll say that I've been ordered back.

NINA KONSTANTINOVNA. That sounds great, honey.

PYOTR. The main thing is, we have to part on good terms. (*Pensively.*) There's not much good in ruining our relations with my father, Ninok.

NINA KONSTANTINOVNA. Yes, yes, I understand....

PYOTR. Don't pretend to agree. You can't understand this. You need to understand my father. You think this is a quiet old man living out his life?

Like Diocletian on the farm? I've been with him for three days, and I can see already—he's the same as ever.

NINA KONSTANTINOVNA. Well, yes.... You didn't have to interrupt me. I really respect Aleksey Petrovich....

PYOTR (*impatiently*). Ugh.... That's not what I mean.

(*Pause.*)

NINA KONSTANTINOVNA (*warily*). Zernov's going to talk business with you? It has to do with that... Ptitsyn... right?

PYOTR. Well, yes.... (*With irony.*) Trubin's pal. (*Knitting his brow.*) You know, anything could happen there.

NINA KONSTANTINOVNA (*warily*). But listen, Petya, in this business with that... Shevtsova, you acted fairly... and reasonably....

PYOTR (*interrupting her*). Acted.... (*Gets angry.*) Silly.... The local authorities acted... I—expressed my opinion.... (*Slowing slightly.*) Who knows, maybe there *were*... infractions... something you could latch onto. That's how Ptitsyns exist. They and their dear colleagues. (*Bitterly.*) But, basically, what can you say?... It seems like you trust someone, tried and true, you think you can rely on him, and then... Krasnoshchekov, too.... Ugh.... (*Spreads his hands.*)

NINA KONSTANTINOVNA. Yes, honey, yes.... You always see things... through rose-colored glasses.

(PYOTR *nods affirmatively.*)

How stressful our life is, though. (*Nestles closer to him.*) But everything will be okay—won't it, Petya?

PYOTR (*weightily*). Things will turn out alright. We're a tough people. Bathed in lye.

NINA KONSTANTINOVNA. You just be smart, honey. Remember, you read to me once: Being smart doesn't mean not making mistakes; it means admitting them.

PYOTR. Correcting them....

NINA KONSTANTINOVNA. Well, yes.... Admitting—correcting. Isn't it the same thing?

PYOTR (*smiles*). How can I put it?...

NINA KONSTANTINOVNA. How wonderful life could be if people didn't complicate it.

PYOTR. It's you who oversimplify....

NINA KONSTANTINOVNA. Yes, yes! That's just what I say: simpler, simpler! We women know a thing or two ourselves....

PYOTR. No one's arguing with that....

NINA KONSTANTINOVNA. Don't laugh. That's why I'm so uneasy.... (*Tired.*) Who do I have, besides you....

PYOTR. Let's go to sleep, honey. Everything will be alright. (*Pensively.*) I'd like to know why my old man isn't going to bed. (*Indecisively.*) Should I drop in on him? (*Spreads his hands.*) I'll see things better in the morning.

(PYOTR *and* NINA KONSTANTINOVNA *exit into the rooms. The gate creaks.* VARVARA *and* TRUBIN *appear.*)

VARVARA (*listens for a while to the melody which wafts in again*). Quiet. Everyone's sleeping.

TRUBIN. Not everyone.

VARVARA. The prodigal daughter's not sleeping. But she's not the only one. There's a light on in my father's room.

TRUBIN. Well, then—is it time to part?

VARVARA. It is, it is. This day has tired both of us out.

TRUBIN. I haven't even thought of getting tired.

VARVARA. You and I have walked around the whole city. Every back alley and street corner. To top it all off, at night you dragged me to the telephone exchange. No Juliet would accompany Romeo on his inter-city negotiations....

TRUBIN. Romeo's received permission from his office to go to Voronezh.

VARVARA. I heard. And why do you need Ptitsyn so urgently? What would be the difference if you hadn't called him today?

TRUBIN. I wouldn't know something, he wouldn't know something.

VARVARA. At sixteen I really loved mysterious men. Too bad I'm not sixteen.

TRUBIN. Not bad at all. If you were sixteen, I definitely wouldn't know what to do with you.

VARVARA. Esteemed sir, you're starting to babble. Go to sleep.

TRUBIN. I don't want to sleep.

VARVARA. Well, I want to. I didn't get enough sleep last night. Early in the morning a bouquet of flowers flew in my window, knocked a pitcher of water over, and whisked the mirror off the table. I'd like to know whose skillful hand flung them?

TRUBIN. Actually, it would be nice to know who the ace was. Some people are just masters. Ha-ha!

VARVARA. Some are. And I think I know that discus-thrower. And you do too. Ha-ha.

TRUBIN (*sadly*). How well it's described in books: "He greeted her as she woke with an armful of fragrant, fresh flowers. She delightedly buried her face in the moist petals...."

VARVARA. There was plenty of moisture alright. Especially when the water spilled.

TRUBIN. Now it's all destroyed. With my own hands I shattered...

VARVARA. My mirror. Nothing more. (*Strokes his head with her hand.*) Cheer up. As an idea, it was splendid.

TRUBIN (*accompanying every adjective with a kiss*). My sweet, kind, forgiving...

VARVARA. Too many virtues for one engineer. Let's talk about you instead.

TRUBIN. Me? I'll be damned. (*Hugs her.*)

VARVARA (*not removing his hand*). I'm just warning you, someone's coming.

TRUBIN. Why doesn't anyone in this house stay put?

VARVARA. Go away. Quick. Goodnight.

TRUBIN. No, this night won't be good. It can't be. (*Disappears.*)

(NIKA *comes downstairs.*)

NIKA. Varvara Alekseyevna...

VARVARA. Nika? You're not asleep yet?

NIKA. I was waiting for you.

VARVARA. What happened?

NIKA. I don't have anyone to talk to. You're probably not in the mood to talk to me....

VARVARA (*shakes her by the shoulders*). Calm down and talk.

NIKA. We're getting ready to leave....

VARVARA. Really? (*Slowing slightly.*) And?

NIKA. I... don't feel like... going with them....

VARVARA. Don't *feel* like it? Then why did you come?

NIKA (*harshly*). I'm stupid. Is that a good enough answer?

VARVARA (*shrugs her shoulders, somewhat dryly*). No one is safe from her own stupidity. Anyway, go to the station, get a ticket, and get on the train. It's not as fancy as a car, but it will save you from your traveling companions.

NIKA (*blushes*). But I... don't have enough money for a ticket.... I didn't know it would turn out like this, and...

VARVARA. Hang on.... I understand. If you had foreseen, you would have turned to your slush fund. I'd like to know what your parents think about all this.

NIKA. I just have a mother.

VARVARA (*her eyes warm up*). Ah, I see.... What does she do?

NIKA. She works... in a government office....

VARVARA (*puts her hand on NIKA's shoulder*). Your father—was killed?

NIKA. Back in forty-one.

(*Pause.*)

VARVARA. May I speak informally with you?

NIKA. Of course.

VARVARA. Is it just you and your mother?

NIKA. I have two sisters. They're still in school. (*With an unhappy smile.*) You thought I was an only child?

VARVARA. Yes, I did.

(*Pause.*)

NIKA. I was so happy when Pyotr Alekseyevich and Tyoma invited me. I sewed myself a dress. (*Decisively.*) I won't go with them. I'll go on foot.

VARVARA. Nonsense. We'll find the money. Leave quietly, without explaining. You're a student at the conservatory?

NIKA. Yes. Do you think I'm wasting my time?

VARVARA. No. On the contrary. (*Takes* NIKA'*s head in her arms.*) You have an excellent voice. It will bring people a lot of joy, and for that joy they'll repay you lavishly. But even when you're rich and famous, remember this summer. Enough. Go to sleep.

NIKA. I won't be able to. (*Exits.*)

VARVARA (*pensively*). A sweet, beautiful life.

(*She glances around. Behind her stands* TRUBIN.)

You haven't left?

TRUBIN. I couldn't.

VARVARA. It must be close to two o'clock.

TRUBIN. Almost. Two thirty.

VARVARA. Have you lost your mind?

TRUBIN. I have.

VARVARA. I thought I could count on you. Typical mistake for women.

(VERA NIKOLAYEVNA *appears on the terrace.*)

VERA NIKOLAYEVNA. Is someone here?

(TRUBIN *sits down on the bench. He's not visible from above.*)

VARVARA. It's me, Mom.

VERA NIKOLAYEVNA. You've been away for a long time.

VARVARA (*hugs her*). I just came.... You couldn't sleep because of me? I'm sorry....

VERA NIKOLAYEVNA. Be still... see? (*Pointing at a light in the window.*) He's still with him.

VARVARA. What? For all this time?

VERA NIKOLAYEVNA. They've been sitting for over four hours. Your father said not to disturb them.

VARVARA. Does Pyotr know?

VERA NIKOLAYEVNA. No. They've already gone to sleep.

VARVARA. Let's go to my room. You're barely standing. Your vacation hasn't gone well this year. I'm also to blame for that.

VERA NIKOLAYEVNA. Stop babbling. Go to bed. I still have a lot to do. (*She walks.*)

VARVARA. To do? At two-thirty in the morning?

VERA NIKOLAYEVNA (*not right away*). Pyotr wanted to talk with your father. But your father said he was sick.

VARVARA (*softly*). Father hasn't been feeling well lately.

VERA NIKOLAYEVNA. True. But when you live your whole life with someone, you can read him by the look on his face. Nothing good will come of this. (*She exits.*)

TRUBIN (*walks up to* VARVARA). You're staring at nothing.

VARVARA (*not right away*). I don't think this night will be good either.

(SERGEY *appears on the terrace. He walks and whistles. Forces himself to sit down, then gets right back up again.*)

Look... Seryozha.... (*Rocks her head in surprise.*) No one's asleep.

TRUBIN. Sit here.

(*Seats* VARVARA *on the bench; she wants to say something—putting his finger to his lips in warning, he walks up to the terrace.*)

Hey!

SERGEY. Who's there?

TRUBIN. Night watchman.

SERGEY. Where from?

TRUBIN. From the telephone exchange. Answering your call. How come you're up?

SERGEY. I can't sleep. Did you speak with Moscow?

TRUBIN. Yes. Tomorrow I'm going to Voronezh. The office has given its blessing.

SERGEY. Really?

TRUBIN. I talked to Ptitsyn, too....

SERGEY. Any news?

TRUBIN. Apparently there will be.

SERGEY. Did you tell him about our project?

TRUBIN (*with a smile*). The call was timely and to the point.

SERGEY (*shakes his hand*). Thank you for coming.

TRUBIN (*glancing around*). No problem. Everything alright with you guys?

SERGEY. Tyoma's all upset. He couldn't find anyone to play cards with.

TRUBIN. Baloney. Young people like him play poker and bridge strictly for self-assurance. It elevates them in their own eyes. (*Listens.*) Someone's walking around....

SERGEY. Grandma can't sleep. (*Quietly.*) Neither can Grampa. See that light?

(*Short pause.*)

I brought Pokrovsky to him. (*Falls silent.*) What do you think, what's he talking about for so long?

TRUBIN. He knows how to listen as well as talk.

(*Sharp, intermittent telephone ringing.* VERA NIKOLAYEVNA *appears on the terrace.* TRUBIN *backs off to his old spot.*)

VERA NIKOLAYEVNA (*grabs the receiver, softly, afraid of waking the sleepers*). Yes? That's right. Yes, the Kirpichovs. Is this Moscow calling? (*After a short silence.*) Please, don't worry about it. Pyotr Alekseyevich? Just a minute.

(SERGEY *backs off to the side.*)

Seryozha...

(SERGEY *does not answer.*)

Where'd he go? I'll just do it myself.... (*Exits into the room.*)

SERGEY. Pavel?... Are you here? There's a call from Moscow for my father....

(TRUBIN *wants to answer, but* PYOTR KIRPICHOV's *cough is already heard in the room, and* VARVARA *holds her finger up to her lips.*)

VARVARA (*quietly*). Not a sound.

(*Enter the sleepy, disheveled* PYOTR. *He's still in pajamas and slippers.* SERGEY *steps back into the corner, where he can't be seen.*)

PYOTR (*takes the receiver, somewhat abruptly, curtly*). Yes! Nikita Vasilievich? Hi. Thanks. I'm enjoying my vacation. Family? Thank you, they're alive and well. So then, give me your report from the battlefield. (*Listens.*) Hang on. That's for later.... Tell me this: What have you heard about... you know what?... (*Listens.*) Ptitsyn and his crowd—aren't mixed up in it? And at the Supreme Soviet? For now—calm? Rotten saying, "for now." Wel-ll keep an eye on it.... So, what's the good news? What—Krasnoshchekov? Wait, wait, slow down.... (*Gets up.*) They're transferring—Krasnoshchekov? From the regional level—to us? Who? You just forget.... What do you mean—are you sure? I understand they're rumors, but there are rumors and there are rumors, after all. Check it out thoroughly. Way to go, Fyodor Ivanovich!... I remember, I remember—you told me. It does honor to your sniffer. What? I say it does honor to your nose. Exactly... you finally sniffed it out.... (*Laughs.*) What? The usual orders—be vigilant! (*Remembers, hurriedly.*) Yes, Nikita Vasilievich... we've got ourselves a complaint... from these Voronezh lawyers. Uh... Pokrovsky and sons.... (*Laughs.*) You finish this off but good. Once and for all. That's the only way. (*Listens to his interlocutor.*) If you sit around flapping your lips, you're just spitting into the wind, I agree with you completely.

VARVARA (*stands up, softly*). Pavel Pavlovich, you have to go.

TRUBIN. And you also—have to. Together with me.

VARVARA. Not at all—I have to stay.

TRUBIN. We'll return later. (*Softly.*) Sergey's here. He's got a right to have a talk with his father. Let's go.

VARVARA (*slowing down*). I won't go far.

(*The gate opens.* VARVARA *and* TRUBIN *exit.*)

PYOTR (*hearing his interlocutor out*). Well, alright, Nikita. We'll see each other soon. Say hi to Anna Kondratievna. From me and Nina Konstantinovna. Thank you, I'll pass it on. Oh yeah... if you see Krasnoshchekov, give him my regards.... Warm congrats and all that.... Well, you know

yourself.... Okay. Take care. (*Lowers the receiver, frowns.*) Bringing Krasnoshchekov... to us... go-getter. Hmm.... (*Hangs up the phone.*)

(*Toward him walks* SERGEY.)

Seryozha, is it you? You know what—your dad's been called to
Moscow.... At our level, you never get a moment to yourself. But how
come you're not sleeping at night? Sleep while you can, silly, before you
get to be the boss.... (*Laughs.*)

(SERGEY *is silent.*)

What are you so serious for? You're not in love, are you? People in love...
don't sleep. Well, fess up.... A father has to know everything.... (*Walks up
to him, wants to take his head in his hands.*)

SERGEY. Don't come any closer. I'll hit you.

PYOTR. Wha-at? Who do you think you're talking to? Who, you little
whelp!...

SERGEY (*shoving him aside*). I've been here since the start of your... conversation.

(*A short pause.*)

PYOTR. You were eavesdropping? Is that right? Spying on your father?
Who ordered you to do that? Answer!

SERGEY. Ordered? I've been waiting for that call. I was afraid I'd miss it. I
was still hoping...

PYOTR. Hoping? That I'd intercede?

SERGEY. Hoping. In case you were actually... human....

PYOTR. Stop it!...

SERGEY. I was just fooling myself. I didn't believe you and still don't. I
don't believe a single word of yours.

PYOTR. Stop it, I'm telling you. I'm not going to wallow around in your
psychology. I'm holding you accountable.

SERGEY. I don't believe your anger, your indignation, your peasant-
worker accent. It's a game! I only believe in your spite.

PYOTR (*stunned*). Wretch....

SERGEY. If only Grandfather had heard your conversation. If he had heard...

(ALEKSEY PETROVICH *appears*.)

ALEKSEY PETROVICH. I heard.

PYOTR. Father?... You're here.... Just look at your grandson....

ALEKSEY PETROVICH. No, I'm going to look at my son. Some... son you are. My son...

PYOTR. Ugh.... What a spectacle.

ALEKSEY PETROVICH. Sit down.

PYOTR. Drop it, Father. It's too late at night to make a scene. Let's talk tomorrow instead.

ALEKSEY PETROVICH. Tomorrow you'll be gone from this house. We're going to talk right now.

PYOTR. I've been summoned to Moscow—that's true. But maybe I won't go tomorrow. They'll wait.

ALEKSEY PETROVICH. They'll wait—but I won't. You're leaving tomorrow.

PYOTR (*smiling*). Banishment?

ALEKSEY PETROVICH. That's a big word. Find a simpler one.

PYOTR. I see-ee. So, because of a scoundrel, who you didn't even know yesterday...

(*Pause. On the threshold is* VERA NIKOLAEVNA.)

ALEKSEY PETROVICH. A minute ago you crushed a man, offhandedly, without stopping even a minute to think. You trampled his future without even batting an eyelash. And as if that weren't enough, you called him a scoundrel. (*With angry irony.*) He's a scoundrel, but you're a moral person!

PYOTR (*soft, conciliatory*). Let's leave it be.... There's a lot you don't know. When I do something, there are reasons for it.

ALEKSEY PETROVICH. Baloney. There can't be any reason for dealing with a man that way, if he's honest.

PYOTR (*smiling*). If...

ALEKSEY PETROVICH. As for that, I know he's honest. And I'm taking this matter into my own hands. I've come to know it *thoroughly*. Although, between us, it doesn't take long to figure it out. The sort of thing where it's written on his face. I've spent several hours with him now. He told me his whole life story. (*Draws nearer to him.*) I've never seen your Krasnoshchekov, though; I've only heard that he's high-ranking, but if I'd seen him, too... I'd see soon enough what a monster he is.

PYOTR (*after a pause*). If it weren't you who said that...

ALEKSEY PETROVICH. Then what?

PYOTR (*softly*). I might think all sorts of things....

ALEKSEY PETROVICH. I believe it. Your thoughts are vulgar enough.

PYOTR (*bangs the table*). Father!

ALEKSEY PETROVICH (*softly, but imperiously*). Be quiet.

(*And* PYOTR *falls silent.*)

Be quiet when I speak with you.

VERA NIKOLAYEVNA (*steps forward*). Alyosha, please, spare yourself.

ALEKSEY PETROVICH. It's too late for that. It won't help. There he is—Pyotr Kirpichov. (*Mournfully.*) It's our fault.

PYOTR. Father, you and I aren't alone. My son is here!

ALEKSEY PETROVICH. All the better that he's here. He's young—let him hear. It's our fault.

VERA NIKOLAYEVNA (*indistinctly*). Calm down, Alyosha. Everything's already been talked over.

ALEKSEY PETROVICH. No, wait. It shouldn't all be under our breath.

PYOTR (*nervously*). Mom, you understand, at least....

VERA NIKOLAYEVNA. The most terrible thing, my firstborn, is when a mother does understand. Mothers don't want to understand. Then one day—they have to. That's the most terrible thing.

ALEKSEY PETROVICH. I became, as they say, a big man; what in our life—in hers, in mine—changed? Nothing. We started working more. The blessings—they fell to you. I thought that was how it was supposed to be—we got the thunderstorms, but then he gets the sun. I was given various honors—I wasn't able to receive them on account of work; they all came to you. People ingratiated themselves before you; you liked that....

PYOTR (*indignantly*). Please...

ALEKSEY PETROVICH (*not listening to him*). I was just working for the good of our land; I worked and never thought about how power smells, but you experienced its taste from childhood, and it poisoned you.... It's our fault....

PYOTR (*grins, clasps his hands*). It's come out; you finally see.

ALEKSEY PETROVICH. Yes.... It's a little late. What can we do? You left us early—for an independent life. I thought your blood was racing, passion, unspent strength; but now I see—it was more convenient for you that way....

PYOTR. What was more convenient?

ALEKSEY PETROVICH. More convenient to live far away. Up close, we got in your way, your mother and I, but farther away we were even useful. You know, all your life I propped you up, unseen, all your life I made your resumé, thanks to no small number of blockheads in love with paperwork.

PYOTR (*through his teeth*). Somehow I don't like your talk....

ALEKSEY PETROVICH (*not listening to him*). You do have a knack... you worked on your demeanor from childhood, you have a good last name— you went right up the ladder. Still, I've seen you for what you are.

PYOTR. You've seen squat! You've gone blind in your old age. So much for your eagle eyes. They wrapped you around their finger, cried a little bit on your shoulder, and it's all over! You're waging war for some shady man (*sorrowfully*), chastising your one and only son....

ALEKSEY PETROVICH (*interrupts*). Wait... my one and only. "For a shady man"?... But you didn't tell him to his face what you thought of him....

PYOTR (*impatiently waving his hand*). In my position you don't tell people to their face....

ALEKSEY PETROVICH. Well you just give it a try. (*Flings open the door.*) Come here, Mikhail Aleksandrovich.

(*Enter* POKROVSKY.)

POKROVSKY. Thank you for calling me in. It was getting hard for me to stay out there.

PYOTR. What is this? A screenplay? Fantastic! Everything played out according to plan.

SERGEY. No. The playing is over.

PYOTR. Mom! What's going on? Where am I?

VERA NIKOLAYEVNA. Don't shout, Pyotr. You don't prove anything by shouting.

POKROVSKY. Pyotr Alekseyevich!... How could you?

PYOTR. You and I have nothing to talk about.

POKROVSKY. Yes, we do. We do! Pyotr Alekseyevich, why did you act that way? What have you done with me?

ALEKSEY PETROVICH. Nothing to say?

POKROVSKY. You spoke so kindly with me. I flew straight to my wife to cheer her up. For the first time in half a year we joked and laughed.... So, you were brushing me off?

(PYOTR *silently drums his fingers on the table.*)

ALEKSEY PETROVICH. You've been asked a question—answer it.

PYOTR. You've set up this scene, you perform it. Let me go.

POKROVSKY (*slowly*). I understand.... (*Short pause.*) For you I'm a speck of dirt, one of a thousand petitioners, just any old person.... (*Flaring up.*) But you know, this person has his own life, his own work, his own family.... No, I won't stand for it!

PYOTR. How about that! Won't even "stand for it."

(NINA KONSTANTINOVNA *and* TYOMA *appear on the terrace.*)

POKROVSKY. I won't stand for it. I am a citizen of my country. And the point isn't me, a provincial lawyer. The point is the law of that country, its essence. You just about wrecked me, damn you. There were moments when I felt like throwing it all to hell. So there wouldn't be any more traipsing around, meetings, sniveling, guilty smile. But now it's clear to me: I don't have that right. I'm not the point. I have to keep struggling. (*Leaves quickly.*)

NINA KONSTANTINOVNA. Pyotr! What's going on here?

PYOTR. What? Drama. Tragedy. Farce.

NINA KONSTANTINOVNA. Don't.... This man.... Why is he here?... Why is everyone quiet? Vera Nikolayevna...

VERA NIKOLAYEVNA. Ahh, dear, I've been Vera Nikolayevna for sixty-five years....

ALEKSEY PETROVICH (*slowly*). It's simple—we've asked your husband to leave us. That's it.

PYOTR. Hear that? That's all there is to it. Well, Father, there's a limit to everything. I'm not only your son—I'm a Communist.

SERGEY (*distinctly, not raising his voice*). Communist? You? After everything we've seen?

PYOTR. Don't you dare speak to me, you wretch!...

ALEKSEY PETROVICH. He's right. You—a Communist? With your dealings, with your way of life?

PYOTR. "Way of life?"... (*With a grin.*) What, am I supposed to wear a hair shirt?

ALEKSEY PETROVICH. Get off your high horse.... We understand each other. The country's gotten stronger—for a decent person there's plenty to go around. But not for you and your iron jaws.

NINA KONSTANTINOVNA. Aleksey Petrovich, for God's sake, what are you saying?

ALEKSEY PETROVICH. And that's the worst part. People are unimportant to you, unnecessary. You know the words: the party, the people, communism. But what do you care about the party? What do you care about the people? About communism? What do you care that our whole path is behind these words, from the Vladimir trail[2] to this day? What do you care about the twenty million buried during the war? For you it's just words.

PYOTR. How dare you....

ALEKSEY PETROVICH. Me? I dare. My godchildren toil all across the country; my conscience is clear. But at the bottom of your soul there's only ambition and... ashes. Nothing else is left. Your generation will ask you: What did you give to the era you live in? You'll have nothing to answer.

PYOTR. Time will tell.

ALEKSEY PETROVICH. Have no doubt. And no matter how much you roar, or play games, or disguise yourself as a man of principle, no one will believe you, no one. A lot of arrogant careerists have tried to pontificate in our name—where are they now? Who remembers them?

(*Pause.*)

NINA KONSTANTINOVNA (*quietly*). My God.... This is terrible... terrible.

(NIKA *appears on the terrace. She stops at the back of it.*)

PYOTR (*trying to be calm*). Is that it? Mom, won't *you* say anything? Say something....

VERA NIKOLAYEVNA (*indistinctly*). I have nothing to say to you.

(*Pause.* VARVARA *and* TRUBIN *enter from the street. Seeing the people, they stop behind the elder bushes.*)

PYOTR (*after lingering for an instant*). Pack up! Nina, Tyoma, look alive! We're going immediately. (*Spotting* NIKA.) Nika, you're up? Excellent. We're going.

NIKA. I'm not going with you, Pyotr Alekseyevich....

TYOMA. What?

NIKA. I'm not going. (*Runs into the rooms.*)

NINA KONSTANTINOVNA. Nika!

TYOMA. Listen... what's the deal? (*Rushes after her.*)

PYOTR. Wait. Come here. Did you offend her somehow? Well?

TYOMA. Don't yell at me. I won't stand for it....

PYOTR. What? You too? Milksop!

NINA KONSTANTINOVNA. Pyotr, wait. Nika's not your daughter or your daughter-in-law; you don't have to clear things up. Even if someone did offend her, she could have handled herself differently. Have a talk, work things out.... The most important culture is the culture of relations. But this, without saying a word to anyone...

VARVARA (*stepping forward*). Nika spoke with me.

PYOTR (*with a gloomy smile looks her over*). Now she appears? With you....
Why—with you?

VARVARA. That's her business.

NINA KONSTANTINOVNA. So what did she say?

VARVARA. Not worth asking about. It's not for just anyone's ears. (*To*
NINA KONSTANTINOVNA.) You're right, the main thing is the culture
of relations.

TYOMA. But still... you just can't... so... suddenly.

VARVARA. She realized that she'd gotten into the wrong car.

TYOMA. I'll go up to her. I'll have a talk with her....

PYOTR (*takes him by the shoulder*). You go get ready— and that's it. The
people around here can't wait for us to leave.

NINA KONSTANTINOVNA. Pyotr, I'm begging you, don't aggravate...

PYOTR. To hell with it!

NINA KONSTANTINOVNA. Vera Nikolayevna! Don't you see, he's in
pain.... You're his mother.

VERA NIKOLAYEVNA (*strictly*). Yes, Nina Konstantinovna, I'm his
mother. (*Turns aside.*)

PYOTR (*walks up to his father*). Hear my last word. (*Indicating his chest.*)
I'm burning here!... I hope you're happy. The road to your house is
forbidden to me. You've murdered everything inside me. I have no
father.

SERGEY (*passionately*). And you have no son! But I'll find the road to you.
I, Sergey Kirpichov, declare war on you, Pyotr Kirpichov. And wherever
I meet you, in any office, any chair, however you look, whatever you call
yourself, whatever your name is, I'll recognize you right away and fight
you to the death. You hear? I'll fight you to the death.

PYOTR. Well then, if that's the way it's got to be, we'll fight. I'll forget about
our having the same last name, too. Let's go, Nina, Tyoma, hurry up!

TRUBIN (*walks up to* VARVARA). There's a wise old saying about life:
Guests come and go, but the hosts remain.

PYOTR. Ugh, you're here too? (*Grins.*) Why so late?

TRUBIN. Mikhail Aleksandrovich and I were having a conversation. He
was leaving.

PYOTR. Well, go ahead and converse. As for me, I've had enough conversation. Come to think of it, I've had enough of our acquaintance, too. Bon voyage.

TRUBIN. Thank you. I'll be in Moscow soon. We'll continue our acquaintance there.

PYOTR. That requires my wishes, as well.

TRUBIN. I'm not sure. I won't come alone, but together with Pokrovsky.

PYOTR. Is that a threat?

TRUBIN. We'll get down to the truth. And not just his little truth. No. The big, unmerciful truth.

PYOTR (*coldly*). A word in parting. The Pokrovsky case is closed.

TRUBIN. We'll see.

PYOTR. It's closed, just the same as the Shevtsova case. And remember: We won't allow anyone to cast the slightest shadow on us. Not Ptitsyn. Not Trubin. Not the devil himself. You'll be cursing yourself for your foolishness.

TRUBIN. We'll see.

PYOTR. You'll see. You'll see things better in the morning.

TRUBIN. Morning—there it is! It's right around the corner. They'll be delivering the newspapers soon now. Read Vladimir Ptitsyn's article about the Shevtsova case and the Krasnoshchekov cases.

(SERGEY *and* VARVARA *rush toward* TRUBIN. *But* ALEKSEY PETROVICH *has already outstripped them.*)

(*Curtain.*)

Editors' Notes

1. From "Some Words about the Book *War and Peace*," translated in Gary Saul Morson, *Hidden in Plain View* (Stanford, Calif.: Stanford University Press, 1987), 76.

2. "The Oberiu Manifesto" in *The Man with the Black Coat: Russia's Lost Literature of the Absurd: Selected Works of Daniil Kharms and Alexander Vvedensky*, ed. and trans. George Gibian (Evanston, Ill.: Northwestern University Press, 1987), 253.

SACRED BLOOD

We have elected to translate the Russian word *rusalka* as "mermaid" because we believe this word is more familiar to American audiences than "water nymph," "sprite," or "undine." A familiar figure in Russian folklore, the *rusalka* would have reminded Russian audiences of Alexander Pushkin's unfinished dramatic work "Rusalka."

THE UNKNOWN WOMAN

Both epigraphs come from Fyodor Dostoevsky's novel *The Idiot*. The woman in the photograph, also the first speaker in the second epigraph, is the captivating and hysterical Nastasya Filipovna. The translators added the ellipses after the first paragraph in the second epigraph to indicate a few intervening paragraphs omitted by Blok.

ELIZAVETA BAM

1. "Bobchinsky" refers to one member of a pair of bumbling characters in Nikolai Gogol's famous play *The Inspector General*. (The other character is named Dobchinsky.)

2. "I—I" and "II—I" indicate rhthms to be played by musical instruments.

3. As Peter Nikolaevich and Ivan Ivanovich are telling the same story, this direction probably means that they take turns standing in front of each other, creating the effect that their characters have merged.

4. "Chinar" was another name used by Kharms and his group.

5. In the original performance a poster with these words was paraded around the stage, in effect dividing the play into two acts.

6. Kharms's notebook indicates a chorus of five to ten women and ten to fifteen men. The "orchestra" consisted of a wind instrument, a piano, a violin, a drum, and a "mouth siren."

THE GUESTS

1. Prishibeev is the nosy bully from Anton Chekhov's well-known short story "Sergeant Prishibeyev."

2. The Vladimir trail was a historic route to Siberian exile.